Miranda™

The Craft of Functional Programming

INTERNATIONAL COMPUTER SCIENCE SERIES

Consulting Editor   **A D McGettrick**   University of Strathclyde

SELECTED TITLES IN THE SERIES

Software Development with Z   *J B Wordsworth*

Program Verification   *N Francez*

Performance Modelling of Communication Networks   *P G Harrison and N M Patel*

Concurrent Systems: An Integrated Approach to Operating Systems, Database, and Distributed Systems   *J Bacon*

Introduction to Parallel Processing   *B Codenotti and M Leoncini*

Concurrent Programming   *A Burns and G Davies*

Comparative Programming Languages (2nd Edn)   *L B Wilson and R G Clark*

Functional Programming and Parallel Graph Rewriting   *R Plasmeijer and M van Eekelen*

Object-Oriented Database Systems: Concepts and Architectures   *E Bertino and L D Martino*

Programming in Ada (4th Edn)   *J G P Barnes*

Software Design   *D Budgen*

Ada from the Beginning (2nd Edn)   *J Skansholm*

Programming Language Essentials   *H E Bal and D Grune*

Human–Computer Interaction   *J Preece et al.*

Distributed Systems: Concepts and Design (2nd Edn)   *G Coulouris, J Dollimore and T Kindberg*

Fortran 90 Programming   *T M R Ellis, I R Philips and T M Lahey*

Parallel Processing: The Transputer and its Applications   *M E C Hull, D Crookes and P J Sweeney*

Foundations of Computing: System Development with Set Theory and Logic   *T Scheurer*

Principles of Object Oriented Engineering   *A Eliëns*

Compiler Design   *R Wilhelm and D Maurer*

Miranda™

The Craft of Functional Programming

Simon Thompson
University of Kent at Canterbury

ADDISON-WESLEY PUBLISHING COMPANY

WOKINGHAM, ENGLAND • READING, MASSACHUSETTS • MENLO PARK, CALIFORNIA • NEW YORK
DON MILLS, ONTARIO • AMSTERDAM • BONN • SYDNEY • SINGAPORE
TOKYO • MADRID • SAN JUAN • MILAN • PARIS • MEXICO CITY • SEOUL • TAIPEI

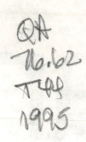

Cover designed by Designers & Partners of Oxford
and printed by The Riverside Printing Co. (Reading) Ltd.
Typeset by CRB Associates, Norwich.
Printed in Great Britain by TJ Press, Padstow, Cornwall.

First printed 1995

ISBN 0–201–42279–4

British Library Cataloguing in Publication Data
A catalogue record for this book is available from the British Library.

Library of Congress Cataloging in Publication Data applied for.

To Jane

Preface

Over the last fifteen years, functional programming has come of age. It has been used successfully on a number of substantial projects. A variety of robust and efficient implementations of functional languages have been developed. A functional language is taught as the first programming language in many university computing courses, and at a later stage in most others. Before examining the reasons for its popularity, we give a short overview of functional programming.

What is functional programming?

Functional programming is based on the simplest of models, namely that of finding the value of an expression. This we meet in our first years at school, when we learn to work out expressions like 8+(3-2) by evaluating the two halves, 8 and (3-2), and adding the results together. Functional programming consists of our defining for ourselves functions like + which we can then use to form expressions.

We define these functions by means of equations, like

$$\text{addD a b} = 2*(a+b) \tag{1}$$

which we use to calculate the value of an expression like addD 2 (addD 3 4). We evaluate this using (1) to replace occurrences of addD with their values, so that we can write down a calculation of its value

```
addD 2 (addD 3 4)
= 2*(2 + (addD 3 4))
= 2*(2 + 2*(3 + 4))
= 32
```

As well as using (1) to calculate, we can read it as a logical description of how the function addD behaves on any values a and b; on the basis of this we can reason about how it behaves. For instance, for any values a and b,

$$\text{addD a b} = 2*(a+b) = 2*(b+a) = \text{addD b a}$$

This equation holds for *all* possible input values, in contrast to the information we gain from testing a function at a selection of inputs.

On top of this simple model we can build a variety of facilities, which give the functional approach its distinctive flavour. These include higher-order functions, whose arguments and results are themselves functions; polymorphism, which allows a single definition to apply simultaneously to a collection of types; and infinite data structures, which are used to model a variety of data objects.

The Miranda[†] language also has support for larger-scale programming, including user-defined algebraic types, such as lists, trees and so on; abstract data types and modules. These contribute to separating complex tasks into smaller sub-tasks, making the components of systems independent of each other, as well as supporting software re-use.

Why learn functional programming?

As a vehicle for learning programming principles a functional language like Miranda has many advantages. As we saw, it is based on a simple model which allows us both to perform evaluation by hand, animating our understanding, and to reason about how the programs behave. In this text, both calculation and reasoning have a central part.

The language is higher-level than most. For example, lists in Miranda are defined directly as a recursive type, and so there is no need to examine their implementation by pointers; indeed, the functional language can be used as a design language for the imperative implementation. A second instance is provided by polymorphism; generic definitions are introduced with almost no overhead, in contrast to object-oriented languages such as Modula-3 and C++.

Moreover, the language supports larger-scale programming by means of its abstype and module mechanisms. Again, these have advantages over

---

[†] Miranda is a product of Research Software Limited. The version of Miranda used in this book is release two.

Enquiries about the Miranda system and its availability for various computers should be directed to Research Software Ltd, 23 St Augustines Road, Canterbury CT1 1XP, UK, or to the electronic mail address *mira-request@ukc.ac.uk*.

traditional languages: module versions are kept consistent automatically, for example.

For these reasons we see Miranda as providing a sound introduction to programming principles, which can be complemented later by learning an imperative language. Equally valuable is to learn Miranda after using a more traditional language, since it can broaden our view of the programming process as well as illustrating many software engineering techniques of general worth.

The approach

The material is grouped into three parts. In the first, we build a foundation, focusing on programming over basic types and lists, using first-order, non-polymorphic programs. Only when readers are fluent with the basics of functions, types and program construction do we look at the twin ideas of higher-order functions and polymorphism, which together give modern functional programming its distinctive flavour and power. Based on this, in the final part we look at larger-scale programming, supported also by an exploration of user-defined types, modules and lazy evaluation, and concluding with an analysis of program efficiency.

As we saw above, we can write down calculations of expressions which use our defined functions, and also give proofs of various of their properties; both aspects are emphasized in the text (although it can be read independently of the material on proof).

The crucial test of any programming text is whether it helps the reader to write programs. The book is called 'The *Craft* of Functional Programming' because it aims to give readers help with design of programs right from the start. At each stage we give advice on how functions, types or modules can be designed; in many cases we give a series of steps which aim to simplify the problem by breaking it down into simpler parts.

Software of any importance will be modified during its lifetime; modification and re-use are emphasized when we discuss design, and in the final part of the book we look in particular at how libraries of polymorphic higher-order functions can be re-used in many different contexts.

The advice on design is supplemented by examples and case studies of varying size and complexity. Some, like the Huffman coding example, are free-standing; others, such as the library database, are re-visited a number of times to illustrate how new techniques can be applied to solve existing problems in different ways. This is important in linking together the different parts of the text, and in showing the variety of ways that any problem can be solved in Miranda.

Finally, other case studies are introduced step-by-step. We first see the simulation example when we design algebraic data types in Chapter 9; next it provides realistic examples of abstract data types in Chapter 11, and finally we look at its top level in Chapter 13. Each aspect is separate; together they provide a substantial case study. Other aspects of our approach are:

- Throughout the text, whenever a function is defined we give its type explicitly; the type forms the first and most important piece of documentation for any definition.

- Material is included on how to find proofs by induction; a template to help with setting down the precise goals of an induction proof is included, as is a discussion of how to search for proofs about functions defined by equations.

- Appendices contain support material of various kinds. Common errors and error messages are collected in one; a glossary of programming terms commonly used in another. A third appendix lists a major part of the Miranda standard environment, a fourth examines how functional and imperative programming are linked, and a fifth gives references for further reading. Finally, we give an overview of how to understand an unfamiliar function definition in Miranda.

- Over four hundred exercises of varying difficulty are included.

- Further support material, including some exercise solutions and support material for teachers, can be found on the page

   ```
   http://www.ukc.ac.uk/computer_science/Miranda_craft/
   ```

   of the World Wide Web.

Outline

The material is presented in three parts.

Part I: Basic functional programming

The aim of Part I is to introduce the basic tools of functional programming, and to give detailed guidance about how to *build* programs to solve particular problems.

The technical material covers the basic types of Miranda: numbers, characters and Booleans, and the structured types of tuples and lists. Readers are introduced to function definitions involving guards, pattern matching and local definitions (where clauses) through a sequence of examples and sections.

Throughout the introduction, details are given about how particular problems can be approached, to encourage students to develop their own solutions. Divide and conquer approaches and top-down design are encouraged, and illustrated by means of examples including a small database, the production of supermarket bills, text processing and equation solving.

To animate the programs, calculations of many examples are given, and readers are encouraged to try definitions out using these rewriting sequences. Integrated into this and the other parts of the book are proofs of program properties. These are shown to be written to a template, in the cases of proof over numbers and lists, and many examples of graded difficulty are presented. More traditional approaches to software testing are also discussed and encouraged.

The material in this part is all first-order and non-polymorphic, deliberately. The aim of the part is to give students a firm grounding on which they can make the abstractions which are the subject of the next part.

Part II: Abstraction

This part forms the bridge between the material on basic functional programming, and the larger-scale programs of the final part. The distinctive features of languages like Miranda are that they are higher-order, allowing functions as arguments to and results of other functions, and polymorphic with definitions applying to, for instance, all types of list rather than to lists of a single type.

Higher-order and polymorphic functions are shown in this part to be generalizations or abstractions of definitions familiar from the first part: an example is the map function which applies an operation to every member of a list, irrespective of the operation (it is a parameter) and the type of the list.

These technical ideas are introduced, and many of the examples of Part I are re-examined to show the general higher-order functions they exemplify or use. Libraries of general functions are developed, particularly over the polymorphic list type.

The consequences of these ideas for software design and engineering are also examined: polymorphic higher-order functions are ideal candidates for re-use, and this is illustrated in the examples.

The most technical chapter of the book is the final one of this part, where type checking is presented. This is necessary fully to exploit the features of the language, and also to understand the error messages which result when type checking fails.

Program verification is a continuing theme here, and it is argued that theorems about general functions are re-usable in the same way as the functions themselves.

Part III: Larger-scale programming

The final part of the book brings in the aspects of the language which support larger-scale programming: user-defined concrete (or algebraic) types; modules; abstract data types. In introducing each of these, examples are given, together with general principles for design of systems which contain algebraic and abstract data types, as well as how systems are built top-down and bottom-up using modules.

Amongst the examples we look at are the design and use of Huffman codes, the simulation of multiple queues (as might be found in a bank), finding the difference between two files, simple interactive programs and aspects of a simple arithmetic calculator.

Lazy evaluation is also discussed here. After showing precisely what it means and how it works, the consequences it has for program development are explored. These include data-directed solutions, infinite data structures and interactive streams of input and output. Design principles for interactive programs are explored, and verification is addressed.

The book concludes with an analysis of program behaviour, including the time taken and space used during evaluation. Examples from the text are re-visited, and various strategies for optimizing program performance are introduced.

Appendices, Bibliography and Index

The appendices consist of: a comparison of functional and imperative programming; a glossary of commonly used and technical terms; sources for further reading; a discussion of common error messages, and their possible sources; an annotated listing of some of the built-in functions (the *standard environment*) and a reminder of the ways that unfamiliar definitions can be understood.

Who should read this book?

This text is intended as an introduction to functional programming for computer science and other students, principally at university level. It can be used by beginners to computer science, or more experienced students who are learning functional programming for the first time; either group will find the material is new, challenging and interesting.

The book can also be used for self-study by programmers, software engineers and others interested in gaining a grounding in functional programming.

The text is intended to be self-contained, but some elementary knowledge of commands, files and so on would be needed to use the

Miranda system under Unix. Some logical notation is introduced in the text; this is explained as it appears. In the final chapter it would be helpful to have an understanding of the graphs of the `log`, n^2 and 2^n functions.

To the teacher

Depending upon a teacher's preferences and the context in which the course is taught, different routes through the book exist. The ordering of the text roughly corresponds to the first-year course at the University of Kent, although the material here is much expanded from that given to our students.

The book follows a linear progression, and it makes sense to follow it from Chapter 1 to Chapter 14; if time does not permit, a coherent course on smaller-scale programming is given by the first part; together with the second, students will gain an additional grounding in the novelties of functional programming, whilst more advanced techniques are introduced in Part III.

In Part III it is possible to pick and choose chapters and sections, rather than following the material page-by-page. The case studies illustrate the material, but a teacher could use his or her own examples rather than those of Huffman coding or relations and graphs, for instance. The calculator and simulation examples are distributed through Part III; another approach would be to delay them until all the supporting material has been studied.

Integral to this course is reasoning about programs, but the material on proof in this text stands independently, and so a proof-free course could be given, omitting Chapters 3 and 5, and Sections 7.7, 9.6 and 13.7. It would also be feasible to give the proof material rather later than it appears in the text. Also standing alone is the material on program behaviour; this could be omitted if so desired.

It is impossible to exclude some more technical sections from the book, but some of this material could be deferred, mentioned in passing or given an informal gloss. In the first two parts, Sections 5.4, 8.3 and 8.4 are potential candidates.

Students should be encouraged to use the information in the appendices. Depending upon their backgrounds, the comparison of functional and imperative programming can be illuminating in both directions; at the University of Kent we find that linking the treatment of lists in Miranda and in an imperative language is very helpful for students who are learning the intricacies of pointer-based linked lists.

Also to be recommended to students is the glossary; both for beginners to programming, and to those familiar with other programming paradigms, some of the terminology of functional programming is either new or consists of common terms used in a slightly different way from the norm. In either case, students should be encouraged to look up words they are unsure about. Also in the appendices are a full treatment of common errors, a reminder of the different ways to understand an unfamiliar function and sources for further reading.

Resources for teachers, including the program text, sample solutions to the exercises and a teachers' guide are available on-line from the World Wide Web page mentioned above.

Acknowledgements

I would first like to thank my colleagues in the functional programming group at the University of Kent. I have learned a tremendous amount from them, both about functional programming itself, and about how best to teach it.

The reviewers of this text have provided invaluable help in finding errors and infelicities of presentation. Each of them provided different, but useful, feedback; grateful thanks therefore to Howard Bowman, Allan Grimley, Steve Hill, Ron Knott, Janet Linington, Iain MacCallum, Phil Molyneux and David Turner. Needless to say, any errors which remain are the author's responsibility.

I am very grateful to Nick Riding for the loan of a portable PC on which many of the programs were developed; to Barry Dean for his help in getting the PC to use Linux and to Research Software Limited for permission to include information about the Miranda system and to quote from the manual.

Final and most heartfelt thanks to Jane, Alice and Rory, for their unfailing support over the last year during which this book has come to fruition.

Simon Thompson
Canterbury, April 1995

Contents

Appendices

Part I

Basic Functional Programming

Introducing functional programming

This chapter introduces the fundamental ideas of functional programming in Miranda™†, including how to use the Miranda system itself, and how to write, test and use functional programs.

---

† Miranda is a trademark of Research Software Limited

1.1   What is functional programming?

This section introduces the fundamental ideas behind functional programming, some of which are familiar from our first introduction to arithmetic at school. It also brings in some of the terminology we will be using in the rest of the book.

Computer programs

Computers are machines to perform tasks which can be automated; some of these are jobs which we could do if we so wished, like calculating the total cost of a basket of shopping at the supermarket, whilst others, like producing accurate weather forecasts, are only possible because of the speed at which present-day computers operate.

Common to all these systems is the **program**, which describes how the system is to behave. We can describe programs to each other in ordinary language:

```
Take a number, subtract three, double it and add six.

Take the total cost of the items in the bill, then add VAT
at the standard rate.

Lay out the words of the book so that each line of the book
is of length exactly eighty letters.
```

Although these programs appear clear, they are ambiguous. We can interpret what should be done in more than one way: do we round up or down in the VAT calculation; what do we do with lines at the end of a paragraph? Even if we were able to *write* our programs in English, present-day computers would be unable to interpret what we had written; instead we have to use a computer **programming language.**

Programming languages are formal languages which are used for describing programs. This book describes **functional** programming, in the programming language Miranda. During the short history of computing, languages have become more **high-level**: the first languages were simply a shorthand for operations on the hardware of the computer; since then the trend has been to make languages which express directly ideas at a level closer to the way we think. Functional languages are amongst the highest-level languages in present-day use.

Since programming languages are precisely defined there is no possibility of the ambiguities we saw with English. To anticipate a little, we could re-write our first program in Miranda thus:

```
((n - 3) * 2) + 6
```

where the n stands for the unknown number over which this program works.

Functions

Despite their variety, computer programs can all be seen to be behaving in a similar way. Programs take **input** data, and transform them into the **output** data. A functional program *describes* directly how the data are analysed, manipulated and re-assembled. The most common way of describing a transformation is as a **function**. A function is something which will return an output which depends upon one or more inputs.

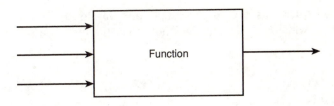

We will often use the term **result** for the output, and the terms **arguments** or **parameters** for the inputs. Examples of functions include:

- A function giving the distance by road (*output*) between two cities (*inputs*).

- A supermarket check-out program, which calculates the bill (*output*) from a list of bar codes scanned in (*input*).

- Mathematical functions, like *sin, cos,* $\sqrt{\ }$ and so on, whose inputs and outputs are numbers.

- A text formatting program, such as the one used to prepare this book. The input is the unformatted text, together with instructions about how exactly it is to be processed; the output consists of the appropriate printing instructions.

- A database system, which gives a reply (*output*) to a question concerning the information it contains (*input*).

- A process controller which controls valves in a chemical plant. Its inputs are the information from sensors, and its output the signals sent to the valve actuators.

- An interactive program returns a sequence of responses (*output*) in reply to a sequence of commands (*input*).

Calculation

When we first start at school, we learn how to **calculate** the value of **expressions** like ((7 - 3) * 2). Every expression like this has a **value** which is a number. To work out the value of ((7 - 3) * 2) we need to multiply together the left- and right-hand sides. The latter is a number, 2, but the left-hand side needs itself to be calculated. This gives 4, and so the whole expression gives 8. A larger example can be written

```
  ((7 - 3) * 2) + 6
= (4 * 2) + 6
= 8 + 6
= 14
```

For many expressions, there is more than one way to calculate their value; the order in which we calculate does not affect the result we produce. For instance,

```
  (7-3) * (4+2)                    (7-3) * (4+2)
= 4 * (4+2)                      = (7-3) * 6
= 4 * 6                          = 4 * 6
= 24                            = 24
```

To help us with arithmetic we can use a calculator; we key in an expression such as (7-3)*(4+2), which involves numbers and the operations +, −, *, ..., to get the result 24.

Functional programming

Functional programming is based on the idea of calculation. We define ourselves the functions to be used, and the implementation will calculate the values of expressions which use these functions, just as a traditional calculator will calculate arithmetical expressions like those given above.

A functional program, or **script** as it is called in Miranda, consists of a number of definitions of functions and other values. As an example, suppose assessment marks need to be analysed. Functions in a script could include ones to:

- give the total of a collection of marks,
- sort a list of student names or of numbers,
- calculate the most common value in a sequence of marks, and so on.

Using these functions we can, for instance, produce:

- the total marks awarded to a particular student over a given year,
- the list of students sorted according to their average mark for the term.

In summary, functional programming consists of defining functions and other values. An implementation of a functional language will calculate the **value** of any **expression** which uses the defined functions.

Appendix A contains a comparison of functional and imperative programming as in Pascal and C.

Types

The examples we discussed on p. 5 cover many different areas; data include 2, 1, 3.145, "A piece of text", "Another piece of text", *January*, *July* and so on. We do not expect all these data to be treated in the same way, and they can be grouped into **types** of similar data. Informally,

- 2, 1, 3.145 are numbers,
- "A piece of text", "Another piece of text" are examples of text, and
- *January*, *July* are months.

Once we have divided the data into types, we can see that the functions we define will expect certain types of data. For example, $+, -, *, /$, and so forth, expect numbers and return numbers; the function giving the number of days in a month expects an argument which is of type month, and returns a number. It makes no sense to add together two months, or to ask for the number of days in a bar code.

This informal idea of type is formalized in Miranda (as it is in nearly every programming language in common use). Every value or function defined has a type, and the system will check that functions are applied only to objects of the right type, amongst other **type constraints**.

In the chapters to come we shall explore the types in detail; here we briefly introduce the type bool of Boolean values which is mentioned in the next section. The Booleans, named after George Boole who was one of the founders of modern **logic**, are the two values True and False which we can think of as the two results of a logical test, like 'Is this number greater than that number?'. For instance, 2>1 will have the value True whereas 2>11 has the value False. These values, sometimes called **truth values**, can be combined by the operators 'and', &; 'or', \/ and 'not', ~. A test t_1 & t_2 will be True only if both the tests t_1 and t_2 give True, for instance.

1.2 Miranda

In this section we introduce Miranda programming, and the Miranda system itself, as well as showing how to make calculations using Miranda functions.

An example script

Figure 1.1 gives an example Miranda script. A script contains a number of definitions. Each definition associates a name, like answer or square, with a value, which may be of any type. The script also contains **comments** which are added to a script to make it easier to read, both for the person who has written it and anyone else. The symbol '||' makes the part of the line to its right a comment. The comments at the start of the script indicate its general purpose; those which follow comment on the purpose of the individual definitions.

We now discuss the definitions in the script one-by-one.

```
answer :: num
answer = 42
```

The first line declares the type of a name. The notation '::' is read as 'is of type', and so the first line says that answer is of type num, the Miranda type of numbers. The next line gives the value of 42 to answer. The symbol '=' is used to make a definition.

```
newline :: char
newline = '\n'
```

Here newline is defined to be the newline character, belonging to the type char; a full description of this type and particular special characters like newline is to be found in the next chapter.

```
yes :: bool
yes = True

greater :: bool
greater = (answer>71)
```

Here two Boolean values are defined. First yes is given the value True; then greater is given the value False, since 42 fails to be larger than 71. The definition of greater uses one of the other definitions, answer. In Miranda any definition may use any other definition in the same script; in particular, it can use a definition which occurs after it in the script.

```
||------------------------------------------------------------||
||          example.m                                         ||
||                                                            ||
||          Some example definitions, to illustrate          ||
||          the form of Miranda scripts.                     ||
||------------------------------------------------------------||


answer :: num               || A number constant
answer = 42


newline :: char
newline = '\n'


yes :: bool                 || The answer yes is represented
yes = True                  || by the Boolean value True.


greater :: bool             || Uses the value of answer
greater = (answer>71)


||-----------------------------------------------------------||
||          To square two numbers                            ||
||-----------------------------------------------------------||
square :: num -> num
square x = x*x


||-----------------------------------------------------------||
||          Are three numbers equal?                         ||
||-----------------------------------------------------------||


allEqual :: num -> num -> num -> bool
allEqual n m p = (n=m) & (m=p)


||-----------------------------------------------------------||
||          The maximum of two numbers                       ||
||-----------------------------------------------------------||


maxi :: num -> num -> num
maxi n m
  = n       , if n>=m
  = m       , otherwise
```

Figure 1.1 An example script.

In this script each definition is preceded by a declaration of its type. The type of a definition is the most important piece of documentation we can supply. It tells us how a definition can be used: we can only use yes where a Boolean value is expected, for example. Because of this, we always give type declarations at the same time as our definitions, even though it is not compulsory in Miranda.

Scripts can also contain function definitions:

```
square :: num -> num
square x = x*x
```

The type declaration says that square is a function from numbers to numbers, since num -> num is the type of functions from num to num. We can read '->' as 'to', so the declaration of the type of square reads 'square is of type num to num'.

The definition itself is an **equation**. It gives the result, x*x, of applying square to x. x is a **variable**, which stands for the input of the function. The output is defined, using this input, on the right-hand side of the defining equation.

It is worth stressing the syntax here: to apply a function f to the arguments a, b and c, we write f next to the arguments, thus

```
f a b c
```

This way of writing function application is called **juxtaposition**.

```
allEqual :: num -> num -> num -> bool
allEqual n m p = (n=m) & (m=p)
```

allEqual is a function which takes three numbers to a Boolean. Formally it has the type num -> num -> num -> bool. Its value, when applied to the three numbers n, m and p, is a combination of two tests: the test that n equals m and the test that m equals p. The result will be True if both tests give True, and will be False if not. A final example is given by

```
maxi :: num -> num -> num
maxi n m
  = n      , if n>=m
  = m      , otherwise
```

The definition of maxi is an equation with more than one **clause** on the right-hand side. Following the clauses on the right-hand side are tests or **guards** which are Boolean expressions. The definition has two **cases**, corresponding to whether or not n is greater than or equal to m. If so, n is the answer; if not m is.

The full details of scripts and the syntax of definitions will be covered in later chapters.

Calculation in Miranda

We explained that functional programming was like calculation (or evaluation) in arithmetic, except that we use our own functions and other definitions. How is evaluation done with the definitions we saw in Figure 1.1?

The definition of answer is clear: answer has the value 42, so in evaluation we can replace it by 42. Function definitions can be interpreted similarly. We can, for example, read the definition

```
allEqual n m p = (n=m) & (m=p)
```

as giving the value of allEqual n m p for any values of n, m and p. We get *particular* values of allEqual by replacing the variables with the values in the defining equation, thus:

```
allEqual 2 3 3                  allEqual 5 5 5
= (2=3) & (3=3)                 = (5=5) & (5=5)
```

We continue the calculations by working out the component Boolean values, and then combine them using &.

```
allEqual 2 3 3                  allEqual 5 5 5
= (2=3) & (3=3)                 = (5=5) & (5=5)
= False & True                 = True & True
= False                        = True
```

Examples can involve more than one definition:

```
allEqual (square 3) answer (square 2)
= ((square 3) = answer) & (answer = (square 2))
= ((3*3) = 42) & (42 = (2*2))
= (9 = 42) & (42 = 4)
= False & False
= False
```

The definition of maxi contains two cases, given by the two clauses on the right-hand side of the equation.

```
maxi n m
    = n     , if n>=m
    = m     , otherwise
```

To work out which of the values to use, we have to work out the values of the guards one by one from top to bottom until one is found which gives the value `True`. In writing out the calculation, '??' is used to signal the calculation of a guard. For instance,

```
maxi 3 1
  ?? 3>=1 = True
= 3
```

Here we have to judge whether 3>=1 to tell which clause applies. Since 3 is greater than 1, the first clause is used; on the other hand,

```
maxi 3 4
  ?? 3>=4 = False
  ?? otherwise = True
= 4
```

As 3>=4 is `False`, the second clause is examined. This is an `otherwise` clause which always applies if it is reached. A more complicated example of evaluation is now given.

```
allEqual (maxi 1 5) 5 (maxi 4 2)
= ((maxi 1 5) = 5) & (5 = (maxi 4 2))
    ?? 1>=5 = False
    ?? otherwise = True
= (5 = 5) & (5 = (maxi 4 2))
    ?? 4>=2 = True
= (5 = 5) & (5 = 4)
= True & False
= False
```

When we perform a calculation, we can choose to evaluate things in a different order. It is most important that *this will not change the final answer we produce*, although it may mean that no answer is found; this is explored in detail in Chapter 12. For instance,

```
allEqual (maxi 1 5) 5 (maxi 4 2)
= ((maxi 1 5) = 5) & (5 = (maxi 4 2))
    ?? 4>=2 = True
= ((maxi 1 5) = 5) & (5 = 4)
    ?? 1>=5 = False
    ?? otherwise = True
= (5 = 5) & (5 = 4)
= True & False
= False
```

It can be helpful to show in a calculation which part of the expression we are going to evaluate next. We do this now for the previous example, by underlining at each stage the part of the expression to be evaluated next.

```
  allEqual (maxi 1 5) 5 (maxi 4 2)
= ((maxi 1 5) = 5) & (5 = (maxi 4 2))
  ?? 4>=2 = True
= ((maxi 1 5) = 5) & (5 = 4)
  ?? 1>=5 = False
  ?? otherwise = True
= (5 = 5) & (5 = 4)
= True & False
= False
```

The double underlining in $(5 = 5)$ & $(5 = 4)$ shows that we have really done two steps in one here, by evaluating both sides of the '&' at once.

The Miranda system

The Miranda system is invoked by typing

```
mira
```

which returns the Miranda prompt

```
Miranda
```

after an initial message giving details about the version of the system and so on. Invoking Miranda begins a Miranda **session**, which continues until the system is quit.

The system acts like a calculator; the prompt indicates that the system is ready to read an expression. The expression is evaluated, and then its value is printed. This behaviour, which is shared by many computer systems, is often called a 'read–evaluate–print loop'. An example interaction might look like:

```
Miranda (2+3)
5
Miranda (1*6)=(3 div 5)
False
    ...
```

where the user's input is shown underlined. (We just make this distinction in this introductory section, as generally underlining is distracting.)

Miranda scripts are stored in **files**, carrying the suffix '.m'. Suppose that the script from the previous section is stored in the file example.m. This can be loaded into the system in two ways. During a session, it is loaded by typing

```
Miranda /f example
```

It can be loaded when Miranda is called by typing

```
mira example
```

instead of mira. Once loaded, the definitions given in the file can be used in the expressions to be evaluated.

```
Miranda maxi (square 2) 1
4
Miranda allEqual answer 3 $$
False
```

In the second example $$ is used as shorthand for the last expression evaluated, in this case maxi (square 2) 1.

Typing an expression followed by '::' will give its type:

```
Miranda (2+3)::
num
Miranda maxi::
num -> num -> num
```

Instead of typing an expression, one of a number of **commands** can be issued. The most important commands include:

/e   Invoke the built-in editor on the current script. This is by default the editor vi, but it can be changed using the command /editor; see the manual, Section 6.

/e parrot   Edit the file parrot.m.

/f rabbit   Change the current script to rabbit.m.

/m   Enter the on-line manual for Miranda – see below.

/q   Quit the session.

!blah   Escape to perform the Unix command blah.

The manual contains information on the Miranda language and system. It is invoked by the command /m. Among its numbered sections are:

5   Brief descriptions of the main commands, including those listed above.

6	The rest of the commands.
28	A listing of the built-in functions, called the **standard environment**. These can also be found in Appendix G.
100	A paper giving an overview of the language.

The numbers here relate to release 2.014 of the Miranda system, and may not apply in other versions of the system.

After using a script like macaw.m, a file macaw.x will appear in the same directory. It contains information which the system has deduced about the script, and should not be removed. If it is removed, the system will have to re-analyse the script when it is loaded; for a large program the time taken to do this could be significant.

Examples from this book and other backup resources are to be found on the World Wide Web at

```
http://www.ukc.ac.uk/computer_science/Miranda_craft/
```

where further details can be found about how to access particular items.

1.3   Practical work

Learning a programming language is like learning any other craft; you can learn part of the skill by reading about it, but you only learn fully by *doing* it. Each chapter of the book contains exercises of various sorts, together with hints about how to do some of them, and tips about functional programming in general.

Using Miranda

The last section gives an introduction to the Miranda system. To see it in practice, begin a Miranda session by typing mira and then type the following expressions. Before you type an expression in, write down what you expect its result should be.

```
(2+3)
$$-1
5-4-3
7/3
7 div 3
4 div $$
7 mod 3
True \/ False
~ False & False
```

Now make a new file by typing

```
/f myExamples
/e
```

which will take you into the editor (usually vi) on the file myExamples.m.
Type in the definitions from the file examples.m (excluding the comments if
you wish) and then type

```
answer + 42
greater
square answer
square $$
allEqual 2 3 3
allEqual 5 5 5
allEqual (square 5) answer (maxi (-4) 2)
```

Miranda errors

The system cannot guarantee that what you type is sensible; if something is
wrong, you will receive an **error message**. Try typing

```
2+(3+4
2+(3+4))
```

These errors are in the **syntax**, and are like sentences in English which do not
have the correct grammatical structure, such as 'Fishcake our camel'. The
first Miranda expression has too few parentheses, the second too many.
After the '4', a closing parenthesis is expected, to match with the opening
parenthesis before '3'. The error messages reflect this by saying that what
follows '4' is unexpected:

```
syntax error - unexpected newline
syntax error - unexpected token ')'
```

Now try the following expression:

```
True + 4
```

This gives a **type** error, since '+' is applied to a Boolean value, rather than a
number:

```
type error in expression
cannot unify bool with num
```

The message 'cannot unify t_1 with t_2' indicates that something of type t_2 was expected, but something of type t_1 was present instead. Here '+' expects something of type num, but True of type bool is found in its place.

When you get an error message like 'cannot unify t_1 with t_2', you need to look for

- a function or operator expecting an argument of type t_2, applied to
- an expression of type t_1.

Now try to predict the effect of typing the following expressions:

```
4 & True
4 5
7 did 4
```

In the last case a mis-typing of div has turned into a type error. This can often happen, so whenever you get an error you do not understand, first check your typing!

The last kind of error we will see are **program** errors. Try the expression

```
4 div (3*2-6)
```

We cannot divide by zero (what would the result be?) and so we get the message

```
program error: attempt to divide by zero
```

More details about the major error messages produced by the Miranda system can be found in Appendix F.

Writing scripts

One of the first tasks you will be asked to do is write new programs, or in the Miranda terminology, scripts. When you are starting to program (or indeed, when you have more experience too) it is often useful to ask what you can build on. There are three ways you can do this.

First, you can build on what you have already written or seen. Suppose you are asked to write a function

```
allFourEqual :: num -> num -> num -> num -> bool
```

which gives the answer `True` if its four arguments are all equal to each other. We have already written a similar function, `allEqual`, and you could modify that definition to get the new function definition.

Second, you could think of solving a *simpler* problem first. Suppose you are asked to write a function

```
howManyEqual :: num -> num -> num -> num
```

which, when given three numbers, returns how many of them are equal to each other; the answers will be 1, 2 and 3. Instead of solving that problem, ask yourself how you could simplify it? An obvious simplification would be to instead write

```
howManyOfTwoEqual :: num -> num -> num
```

which when given *two* numbers returns how many of them are equal. Once you have solved this, you have a model to work on for defining `howManyEqual`.

Finally, you could *use* a function already defined. You could, if asked to write a function to cube a number, use the function you know for finding the square of a number:

```
cube :: num -> num
cube x = x * square x
```

Testing

Once you have written a function which does not cause any errors as seen above, you need to assure yourself that it has the effect it is supposed to. One way you can find that it does *not* do what it should is to test it with representative test data.

Suppose you have to write a function `allEqual` testing whether three numbers are equal. What would be suitable test data? You need to think about the different kinds of input you could give to a function like this. It splits three ways, to start with:

- all three inputs are equal;
- two of the inputs are equal;
- all three inputs are different.

You should test each of these different kinds of input. You might stop there, or decide that the ordering of the inputs might matter, so you could test the three different numbers in different orders. Again, you might want to check zero and negative numbers separately, or make even more different cases.

If you have the definition of the function `allEqual` in the file eq.m, to test it you need to load the file into Miranda as explained above and then evaluate the test expressions:

```
allEqual 3 3 3
allEqual 3 4 3
allEqual 4 3 5
```

This is one of the cases where Miranda behaving like a calculator makes program development very straightforward.

Whatever the approach you take to testing, you can never test *all* the possible inputs, and errors can slip through quite thorough tests. One way out of this problem is to take a different approach and to *prove* that a function behaves as it ought to on all its inputs. This we address in Chapter 3.

EXERCISES

1.1   Give a definition of the function `allFourEqual` of type

    num -> num -> num -> num -> bool

which gives the result `True` if its four arguments are equal.

1.2   Can you give a definition of `allFourEqual` which *uses* the function `allEqual`?

1.3   Give definitions of the functions

    howManyEqual :: num -> num -> num -> num

and

    howManyOfTwoEqual:: num -> num -> num

which count how many of their arguments are equal.

1.4   Give a definition of a function

    allDifferent :: num -> num -> num -> bool

which gives the value `True` if the three arguments are all different. You might need to use the function '~=' with the property that m ~= n is `True` if m and n are not equal.

1.5   Design test data for the function `allDifferent`.

1.6 What is wrong with the following definition of `allDifferent`?

    allDifferent n m p = ((n ~= m) & (m ~= p))

Does this definition pass your test data?

1.7 Give a definition of `howManyEqual` which *uses* the functions `allEqual` and `allDifferent`.

1.8 Give the definition of a function

    fourPower :: num -> num

which returns its argument to the power four. Give a definition which uses the function `square`.

1.9 Design what you consider to be adequate test data for the function `allEqual`. Consider the function

    tester n m p = ((n+m+p) = 3*p)

Does is behave in exactly the same way as the `allEqual` function does for your test data? What do you think this implies for testing in general?

1.10 Do calculations of the following expressions

    maxi ((2+3)-7) (4+(1-3))
    howManyOfTwoEqual 3 3
    howManyEqual 3 4 3

Your answers should use underlining to show the next expression to be evaluated, and should show tests being calculated.

1.11 Do calculations of the following expressions

    allFourEqual 5 6 4 5
    howManyOfTwoEqual 3 4

Your answers should show tests being calculated.

SUMMARY

This chapter has laid the foundations for the rest of the book. We have seen the fundamental ideas behind functional programming:

- a function is an object which transforms input(s) to an output;
- a script is a collection of definitions;

- a type is a collection of objects of similar sort, such as the numbers, or the calendar months;

- every object has a clearly-defined type, and we state this type on making a definition;

- these definitions are used in writing expressions to be evaluated by the implementation; and

- the values can be found by performing calculations by hand.

We have also seen how definitions are written in Miranda, and how the system is used to perform calculations involving them. Finally, we saw how to test definitions we have written, following the advice on finding definitions also contained in the final section of the chapter.

2 Basic types and simple programs

This chapter explores the basic types of Miranda – numbers, Boolean values, characters, strings and tuples – and straightforward forms of function definition. The basic types are common to almost all programming languages.

2.1   The numbers: Integers

The Miranda type num contains the integers. The integers are the whole numbers, used for counting; they are written thus:

```
0
45
-3452
329423479132545375847584789578787387427487234
```

As can be seen from the last example given, an integer in Miranda can be of unlimited size. Arithmetic over integers in Miranda is accurate, which does not happen when a programming language uses a fixed-size representation for integers, as is usually the case. You can see the problem from doing sums by hand: if you restrict your numbers to those you can write on one page, there will come a point when, for instance, adding two numbers would require more than a page to write the answer down.

We do arithmetic on integers using the following operators and functions:

+	Add two integers
*	Multiply two integers
-	Subtract one integer from another, when infix: a-b; change the sign of an integer, when prefix: -a
div	Whole number division; for example 14 div 3 is 4
mod	The remainder from whole number division; for example 14 mod 3 is 2
abs	The absolute value of an integer; remove the sign

N.B. A common pitfall occurs with negative numbers. For example, the number minus twelve is written as -12, but the prefix '-' can often get confused with the infix operator to subtract one number from another, and can lead to unforeseen and confusing type error messages. If in any doubt, you should enclose negative numbers in parentheses, thus: (-12).

There are ordering and (in)equality relations over the integers, as there are over all basic types. They take two integers as input, and return a bool. The relations are:

>	greater than (and not equal to)
>=	greater than or equal to
=	equal to
~=	not equal to
<=	less than or equal to
<	less than (and not equal to)

In what follows will use the term the **natural numbers** for the non-negative integers: 0, 1, 2, ...

2.2   Programming with integers

We begin to look at programming with integers by looking at some examples. Suppose we are given a function

```
sales :: num -> num
```

which gives the weekly sales from a shop, when weeks are numbered in sequence 0, 1, 2, ... We are asked to find the following data:

- total sales for the period week 0 to week n;
- the maximum weekly sale during weeks 0 to n;
- the week in which the maximum sale took place;
- whether there is a week between week 0 and week n in which no sales took place;
- a week between week 0 and week n in which no sales took place (if there is such a week).

How should we begin? If we were asked, for instance, for the total sales for the period week 0 to week 2, we could simply write

```
sales 0 + sales 1 + sales 2
```

However, we have to give the answer for each possible value of n. In other words, we need to write a *function* whose input is n and whose output is the total sales for the period up to week n. To solve the other problems we will also need to write functions.

If we are asked to write a function, the first thing we should do is to choose a name for it and to write down its type. Here we have

```
totalSales :: num -> num
```

as we take as input a week number n and give as the output the total of the sales during the period up to and including week n. How does the definition look? It can be split into two cases.

- The sales up to week 0 are going to be just sales 0.

- What about the case of week n when n>0? The total will be

$$\underline{sales\ 0\ +\ sales\ 1\ +\ \ldots\ +\ sales\ (n-1)}\ +\ sales\ n$$

where the underlined part is the total sales up to week (n-1). We therefore get the total we seek by adding this underlined value, totalSales (n-1), to the sales in week n.

The definition in Miranda is then going to be

```
totalSales n
  = sales 0                       , if n=0
  = totalSales (n-1) + sales n    , otherwise
```

Suppose that the sales in weeks 0, 1 and 2 are 7, 2 and 5. The definition gives

```
totalSales 2
= totalSales 1 + sales 2
= (totalSales 0 + sales 1) + sales 2
= (sales 0 + sales 1) + sales 2
= (7 + 2) + 5
= 14
```

We can tackle the problem of finding the maximum sales in weeks 0 to n in a similar way. The function will have type

```
maxSales :: num -> num
```

and again we can make two cases in the definition:

- The maximum in the weeks up to week 0 must be sales 0.
- What about the case of week n when n>0? The maximum can occur in two places. It can either be in the weeks up to (and including) week (n-1), or it can be week n itself. The maximum for the weeks up to (n-1) is maxSales (n-1), and this has to be compared to sales n.

The Miranda definition of the function is

```
maxSales n
  = sales 0          , if n=0
  = maxSales (n-1)   , if maxSales (n-1) >= sales n
  = sales n          , otherwise
```

There is, in fact, a neater solution of the problem. In the general case, what we have to do is find the maximum of maxSales (n-1) and sales n. We can therefore use the function maxi defined in the previous chapter, thus:

```
maxSales n
   = sales 0                         , if n=0
   = maxi (maxSales (n-1)) (sales n)  , otherwise
```

Why is this solution preferable?

- The two cases of n being 0 and being greater than 0 are clearer in this solution.

- Finding the maximum of two values is a separate calculation, and so the program should make it a separate function definition. Any problem is made easier to solve if it is split into two problems which can be solved separately. This is sometimes called the 'divide and conquer' principle.

- Because of this separation, the solution is easier to read and understand.

The solutions to the other problems follow a similar pattern, which is a pattern that we shall see repeated throughout this book. To define a function (call it fun) over 0, 1, 2, ... we should:

- Give the value fun 0. This is the **base case** or starting value;

- Give the value fun n using the value of fun at (n-1). This is the **recursive** case.

This form of definition is called **primitive recursion.**

As this explanation makes clear, functions defined this way work over the natural numbers. If we apply totalSales to a negative number, what will happen?

```
totalSales (-2)
   = totalSales (-3) + sales (-2)
   = (totalSales (-4) + sales (-3)) + sales (-2)
   = ...
```

The calculation will carry on forever, or at least until the system has exhausted its available resources! It would be better to check for a negative argument and to return the result 0, say, in that case:

```
totalSales n
  = sales 0                        , if n=0
  = totalSales (n-1) + sales n     , if n>0
  = 0                              , otherwise
```

As can be seen from the calculation above, calculation of these functions works just as we saw in Chapter 1.

To summarize this section, we have now seen three ways of defining functions on numbers:

- In Chapter 1 we saw a direct definition of the square function, by a single equation

  ```
  square x = x*x
  ```

- In the same chapter we saw the definition of maxi which used two clauses in the equation corresponding to two cases in the definition

  ```
  maxi n m = n     , if n>=m
           = m     , otherwise
  ```

- In this chapter we have seen the use of the function at a smaller value, for example totalSales (n-1), in defining the value totalSales n. If we want to use this principle in defining a function, we should ask the question: 'How could I solve the problem for n if I had already solved it for n-1?'

  An example of this is in defining the factorial function, which takes n to the product 1*2*...*(n-1)*n. If we have factorial n-1, 1*2*...*(n-1), we only have to multiply it by n to get factorial n.

EXERCISES

2.1 Add a check for the argument being positive to the maxSales function defined above.

2.2 Define the function to find the week in which maximum sales occur during weeks 0 to n. What does your solution do in the case that the maximum value happens in more than one week? On the basis of the answer to this question, give a more precise description of your function.

2.3 Define the function to find a week in which there are zero sales in weeks 0 to n. Your function should return (n+1) if there is no week in weeks 0 to n with zero sales.

2.4   Define a function which returns the number of weeks during the period week 0 to week n in which there are zero sales.

2.5   Using your answer to Exercise 2.4 as a guide, define a function which when given a number s and a week number n returns the number of weeks during the period week 0 to week n in which there are sales of s.

2.6   How would you use your answer to Exercise 2.5 to solve Exercise 2.4?

2.7   To test the functions which use `sales` use the definition

```
sales n = n mod 2 + (n+1) mod 3
```

Design test data for the functions using this `sales` function. Your answers should explain how the test data have been selected.

2.8   The functions defined so far operate over the period 0 to n. Generalize them so they work over the period week m to week n, where you can assume n is greater than or equal to m. You should first write down the types of the new functions, and then give their definitions.

2.9   The factorial of a positive integer n is the product $1*2*\ldots*(n-1)*n$, and the factorial of 0 is usually defined to be 1. Give a Miranda definition of the factorial function.

2.10 Give a definition of the function of m and n which returns the product $m*(m+1)*\ldots*(n-1)*n$.

2.11 The Fibonacci numbers are the sequence 0, 1, 1, 2, 3, 5, ... whose first two values are 0 and 1, and whose subsequent values are calculated by adding together the previous two values (0+1=1, 1+1=2, 1+2=3, ...).
    Write a definition of a Miranda function `fib` so that `fib n` is the nth number in the sequence.

2.12 Suppose you are given a function

```
stock :: num -> num
```

which gives the flow of stock in and out of a warehouse week-by-week. A positive number is a flow out of the warehouse, a negative a flow in. Write functions which find the total outflow and inflow over the period of weeks 0 to n: the outflow function finds a total of the positive values, and the inflow function a total of the negative values.

2.13   Give a definition of the function

```
power :: num -> num -> num
```

so that power k n is k to the power n. You can assume that n is positive.

2.14   Using the facts that

```
power k (2*n) = square (power k n)
power k (2*n+1) = square (power k n) * k
```

write an alternative definition of the power function.

2.3   Syntax

The syntax of a language describes the properly-formed programs. This section looks at various aspects of the syntax of Miranda, and stresses especially those which might seem unusual or unfamiliar at first sight.

Definitions and layout

A script contains a series of definitions, one after another. How is it clear when one definition ends and another begins? In writing English, the end of a sentence is signalled by a full stop, '.'. In Miranda the **layout** of the program is used to say where one definition ends and the next begins.

In writing an equation, the first characters on the right-hand side open up a box, which will hold the right-hand side of the equation, thus

```
square x = x*x
```

Whatever is typed in the box forms part of the right-hand side ...

```
square x = x*x

       +2
```

... until something is found which is to the left of the line. This closes the box, thus

```
square x = x*x


               +2

cube x = ...
```

This rule for layout is called the **offside rule** because it is reminiscent of the idea of being 'offside' in soccer. The rule also works for equations with more than one clause on the right-hand side.

```
square x = x*x          , if x>0
```

Each clause is ended by an 'offside' character,

```
square x = x*x          , if x>0



         = 0            , otherwise
```

as is the equation itself.

```
square x = x*x          , if x>0



         = 0            , otherwise


cube x = ...
```

The same offside rule applies to guards, which can also extend over a number of lines. When the offside rule is broken, as in the definition

```
funny x

     = x +


     x
```

the system replies with the error message

```
syntax error - unexpected token "OFFSIDE"
```

which can be interpreted as saying that the expression or guard that is being given has ended too soon because part of it, here the second 'x', was offside.

Recommended layout

The offside rule permits various different styles of layout. In this book for definitions of any size we use the form

```
fun v₁ v₂ ... vₙ
   = e₁     , if  g₁
   = e₂     , if  g₂
   ...
   = eᵣ    , otherwise      (or    = eᵣ    , if  gᵣ)
```

with each clause starting on a new line, and the guards lined up. If any of the expressions e_i or guards g_i is particularly long, then the guard can appear on a line (or lines) of its own, like this

```
fun v₁ v₂ ... vₙ
   = very long expression which goes
      over a number of lines
                    , if    a long guard which
                            also goes over many
                            lines
    = e₂         , if    g₂
    ...
```

Names in Miranda

Thus far in the book we have see a variety of uses of names in definitions and expressions. In a definition like

```
pair == (num,num)

addTwo :: pair -> num
addTwo (first,second) = first+second
```

the names or **identifiers** pair, addTwo and first are used to name a type, a function and a variable. Identifiers in Miranda must begin with a letter – small or capital – which is followed by an optional sequence of letters, digits, underscores '_' and single quotes '' '.

There are some restrictions on how identifiers can be chosen. First, there is a small collection of **reserved words** which cannot be used; these are

```
abstype div if mod otherwise readvals show type
where with
```

Secondly, a certain collection of identifiers are predefined, and they cannot be redefined. These are listed in the standard environment, but include such as

```
True False or and abs ...
```

These identifiers can be used as variable names, or in the `where` clauses introduced below; this is to be avoided, since only confusion can result!

The final constraint on the choice of names is that only names of constructors, the only examples of which we have met so far are the Booleans `True` and `False`, can begin with capital letters. All other identifiers must begin with a small letter. An attempt to define a function which begins with a capital letter, such as

```
Fun x = x+1
```

gives the error message 'undeclared constructor "Fun"'.

Operators

The Miranda language contains various operators, like +, # and so on. In principle it is possible to write all applications of an operator with enclosing parentheses, thus

```
(((4+8)*3)+2)
```

but expressions rapidly become difficult to read. Instead, two extra properties of operators allow us to write expressions uncluttered by parentheses.

Associativity

If we wish to add the three numbers 4, 8 and 99 we can write either `4+(8+99)` or `(4+8)+99`. The result is the same whichever we write, a property we call the **associativity** of addition. Because of this, we can write

```
4+8+99
```

for the sum, unambiguously. Not every operator is associative, however; what happens when we write

```
4-2-1
```

for instance? The two different ways of inserting parentheses give

$$(4-2)-1 = 2-1 = 1 \qquad \text{left associative}$$
$$4-(2-1) = 4-1 = 3 \qquad \text{right associative}$$

In Miranda each non-associative operator is classified as either left or right associative. If left associative, any double occurrences of the operator will be bracketed to the left, if right associative, to the right. The choice is arbitrary, but follows custom as much as possible.

Binding powers

The way in which an operator asscociates allows us to resolve expressions like

```
2^3^2
```

where the same operator occurs twice, but what is done when two different operators occur, as in the following expressions?

```
2+3*4
3^4*2
```

For this purpose the 'stickiness' or **binding power** of the operators needs to be compared. * has a higher binding power than +, so that in 2+3*4 the 3 sticks to the 4 rather than the 2, giving

```
2+3*4 = 2+(3*4)
```

In a similar way, ^ binds more tightly than *, so

```
3^4*2 = (3^4)*2
```

A full table of the associativities and binding powers of the Miranda operators is given in Appendix E.

A pitfall – function application

Binding most tightly is function application, which is given by writing the name of the function in front of its argument(s), thus: $f\ v_1\ v_2\ \ldots\ v_n$. This binds more tightly than any other operator, so that f n+1 is interpreted as f n added to 1, rather than f applied to n+1. If in doubt, bracket the arguments to function applications must be the advice here.

Similarly, as '−' is both an infix and a prefix operator, there is scope for confusion. f -12 will be interpreted as 12 subtracted from f, rather than f applied to -12; the solution again is to bracket the argument.

EXERCISES

2.15 Rewrite your solutions to the earlier exercises to use the recommended layout.

2.16 Given the definition

```
funny x = x+
          x
```

explain what happens when you change the name of the function from funny to peculiar. Can this happen if you use the recommended layout?

2.4 Definitions: Patterns

The function definitions we have seen so far have consisted of a single equation, possibly having more then one clause on its right-hand side. On the left of the equation there is

```
fun v₁ v₂ ... vₙ
```

the function name fun applied to the *variables* v_1 to v_n.

Instead of a single equation, we can supply two or more equations. These equations describe how the function behaves when it is applied to *patterns* rather than variables. The simplest patterns are variables and *constants*. As a first example, the definition of totalSales from Section 2.2 can be rewritten as

```
totalSales 0 = sales 0
totalSales n = totalSales (n-1) + sales n
```

The first equation applies to the 0 case; the second equation will apply in all other cases.

This is the general behaviour when a function is defined using more than one equation. In finding the value of the function on a particular input, we use the *first* equation for which the input matches the pattern on the left-hand side.

The argument a matches the pattern p if

- p is a constant and a=p, or
- p is a variable.

Over numbers there is a third form of pattern. Looking at the totalSales example again, it can also be defined by

```
totalSales 0     = sales 0
totalSales (n+1) = totalSales n + sales (n+1)
```

where a number a matches the pattern n+1 if a is an integer greater than or equal to 1. When n+1 matches 5, say, then n will get the value 4, so that

```
totalSales 5 = totalSales 4 + sales 5
```

The function defined this way is not defined for negative integers, so to cover that case, we could add a third equation:

```
totalSales 0     = sales 0
totalSales (n+1) = totalSales n + sales (n+1)
totalSales n     = 0
```

The first equation gives the zero case, the second covers the positive integers, and the final case covers the remaining values, since pattern matches are attempted in sequence from the first equation to the last.

Another example using pattern matching is the sequence of Fibonacci numbers 0, 1, 1, 2, 3, 5, ... whose first two values are 0 and 1, and whose subsequent values are calculated by adding together the previous two values:

```
fib :: num -> num
```

```
fib 0     = 0
fib 1     = 1
fib (n+2) = fib n + fib (n+1)
```

To the definition of pattern matching we add a third clause to explain n+k patterns:

- a matches the pattern n+k, where k is a constant, if a is an integer greater than or equal to k.

EXERCISES

2.17 Give a definition using pattern matching of the maxSales function from Section 2.2.

2.18 The factorial function returns the product of 1 to n for a positive integer n, and has value 1 at 0. Give a definition of the factorial function using pattern matching.

2.5   Programming with Booleans

The Boolean values True and False represent the results of tests, which might, for instance, compare two numbers for equality, or might check whether the first is smaller than the second. The Boolean type in Miranda is called bool.

The Boolean operators provided in the language are

&	and
\/	or
~	not

We can explain the behaviour of the operators by truth tables

t_1	t_2	t_1 & t_2	t_1 \/ t_2	t_1	$\sim t_1$
T	T	T	T	T	F
T	F	F	T	F	T
F	T	F	T		
F	F	F	F		

Booleans can be arguments to or results of functions. We now look at some examples. Exclusive or is the function which returns True if one of its arguments is True and the other False; exclusive or is like the 'or' of a restaurant menu: you may have chicken or fish, but not both! The built-in or is 'inclusive' because it returns True if one or both of its arguments are True.

```
exOr :: bool -> bool -> bool
exOr x y = (x \/ y) & ~ (x & y)
```

We can use the constants True and False as arguments, in defining 'not' for ourselves.

```
myNot :: bool -> bool
myNot True  = False
myNot False = True
```

We can also use a combination of constants and variables to re-define exOr.

```
exOr True  x = ~x
exOr False x = x
```

Section 2.2 has examples which analyse weekly sales from a shop, where the function sales :: num -> num records the sales.

One further question we can ask is whether there are zero sales in a particular week. We make this test in week n by writing (sales n = 0). We can write a function which does this test now:

```
isZeroWeek :: num -> bool
```

```
isZeroWeek n = (sales n = 0)
```

On the right-hand side is the Boolean expression, so that the value for week 0, say, will be (sales 0 = 0).

One of the original tasks in Section 2.2 was to decide

- whether there is a week between week 0 and week n in which no sales took place.

The function to make this decision will have the type

```
zeroInPeriod :: num -> bool
```

so that zeroInPeriod n has the value True if there are zero sales in one of the weeks 0, . . . , n.

Once we know the type of a function, how do we start to write its definition? We can do it in stages

- First design the left-hand side. We decide on what the arguments should be: are they to be variables, or general patterns? If they are patterns, what exactly should they be? To do this we need to think about the cases the definition will divide into.

- Once we have decided the left-hand side, we can fill in the details on the right. In filling in these details we may choose to write or use some other functions.

The `zeroInPeriod` function will have two cases, depending on whether the argument is zero or positive, so the left-hand sides will look like

```
zeroInPeriod 0     =
zeroInPeriod (n+1) =
```

Now to look at the right-hand sides. In the first case, the only week we are looking at is week 0, so we have to check whether sales that week are zero:

```
zeroInPeriod 0     = isZeroWeek 0
```

In the case of (n+1) we can find a zero in either of two places

sales 0	sales 1	$\cdots$	sales n	sales $(n+1)$

$\lhd$ ...... zeroInPeriod n ...... $\rhd$

It can be in the weeks up to n, which is tested by `zeroInPeriod n`, or it can be in week (n+1), tested by `isZeroWeek (n+1)`. This gives the full definition:

```
zeroInPeriod :: num -> bool

zeroInPeriod 0     = isZeroWeek 0
zeroInPeriod (n+1) = zeroInPeriod n \/ isZeroWeek (n+1)
```

A pitfall

Boolean values and expressions can be used in just the same way as numbers. However, it is not hard to write definitions like

```
isZeroWeek n
   = True    , if sales n = 0
   = False   , otherwise
```

where the Boolean expression is placed in a guard.

When the expression `sales n = 0` has the value `True`, the function has value `True`, and when the expression has the value `False`, the function has value `False`. Instead of doing this, we should simply write

```
isZeroWeek n = (sales n = 0)
```

just as we did earlier. In a similar way, we could have defined the zeroInPeriod function thus:

```
zeroInPeriod (n+1)
    = True              , if isZeroWeek (n+1)
    = zeroInPeriod n    , otherwise
```

but it is clearer to use the 'or' operator, '\/', to combine the two. We can read off how the function behaves from the original definition: there is a zero in weeks 0 to (n+1) if there is a zero in weeks 0 to n *or* if week (n+1) is itself zero. This is not so clear from the definition given here.

EXERCISES

2.19 Give a definition of the nAnd function

```
nAnd :: bool -> bool -> bool
```

which gives the result True except when its two arguments are both True.

2.20 Give a definition of the function allZeroPeriod so that allZeroPeriod n tests whether the sales for every week in the period 0 to n are zero.

2.21 Give definitions of functions

```
isAbovePeriod  :: num -> num -> bool
allAbovePeriod :: num -> num -> bool
```

so that isAbovePeriod target n is True if at least one of the sales in weeks 0 to n exceeds the value target. allAbovePeriod checks whether sales exceed the target in all the appropriate weeks.

2.22 Design test data for these functions, using your own definition of the sales function. You can define the function to have the values you choose thus:

```
sales :: num -> num
sales 0 = 345
sales 1 = 32
sales 2 = 0
  ...
```

Explain for each of the functions why you have defined the sales function and chosen the test data in the way you have.

2.23 Using your own definition of sales, give calculations of zeroInPeriod n for two values of n, one leading to the value True and the other to False.

2.24 Define the function

```
numEqualMax :: num -> num -> num -> num
```

so that numEqualMax n m p is the number of n, m and p which are equal to the maximum of the three. For instance,

```
numEqualMax 1 1 1 = 3
```

This is an exercise in defining guards properly; you need to be careful to cover all the cases.

2.25 Give test data for the function numEqualMax, explaining how you made your choices.

2.26 How could you simplify this definition to one with a single clause on the right-hand side?

```
funny x y z
    = True      , if x>z
    = False     , if y>=x
    = True      , otherwise
```

2.6   Characters and strings

People and computers communicate using keyboard input and screen output, which are based on sequences of **characters**; that is, letters, digits and 'special' characters like space, tab, newline and end-of-file. Miranda contains a built-in type of characters, called char.

Individual characters are written inside single quotes, thus: 'd' is the Miranda representative of the character d. Similarly '3' is the character three. Some special characters are represented as follows:

tab	'\t'
newline	'\n'
backslash (\)	'\\'
single quote (')	'\''
double quote (")	'\"'

There is a standard coding for characters as integers, called the ASCII coding. The capital letters 'A' to 'Z' have the sequence of codes from 65 to

90, and the small letters 'a' to 'z' the codes 97 to 122. The character with code 34, for example, is written '\34'. There are also the conversion functions

```
decode :: num -> char
code :: char -> num
```

which convert a number to a character, and vice versa.

The coding functions can be used in defining functions over char. To convert a small letter to a capital an offset needs to be added to its code:

```
offset = code 'A' - code 'a'

capitalize :: char -> char
capitalize ch = decode (code ch + offset)
```

Note that the offset is defined as a constant. This is standard practice, making the program both easier to read and to modify. To change the offset value, we just need to change the definition of offset, rather than having to change the function (or functions) which use it.

Characters can be compared using the ordering on their codes. So, since the digits 0 to 9 occupy codes 48 to 57, we can check whether a character is a digit, thus:

```
isDigit :: char -> bool
isDigit ch = ('0' <= ch) & (ch <= '9')
```

Strings of characters are enclosed in double quotes, thus:

```
"baboon"
""
"\99a\116"
"gorilla\nhippo\nibex"
"1\t23\t456"
```

Try evaluating these strings in Miranda. On screen you will see the strings without the quotes, and with the special characters expanded out, as follows:

```
baboon

cat
gorilla
hippo
ibex
1       23      456
```

Strings can be joined together using ++, so that "cat"++"\n"++"fish" prints

```
cat
fish
```

Strings in Miranda are a special case of the type of lists; they are lists of characters, and the type is written [char]. In Chapter 4 many more operations on lists are given, and all these are available for manipulating strings. In particular, # will give the length of a string.

Miranda allows us to give our own names to types: to give them **synonyms**. We will take string to be a synonym for [char] throughout the book; this is achieved in Miranda by typing

```
string == [char]
```

A pitfall

It is easy to confuse a, 'a' and "a". To summarize the difference,

a	is a name or a variable, if defined it may have any type whatever;
'a'	is a character;
"a"	is a string, which just happens to consist of a single character.

Similarly, there is a difference between

emu	a Miranda name or variable;
"emu"	a string.

EXERCISES

2.27 Define a function to convert small letters to capitals which leaves alone characters which are not small letters.

2.28 Define the function

```
charToNum :: char -> num
```

which converts a digit like '8' to its value, 8. The value of non-digits should be taken to be 0.

2.29 Define a function

```
printDigit :: char -> string
```

which converts a digit to its representation in English, so at 6 it will have the value "Six", for instance.

2.30 Define a function

```
romanDigit :: char -> string
```

which converts a digit to its representation in Roman numerals, so at 7 it will have the value "VII" and so on.

2.31 Define a function

```
onThreeLines :: string -> string -> string -> string
```

which takes three strings and returns a single string which when printed shows the three strings on separate lines.

2.32 Give a function

```
duplicate :: string -> num -> string
```

which takes a string and a natural number, n. The result is the string joined to itself n times. If n is 0, the result should be the empty string, "".

2.33 Using the last answer, or otherwise, give a function

```
makeSpaces :: num -> string
```

so that makeSpaces n is a string of n spaces.

2.34 Using the previous answer, give a function

```
pushRight :: string -> string
```

which takes a string and forms a string of length linelength by putting spaces at the front of the string. If linelength were 12 then pushRight "crocodile" would be "   crocodile".

2.35 Can you criticise the way the last function is specified? Look for a case in which it is not defined what it should do – it is an exceptional case.

2.7   The numbers: Fractions

In Section 2.1 we said that the Miranda type num contains the integers; this is true, but it also contains **fractions**, which are represented internally by fixed-size **floating-point numbers**.

Because of the fixed size of floating-point numbers, not all fractions can be represented by them, and arithmetic over them will not be always be accurate. For this reason, it is best whenever possible to use the integer operations over integers, +, -, *, div, mod as these are completely precise.

Fractions in Miranda can be given by decimal numbers, such as

```
0.31426
-23.12
567.347
4523.0
```

The numbers are called floating point because the position of the decimal point is not fixed: depending upon the particular number, more of the space can be used to store the integer or the fractional part; the decimal point 'floats', in other words.

Miranda also allows numbers in **scientific notation**. These take the form below, where their values are given in the right-hand column of the table:

```
231.61e78        231.61×10⁷⁸
231.6e-2         231.61×10⁻² = 2.3161
-3.412e03        -3.412×10³  = -3412
```

This representation allows larger and smaller numbers than the decimals above. Consider the number 2.1^{444}. This will need well over a hundred digits before the decimal point, and this would not be possible in decimal notation of limited size (usually 20 digits at most). In scientific notation, it will be written as 1.162433e+143.

Miranda provides a range of operators and functions over numbers in the standard environment. Figure 2.1 gives their name, type and a brief description of their behaviour. Included are the following:

- standard mathematical operations: exponential, logarithm and trigonometric functions;

- printing functions: shownum, showfloat and showscaled;

- constants of particular systems: hugenum and tinynum; and

- functions relating integer and fractional numbers: entier, integer.

+ - *	num -> num -> num	Add, subtract, multiply.
/	num -> num -> num	Fractional division.
^	num -> num -> num	Exponentiation $x{\char`\^}y = x^y$.
abs	num -> num	Absolute value.
arctan	num -> num	The inverse of tangent.
cos	num -> num	Cosine.
e	num	The base of natural logarithms, 2.718....
entier	num -> num	Converts a fraction to an integer by rounding down.
exp	num -> num	Powers of e.
hugenum	num	The largest number representable as a num.
integer	num -> bool	Tests whether a num is an integer.
log	num -> num	Logarithm to base e.
log10	num -> num	Logarithm to base 10.
neg	num -> num	Change the sign of a number.
numval	string -> num	Converts a string representing a num to its value.
pi	num	The constant pi.
shownum	num -> string	Convert a number to a string.
showfloat	num -> num -> string	Convert a number to a string. The first argument gives the number of decimal places.
showscaled	num -> num -> string	Convert a number to a string, in scientific format. The first argument gives the number of decimal places.
sin	num -> num	Sine.
sqrt	num -> num	(Positive) square root.
subtract	num -> num -> num	Subtraction as a function.
tinynum	num	The smallest positive number representable as a num.

Figure 2.1   Numeric operations and functions.

integer is a test which is True for integer arguments, and entier converts a fraction to an integer; the function rounds down, so that

```
entier 4.3    = 4
entier (-4.3) = -5
```

For any a and non-zero b, entier obeys the law

```
entier (a/b) = a div b
```

When a function is applied to an integer, the integer will be converted to a fraction if necessary before applying the function. This happens, for instance, in 4 + 5.6, which has the result 9.6. Fractions are only converted to integers *explicitly* using the function `entier`.

EXERCISES

2.36 Miranda can be used as a numerical calculator. Try typing the expressions which follow to the Miranda prompt:

```
sin (pi/4) * sqrt 2
exp 7 + log10 100
```

2.37 Give a function

```
averageSales :: num -> num
```

so that `averageSales n` is the average of the values `sales 0` to `sales n`.

2.38 Define a function

```
salesExceed :: num -> num -> num
```

so that `salesExceed val n` gives the number of weeks in the period 0 to n in which sales exceed `val`.

2.39 Define a function

```
aboveAverageSales :: num -> num
```

which returns the number of weeks 0 to n in which sales exceed the average for that period. Do you see how you can use the answers to the two preceding questions?

2.8 Programming with numbers and strings

This section covers a longer example, that of giving sales information in a readable form, using the functions `totalSales`, `averageSales` and so on. The sales are to be printed in a table, with summary information (total and average sales) appearing below.

Suppose that the sales for weeks 0, 1 and 2 are 12, 14 and 15; the output from printTable 2 should look like

```
        Week      Sales
         0         12
         1         14
         2         15

        Total      41
       Average     13.67
```

Top-down

We begin by working through the solution *top-down*; that is, by defining the auxiliary functions we need as we go along. At the top level, we have to define

```
printTable :: num -> string
```

which outputs the whole table. The table itself has four parts: the heading, the week-by-week values, the total and the average. The solution also has these parts, which are joined together by ++:

```
printTable n
   = heading ++ printWeeks n
       ++ printTotal n ++ printAverage n
```

The heading has an immediate definition

```
heading :: string
heading = "       Week        Sales\n"
```

To print the values for the weeks 0 to n we have to print the line for each week. We therefore need to define a function

```
printWeek :: num -> string
```

which is used in defining printWeeks using recursion much as we have done before.

```
printWeeks :: num -> string

printWeeks 0     = printWeek 0
printWeeks (n+1) = printWeeks n ++ printWeek (n+1)
```

The top-down approach has now reduced the problem to one of defining the functions printWeek, printTotal and printAverage.

Bottom-up

Now we look to building the functions printWeek and printAverage from their parts. In doing this we use some of the Miranda built-in functions. To print numbers we use

```
shownum    :: num -> string
showfloat :: num -> num -> string
```

shownum converts a number to a string, whilst showfloat's first argument allows us to specify the number of decimal places used in displaying the other argument.

We also use some Miranda functions designed to help with position-ing text; these will help us to put the numbers into columns. The functions are

```
ljustify :: num -> string -> string
cjustify :: num -> string -> string
rjustify :: num -> string -> string
```

Typical examples follow:

```
ljustify 12 "elephant" = "elephant    "
cjustify 12 "elephant" = "  elephant  "
rjustify 12 "elephant" = "    elephant"
```

The functions are designed to pad out text into the length given. The spaces can be added to justify the text to the left, centre or right, hence the first letters of the names. If the text is longer than the given length, the functions return it unchanged; it is *not* cut to fit the space.

Now we can write the function to print a week's values:

```
printWeek n
  = rjustify offset (shownum n) ++
    rjustify offset (shownum (sales n)) ++ "\n"
```

where

```
offset :: num
offset = 10
```

In the definition, we twice use `shownum` followed by `rjustify`. A clearer solution makes this into a function, and *uses* the function twice:

```
rPrintNum :: num -> string
rPrintNum n = rjustify offset (shownum n)

printWeek n
  = rPrintNum n ++ rPrintNum (sales n) ++ "\n"
```

The final task is to define the last lines of the table. The weeks have the numbers printed in columns of width ten; to align the integer part of the average with the sales figures, we define

```
printAverage :: num -> string

printAverage n
= "\n     Average " ++
  rjustify offset (showfloat 2 (averageSales n))
```

where again we can make the definition clearer by defining an auxiliary function `rPrintFloat` which prints a floating-point number with a given width. This gives the definition

```
printAverage n
= "\n     Average " ++ rPrintFloat (averageSales n)
```

The system is complete once `rPrintFloat` and `printTotal` are defined. We leave these, which are variants on what we have already done here, as exercises.

The full solution can be seen in Figure 2.2. The development of the solution here is typical of many. A top-down solution takes us from the original problem `printTable` to smaller problems like `printWeeks` and `printAverage`. These in turn can either be solved directly, like `heading`, or give rise to other problems, like `printWeek`. Once we get closer to a solution, it is worth asking ourselves how we can use what we already have in pre-defined functions to build a solution bottom-up. Here we used the built-in facilities for printing numbers and positioning strings.

Another important step in the strategy was to recognize parts of the solution which could be themselves described by functions, making the solution easier to read and understand, as well as making it easier to modify, if this were needed. In this solution, we made printing a number in a space of ten characters a separate function, `rPrintNum`, after seeing it used twice in defining `printWeek`.

```
printTable :: num -> string
printTable n
  = heading ++ printWeeks n
    ++ printTotal n ++ printAverage n

heading :: string
heading = "         Week       Sales\n"

printWeeks :: num -> string
printWeeks 0     = printWeek 0
printWeeks (n+1) = printWeeks n ++ printWeek (n+1)

printWeek :: num -> string
printWeek n
  = rPrintNum n ++ rPrintNum (sales n) ++ "\n"

offset :: num
offset = 10

rPrintNum :: num -> string
rPrintNum n = rjustify offset (shownum n)

printAverage :: num -> string
printAverage n
  = "\n    Average " ++ rPrintFloat (averageSales n)

rPrintFloat :: num -> string
printTotal  :: num -> string
```

Figure 2.2   Printing sales information.

EXERCISES

2.40   Define the functions rPrintFloat and printTotal specified in the example.

2.41   Explain how you would define the functions ljustify etc. yourself, using the ideas introduced in the exercises of Section 2.6.

2.42   Show how to modify the table so that

- the number of weeks of zero sales is listed;

- the number of weeks of above-average sales is listed;
- [*harder*] each week with above-average sales has its entry marked by a star.

2.43   Give a definition of a function

```
factorialTable :: num -> num -> string
```

so that `factorialTable` m n tabulates the values of factorial from m to n inclusive. You should make sure that your answer outputs something sensible if either of m or n is not a natural number, or if m is larger than n.

2.9   Data structures: Tuples

In writing programs, we model items in the real world by values of particular types. We can represent a temperature by a number, a telephone number by a string (why not a number?), a person's name by a string, and so forth. The types we have seen so far just contain single values, while real-world objects can be complex. Many real-world objects can be modelled by a collection of data items; for instance, a person in a mailing list may be specified by their name, telephone number and age.

Miranda provides composite types, called *tuples*,[†] which are built up from components of simpler types. The type

```
(t₁, t₂, ..., tₙ)
```

consists of values

```
(v₁, v₂, ..., vₙ)
```

in which $v_1 :: t_1, \ldots, v_n :: t_n$. In other words, each component v_i of the tuple has to have the type t_i given in the corresponding position in the type.

We can model our type of people in the mailing list by

```
(string, string, num)
```

whose members include

[†] The reason for the name is that these objects are usually called pairs, triples, quadruples, quintuples, sextuples and so on. The general word for them is therefore 'tuple'. In other programming languages, these types are called records or structures; see Appendix A for a more detailed comparison.

```
("Joe Grundy","0000-000000",73)
```

To record that we want to think of this type as representing people, we can give the following **type synonym** in Miranda:

```
person == (string,string,num)
```

Definitions like this are treated as shorthand in Miranda – wherever a name like person is used, it has exactly the same effect as if (string,string,num) had been written.

Other examples include

```
mary :: person
mary =  ("Mary Poppins","0800-000-000",68)

nump :: (num,num)
nump =  (34,32)
```

As part of the development of programs, we often have to choose types to represent objects we have to model. Tuples are often used to group data together; some representative examples follow:

- A function to return both the minimum and maximum of three numbers can return a pair, and therefore have the type

  ```
  minNmax :: num -> num -> num -> (num,num)
  ```

- A person's name can be represented in many ways. In the example above we used a single string, but it could also be represented by a pair, (string,string), of first and last names.

- When returning a week in which sales are zero, there is a possibility that there may be no such week. One way of dealing with this is for the function to return a (num,bool) pair. If the Boolean part is False, this signals that no zero week was found; if it is like (4,True), it signals that week 4 was such a week.

Functions over tuples are defined by pattern matching. Instead of writing a variable for an argument of type (num,num), say, a **pattern**, (x,y) is used:

```
addPair :: (num,num) -> num
addPair (x,y) = x+y
```

On application the components of the pattern are matched with the corresponding components of the argument, so that

```
addPair nump
  = addPair (34,32)
  = 34 + 32
  = 66
```

Patterns can contain constants, and nested patterns:

```
shift :: ((num,num),num) -> (num,(num,num))
shift ((a,b),c) = (a,(b,c))
```

The functions which pick out particular parts of a tuple are defined by pattern matching. For the person type, the definitions might be

```
name  :: person -> string
phone :: person -> string
age   :: person -> num


name  (n,p,a) = n
phone (n,p,a) = p
age   (n,p,a) = a
```

name mary is "Mary Poppins", for instance. Miranda has these functions on pairs built in. They are

```
fst (x,y) = x
snd (x,y) = y
```

Each element of a given type of tuples will contain the same number and type of components: two strings and a num in the case of person, for example. Types of lists, which are discussed later, contain lists with differing numbers of elements, all of which must have the same type.

A pitfall

It is important to distinguish between the functions

```
addPair :: (num,num) -> num
addPair (a,b) = a+b


addTwo :: num -> num -> num
addTwo a b = a+b
```

addPair has a single argument which is a pair of numbers, and returns the sum of the two parts. addTwo has two arguments, each of which is a number, and returns their sum. We shall see later that the second function can be used in a more flexible way than the first; for the moment it is important to realize that there is a difference, and that type errors will result if we confuse the two thus:

```
addPair 3 4
addTwo (2,3)
```

EXERCISES

2.44 Define the function minNmax which returns both the minimum and maximum of three numbers.

2.45 Give a definition of a function

```
maxOccurs :: num -> num -> (num,num)
```

which returns the maximum of two numbers, together with the number of times it occurs. Using this, or otherwise, define a function

```
maxThreeOccurs :: num -> num -> num -> (num,num)
```

which does a similar thing for three arguments.

2.46 Give a definition of a function

```
orderTriple :: (num,num,num) -> (num,num,num)
```

which puts the elements of a triple of three numbers into ascending order. You might like to solve the simpler problem for pairs first.

2.47 Redefine the function which finds a week of zero sales value, so that it has type

```
num -> (num,bool)
```

and behaves as described above.

2.48 Design test data for the preceding exercises; explain the choices you have made in each case. Give a sample evaluation of each of your functions.

2.10 Function definitions

The definitions of functions we have seen so far consist of a number of equations, each of which can have multiple clauses on the right-hand side. In this section we see how local definitions can be attached to each equation. To recap, the definitions resemble:

```
f p₁ p₂ ... p_k
  = e₁ , if g₁
  = e₂ , if g₂
  ...
  = e_r , otherwise    (or   = e_r, if g_r)

f q₁ q₂ ... q_k
  = f₁ , if h₁
  ...
  = f₁ , if h₁


  ...
```

Here p_1, q_1, ... are patterns; g_1, h_1, ... are Boolean expressions called guards and e_1, f_1, ... are the expressions which give the results of the function in the different cases.

An example is given by the function which gives the highest common factor (hcf) of two natural numbers:

```
hcf :: num -> num -> num
hcf n 0 = n
hcf n m = hcf m n            , if m > n
        = hcf (n-m) m        , otherwise
```

Local definitions

There is one more feature of definitions which we introduce now. Each equation can be followed by a list of definitions which are **local** to the function or other object being defined. These definitions are written after the keyword where. A simple example is given by a function which is to return the sum of squares of two numbers:

```
sumSquares :: num -> num -> num
```

The result of the function will be the sum of two values, sqN and sqM, so that

```
sumSquares n m
  = sqN + sqM
```

The calculation of these two values is done in the `where` clause which follows the equation, thus:

```
sumSquares n m
  = sqN + sqM
    where
    sqN = n*n
    sqM = m*m
```

In such a simple example, it is perhaps hard to see the point of making the local definitions, but if a more complicated function of the two numbers is required, the definition is made much clearer. An example of this is the function `printAverage`, developed in Section 2.8:

```
printAverage :: num -> string

printAverage n
= text ++ averageVal
  where
  text       = "\n      Average "
  averageVal = rPrintFloat (averageSales n)
```

At the top level we see that two strings are joined together; we can then look at each of the two separately. The definition also reflects how it might have been written: first we decide that we print a piece of text saying that the average is being written, then we give the value of the average.

In each case, the layout of the definition is important. For the system to determine the end of each part of a definition, the offside rule is used. The `where` clause must be found in the right-hand side to which it belongs; to that effect it must appear within the offside block associated with the final clause on the right-hand side. In the recommended layout, we suggest writing:

```
f p₁ p₂ ... pₖ
  = e₁ , if g₁
  ...
  = eᵣ , otherwise
    where
    v₁  a₁ ... aₙ = r₁
    v₂ = r₂
    ....
```

This example also shows that the local definitions can include functions – here v_1 is an example of a local function definition. We have given type declarations for all top-level definitions; unfortunately, it is not possible to give type declarations for where-defined objects in Miranda. In cases where the type is not obvious, a declaration should be given in a comment.

If a where clause lies offside, as in

```
fun x = 3.7 + pie
        where
          pie = 22/7
```

we will get the error message

```
syntax error - unexpected token "where"
```

The where has closed the right-hand side of the definition because it lies to the left of the 3.7, and so the where is not attached to the definition of fun as it should be.

Scopes

A Miranda script consists of a sequence of definitions. The **scope** of a definition is that part of the program in which the definition can be used. All definitions at the top-level in Miranda have the whole script they are defined in as their scope: that is, they can be used in all the definitions the script contains. In particular, they can be used in definitions which occur before theirs in the script, as in

```
isOdd, isEven :: num -> bool

isOdd 0     = False
isOdd (n+1) = isEven n

isEven 0     = True
isEven (n+1) = isOdd n
```

Local definitions, given by where clauses, are not intended to be 'visible' in the whole of the script, but rather just in the equation in which they appear. The same is true of the variables in a function definition, their scope is the whole of the right-hand side of the equation in which they appear. Specifically, in the example which follows, the scope of the definitions of sqx, sqy and sq and of the variables x and y is given by the large box; the smaller box gives the scope of the variable z:

```
maxsq x y

  =  sqx      , if sqx > sqy
  =  sqy      , otherwise
     where
     sqx  =  sq x
     sqy  =  sq y

     sq z =   z*z
```

In particular it is important to see that

- x and y can be used in the local definitions; here they are used in sqx and sqy;
- local definitions can be used before they are defined: sq is used in sqx here;
- local definitions can be used in the results and in guards as well as in other local definitions.

It is possible for a script to have two definitions or variables with the same name. In the example, the variable x appears twice. Which definition is in force at each point? The *most local* is the one which is used.

```
maxsq x y

  =  sq x     , if sq x > sq y
  =  sq y     , otherwise
     where

     sq x =   x*x
```

In the example, we can think of the inner box *cutting a hole* in the outer, so that the scope of the outer x will exclude the right-hand side of the definition of sq. When one definition is contained inside another, the best advice is that different variables and names should be used for the inner definitions unless there is a very good reason for using the same name twice.

2.11 Programming with local definitions

We explore in this section how local definitions in where clauses are used in programming, and how calculations are extended to handle local definitions.

Program development

Here we give a sample program which uses where clauses during its development. The problem is to define

```
maxThreeOccurs :: num -> num -> num -> (num,num)
```

which returns the maximum of three numbers paired with the number of times it occurs amongst the three.

A natural solution first finds the maximum, and then investigates how often it occurs among the three:

```
maxThreeOccurs n m p
  = (max,eqCount)
    where
    max     = maxiThree n m p
    eqCount = equalCount max n m p
```

Note that max is used twice: in the final answer (max,eqCount) and in the call of the function equalCount. Working top down, we have used the function equalCount which counts how many of its final three arguments are equal to the first.

Now we have to define equalCount. We want to 'score' one for each of n, m and p equal to the number sought. We could say

```
equalCount val n m p
  = isN + isM + isP
    where
    isN = 1 , if n=val
        = 0 , otherwise
    isM = 1 , if m=val
        = 0 , otherwise
    isP = 1 , if p=val
        = 0 , otherwise
```

This seems repetitive: we compare each value with the value val; we can make this comparison into a function, and then call the function three times:

```
equalCount val n m p
  = isVal n  + isVal m + isVal p
    where
    isVal x = 1 , if x=val
            = 0 , otherwise
```

Observe that the function isVal uses the value val in its definition.

Calculation

Calculations can be extended to deal with where clauses. The sumSquares function in the previous section gives, for example

```
sumSquares 4 3
= sqN + sqM
  where
  sqN = 4*4 = 16
  sqM = 3*3 = 9
= 16 + 9
= 25
```

The values of the local definitions are calculated beneath the where if their values are needed. All local evaluation is indented below the where. To follow the top-level value, we just have to look at the calculation at the left-hand side.

A longer example is given by Figure 2.3, which shows the calculation of maxThreeOccurs 2 1 2, where we assume that maxiThree is given by

```
maxiThree a b c = maxi (maxi a b) c
```

```
                maxThreeOccurs 2 1 2
            = (max,eqCount)
              where
              max = maxiThree 2 1 2
                  = maxi (maxi 2 1) 2
                    ?? 2>=1 = True
                  = maxi 2 2
                    ?? 2>=2 = True
                  = 2
            = (2,eqCount)
              where
              eqCount = equalCount 2 2 1 2
                      = isVal 2 + isVal 1 + isVal 2
                        where
                        isVal x = 1  , if x=2
                                = 0  , otherwise
                        ?? 2=2 = True
                      = 1 + isVal 1 + isVal 2
                        ...
                      = 1 + 0 + 1
                      = 2
            = (2,2)
```

Figure 2.3 Calculation of maxThreeOccurs 2 1 2.

In the calculation of Figure 2.3, we also explicitly calculate the values of guards, using '??' to signal that a guard is being calculated. We also omit some steps of the calculation, signalled by '...'.

The vertical lines which appear are used to link the successive steps of the calculations when these have intermediate where calculations. The lines can be omitted.

EXERCISES

2.49   Compare the definition of maxThreeOccurs used here with your earlier solution, which does not use where clauses.

2.50   Calculate the values of maxThreeOccurs 1 2 1 and equalCount 4 2 1 3.

2.51   Define the function

```
cjustify :: num -> string -> string
```

so that cjustify n st gives a string of length n by adding spaces to both ends of st to centre it in the answer. You should think about what to do when the length of st is greater than n; and also about what to do when n is not a positive integer.

2.52   Define a function

```
stars :: num -> string
```

so that, for example, stars 3 is "***". How do you deal with non-natural numbers?

2.53   Give a table of the sales function, so that if sales in weeks 0, 1 and 2 are 7, 5 and 9, the table will be

```
0    *******
1    *****
2    *********
```

2.54   Look at some of the exercises from earlier sections, and your solutions to them. How can they be made easier to read and understand by using where clauses?

2.12 Example: Quadratic equations

This section concludes the chapter with an example drawing on many of the features introduced so far: numbers, strings, local definitions, pattern matching and guards.

It explores how a larger program is built from smaller components, and how problems can be broken down into separate sections.

The problem

A quadratic equation, like

$$a*X^2 + b*X + c = 0$$

generally has

- two real roots, if $b^2 > 4*a*c$;
- one root, if $b^2 = 4*a*c$, and
- no roots, if $b^2 < 4*a*c$.

This assumes that a is non-zero – the case which we call **non-degenerate**. In the degenerate case, there are three sub-cases:

- one root, if b ~= 0;
- no roots, if b = 0 and c ~= 0;
- every number a root, if b = 0 and c = 0.

Suppose for the moment that we only have to look at non-degenerate cases. We seek a program which when given the coefficients 1, 5 and 6 will print

```
The quadratic equation

    1*X^2 + 5*X + 6 = 0

has two roots: -2.0 -3.0
```

The formula for the roots is

$$\frac{-b \pm \sqrt{b^2 - 4ac}}{2a}$$

The solution

The solution splits naturally into two parts: finding the roots (if any) and printing the outcome. The roots are given by

```
oneRoot :: num -> num -> num -> num
oneRoot a b c = -b/(2*a)
```

and

```
twoRoots :: num -> num -> num -> (num,num)

twoRoots a b c
  = (d-e,d+e)
    where
    d = -b/(2*a)
    e = sqrt(b^2-4*a*c)/(2*a)
```

Note the choice of types: the twoRoots function returns a pair of values, while the oneRoot function returns a single value.

The output consists of two parts; there is a header common to the three cases, whilst the values printed differ in those three. We therefore make two separate definitions:

```
quadAnalyse :: num -> num -> num -> string

quadAnalyse a b c
  = header a b c ++ roots a b c
```

The header of the output is given by

```
header :: num -> num -> num -> string

header a b c
  = "The quadratic equation\n\n\t" ++
    shownum a ++ "*X^2 + " ++
    shownum b ++ "*X + " ++
    shownum c ++ " = 0" ++ "\n\nhas "
```

whilst the roots are printed by

```
roots :: num -> num -> num -> string

roots a b c
  = "two roots: " ++ shownum f ++ " " ++ shownum s
                   , if b^2 > 4*a*c
```

```
    = "one root: " ++ shownum (oneRoot a b c)
                    , if b^2 = 4*a*c
    = "no roots"   , otherwise
      where
      (f,s) = twoRoots a b c
```

One new feature is introduced here. The function twoRoots returns a pair when applied to a, b and c. We want to print the two halves of the pair. One way to obtain them is to use fst and snd, but we can also use the **conformal pattern match** of (f, s) to the result of the function. This makes f be the first half of that value, and s the second. The pattern match is called conformal, as for the definition to be effective, the value on the right needs to conform to the pattern on the left.

Error handling

In writing a function like oneRoot, an assumption is made that it is not to be called with a equal to 0. If oneRoot is called with a equal to 0, the system will give a run-time error, that there has been an attempt to divide by zero.

It is possible to add to the definition a dummy value in that case – often the choice is 0 – or to make the function return an explicit error message and halt evaluation. This is done using the function error thus:

```
oneRoot a b c
  = -b/(2*a)                        , if a ~= 0
  = error "oneRoot called with a=0"  , otherwise
```

If the otherwise case is reached, evaluation of the expression stops and the error message given, "oneRoot called with a=0" is printed. This gives a guide to where the problem has occurred.

EXERCISES

2.55 By modifying the function roots, add the three degenerate cases to the analysis.

2.56 An alternative, better structured, way of adding the degenerate cases is to define a separate function

```
degen :: num -> num -> num -> string
```

which plays the same role as the roots function. A case analysis can be added to the top-level function quadAnalyse to decide which of the functions roots, degen is to be used.

2.57 Extend the definition of twoRoots so that it returns an error message if it is called in either the 'one root' or the 'no roots' cases.

2.58 In the case that (b^2-4*a*c) is negative, it is possible to say that there are two *complex* roots. Modify the functions so the complex roots are returned in this situation, rather than the 'no roots' message.

2.13 Design

Defining a function requires us to think about the particular combination of these features which will best fit what we wish to do. The points which follow offer some guidance on function design.

- In solving a problem it can help to look at similar problems, or simpler problems. A solution to a similar problem might be adapted; a solution to a simpler problem might be generalized to give a solution or be used as a part of the larger solution.

- In looking at a problem area, we need to decide the types to represent the data of the area. For instance, we might decide to represent telephone numbers as strings.

- The first decision to make about a particular definition is the *type* of the object being defined; without being sure about this, it is not possible to make any further progress. A function which takes arguments of type $t_1, \ldots, t_n$ and gives a result of type t has type t_1 -> t_2 -> ... -> t_n -> t.

- Many problems are solved by breaking the problem into a number of parts, with each part having a simpler, separate, solution. This happened in the example of analysing quadratic equations, where finding the solutions and displaying them were identified as separate activities.

- Many other problems are amenable to solutions which are recursive: the solution to a 'smaller' case is used in solving the problem in the 'larger' case. For instance, the total sales for weeks 0 to (n+1) are the sum of the total sales for weeks 0 to n and the sales for week (n+1).

- Once the breakdown of the problem is decided, we can see the cases into which the problem breaks. This helps to design the patterns on the left-hand side of the equations, which we can do before looking at the right-hand side.

- In designing the right-hand sides, there are decisions to make about using `where` clauses. These can help in developing the solution; if we need two strings in the solution we can say

    ```
    ... = front ++ back
    ```

    and then decide the values of `front` and `back` separately. This is another case where breaking the problem down into smaller parts makes it easier to see where the solution is going. The use of `where` clauses also makes it easier to read and modify the final solution.

- If we use a particular sort of expression more than once, it is a candidate for a function definition. We saw this with the script to give a formatted table of sales figures, when we made a definition of a function to print a number at the right-hand end of a block of space.

- A final, slightly different, approach is to work bottom-up. If we know that we have to solve problems to do with a particular area, like lines in geometry or supermarket bills, we might begin by building a *library* of useful functions which handle, for instance, line intersections or pricing items according to bar codes.

A Miranda script is intended to look like a sequence of equations which define functions and other items. The syntax of the language is designed to be straightforward, but there are some traps for the beginner:

- The layout of the equations is significant; we give a recommended layout which makes it easy to read definitions, and to modify them without introducing syntax errors.

- There is a distinction between names beginning with small letters: `name1` etc., and those beginning with capitals: `Name1`. The former are used for defined functions, the latter for another purpose which we come to below.

- The precedence of operators: `*` binding more tightly than `+`, and function application binding most tightly, can cause problems. If in doubt, brackets should be put into expressions to make their purpose clear. In particular, negative numbers like `(-12)` should be bracketed when they are arguments to functions.

- There is a distinction between the name `a`, the character `'a'` and the string `"a"`. Confusing these can give errors stating that a name is undefined, or type errors.

EXERCISES

The sequence of exercises which follows leads up to a solution of the problem of whether two lines on a flat surface intersect. An application of this is in the layout of printed circuit boards, or canals, when lines which do not intersect need to be drawn.

A point is given by two coordinates, and a line by the two points at its ends. We can therefore define

```
point == (num,num)
line  == (point,point)
```

A line could be represented in two different ways, depending upon the order in which the two points specifying it are given. A line $((x_1, y_1), (x_2, y_2))$ is called **sensible** if $x_1 <= x_2$.

2.59   Define functions which return the x (first) and y (second) coordinates of a point.

2.60   Define a function which decides whether a line is vertical.

2.61   If a line is $((x_1, y_1), (x_2, y_2))$, its equation is given by

$$\frac{y - y_1}{x - x_1} = \frac{y_2 - y_1}{x_2 - x_1}$$

Define a function

```
yValue :: num -> line -> num
```

which when given an x-coordinate and a line gives the corresponding y-value on the line. You may assume that the line is not vertical, or include a test for this if you wish: why is this necessary?

2.62   Define a function which makes any line into a sensible one by swapping the end points if necessary.

2.63   If the two sensible lines $((x_1, y_1), (x_2, y_2))$ and $((x_3, y_3), (x_4, y_4))$ are known to be either horizontal or vertical, the following test is sufficient to see whether they intersect:

```
(x₁ <= x₃ <= x₂ &
    y₃ <= y₁ <= y₄) \/
(x₃ <= x₁ <= x₄ &
    y₁ <= y₃ <= y₂)
```

Implement this. Give an example to show that the test does not work when the (sensible) lines can be sloping.

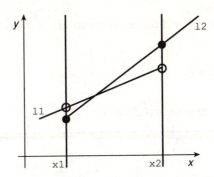

Figure 2.4   Checking line intersections.

2.64   To test for arbitrary lines intersecting, we first check that there is some overlap in their x values; in Figure 2.4 it is the range from x1 to x2. Write a function which checks to see whether for two sensible lines there is such an overlap.

2.65   If there is an overlap, then we can check whether the lines intersect as illustrated in Figure 2.4. The lines intersect if over their common x-values they cross. In the figure, l1 is above l2 at x1, below it at x2. Write a function which checks for intersection in this way. Your definition should be able to deal with the case of either of the lines being vertical.

2.66   Design test data for your function. There are a number of cases to be checked, depending upon whether one or both of the lines are vertical, whether the lines do or do not cross in their overlap and whether they indeed have an overlap. You should also examine extreme cases: where intersection is at one of the ends of the overlap, and where the lines intersect at more than one point.

    Explain the cases that your particular data are intended to test, and how you have covered all possible cases.

SUMMARY

This chapter has covered the basic types in Miranda: numbers – the integers, which are fully precise, and the fractions, represented by floating-point numbers – Booleans, characters, strings and tuples. Together with each type, we gave the operations and pre-defined functions from the standard environment. Information about the operations is found in Appendix E, and the standard environment is discussed in Section 28 of the on-line Miranda manual as well as in Appendix G of this text.

We have also covered the main forms of function definition using

- pattern matching;
- guards;
- local definitions – where clauses.

3 Reasoning about programs

This short chapter introduces the important idea that we can write down logical arguments about functional programs. These **proofs** of program properties have the advantage that they can argue about the behaviour of a program over *all* its inputs, rather than testing which can only look at behaviour on a finite set of inputs, which it is hoped are representative of its behaviour as a whole.

   After introducing **mathematical induction**, the most powerful method for proving properties of functions over the natural numbers, we apply it in a series of examples, and give advice about how to build proofs of program properties.

3.1 Informal proof: An introduction

In this section we look at two straightforward methods of proof used to infer properties of functional programs, before looking at the more powerful method of induction in the next section.

Direct proofs

As a first example, suppose we define the function

```
swap :: (num,num) -> (num,num)
swap (a,b) = (b,a)
```

The program takes a pair of numbers, and swaps them about. As well as being a program, we can read this as an equation which *describes* the behaviour of the function. The equation says that *for all possible values* of a and b, swap (a,b) is equal to (b,a). Using the equation, we can *prove* that the function has various properties. It is not hard to see that swapping twice should have the same effect as making no change; we could see evidence for this from testing, but we can prove it directly from the equation, working just as we do in calculation:

```
swap (swap (a,b))
  = swap (b,a)
  = (a,b)
```

for all a and b. In a similar way, if we define cycle and recycle thus:

```
cycle, recycle :: (num,num,num) -> (num,num,num)
cycle (a,b,c) = (b,c,a)
recycle (a,b,c) = (c,a,b)
```

then we can show that, for all a, b and c,

```
cycle (recycle (a,b,c)) = (a,b,c)
recycle (cycle (a,b,c)) = (a,b,c)
```

As can be seen from the examples here, the properties we prove often summarize part of the behaviour of a function. In the case of swap, we choose to show that it is reversed by applying the function a second time, while in the latter examples we show that cycle reverses recycle, and vice versa.

Proof by cases

In Chapter 1 we saw the definition

```
maxi :: num -> num -> num
maxi n m
  = n     , if n>=m
  = m     , otherwise
```

This is a program to give the maximum of two numbers; it is an equation which says that the value of maxi n m is either n or m, whichever is larger.

We can *deduce* from this equation the important properties of maxi. These are that, for any defined[†] numbers n and m

```
maxi n m ⩾ n
maxi n m ⩾ m
maxi n m = n or maxi n m = m
```

How do we deduce these properties? We know that $m > n$ **or** $n \geqslant m$ for all defined n and m. There are therefore two cases.

- If $n \geqslant m$ holds then from the definition, maxi n m = n and so we get maxi n m ⩾ n.

- If, on the other hand, $m > n$ holds, then maxi n m = m > n and so maxi n m ⩾ n.

Since maxi n m ⩾ n holds in both the possible cases, it will be true in general. Similar arguments prove the other two properties.

It is interesting to see that the proof has a similar structure to the function definition: both use cases depending upon the relative size of m and n. We can also see a relation to testing: instead of picking a typical representative of the two cases, we use the *variables* n and m and look at the two cases that can apply to those variables.

We can use the properties of maxi in proving things about the functions which use maxi. We have, in a variant of the function from Section 2.2,

```
maxSales 0     = sales 0
maxSales (r+1) = maxi (maxSales r) (sales (r+1))
```

[†] We restrict to the *defined* numbers to avoid expressions like the example of totalSales (-2) given in Section 2.2 whose evaluation does not terminate, and so is not defined.

Using maxi n m $\geqslant$ n, which holds for all possible values[†] of n and m, we get

```
maxSales (r+1)
  = maxi (maxSales r) (sales (r+1))
  ≥ maxSales r
```

The inequality follows from maxi n m $\geqslant$ n by replacing n by maxSales r and m by sales (r+1).

For s $\geqslant$ r we can then deduce maxSales s $\geqslant$ maxSales r from the chain of inequalities

```
maxSales s ≥ maxSales (s-1) ≥ ... ≥ maxSales r
```

EXERCISES

3.1 Prove that cycle (recycle (a,b,c)) = (a,b,c) for all a, b and c.

3.2 Prove that cycle (cycle (cycle (a,b,c))) = (a,b,c) for all a, b, c.

3.3 If we define

```
sumThree (a,b,c) = a+b+c
```

give a proof that for integers a, b and c

```
sumThree (cycle (a,b,c)) = sumThree (a,b,c)
```

3.4 Given the following definition

```
swapIf :: (num,num) -> (num,num)
swapIf (a,b)
  = (a,b)     , if a <= b
  = (b,a)     , otherwise
```

prove that for all a and b,

```
swapIf (swapIf (a,b)) = swapIf (a,b)
```

[†] All possible *defined* values. If sales gives defined values, then maxSales will too, since the value at (r+1) only uses maxSales at the smaller argument r. After r steps the base case of the definition, maxSales 0 = sales 0, is reached.

3.2   **Proof by induction**

In the previous section we gave two methods of proof that a property holds for all values – for all natural numbers, for instance. The first one worked directly for all values at once, using a single equation; the second made a proof by cases; for example, depending upon the cases of whether m > n or n ⩾ m. This section introduces a powerful method of proof by **induction** which we use to prove properties for all natural numbers 0, 1, 2, . . ., n, ...

Assumptions in proofs

Before looking at the method of induction, we look at the idea of proofs and formulas which contain **assumptions**. Taking a particular example, it follows from elementary arithmetic that if we *assume* that petrol costs 27 pence per litre, then we can prove that four litres will cost £1.08.

What does this tell us? It does *not* tell us outright how much four litres will cost; it only tells us the cost if the assumption is valid. To be sure the cost will be £1.08, we need to supply some evidence that the assumption is justified: this might be another proof – perhaps based on petrol costing £1.20 per gallon – or direct evidence.

We can write what we have proved as a formula,

1 litre costs 27 pence ⇒ 4 litres cost £1.08

where the arrow or implication, ⇒, suggests that the second proposition follows from the first.

As we have seen, we prove an implication like $A \Rightarrow B$ by assuming A in proving B. If we then find a proof of A, the implication tells us that B is also valid. Yet another way of looking at this is to see a proof of $A \Rightarrow B$ as a *machine* for turning a proof of A into a proof of B.

We use this idea in proof by induction, as one of the tasks in building an induction proof is the induction step, where we prove that one property holds, assuming another. We turn to induction now.

Proof by mathematical induction

To prove the property P(n) for all natural numbers n we have to do two things:

Base case	Prove P(0).
Induction step	Prove P(n+1) assuming that P(n) holds already.

How does this give a proof of P(n) for every n? The base case gives P(0), and the rest of the cases follow from the induction step. As we argued above,

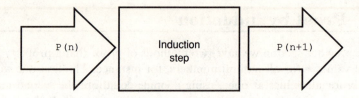

Figure 3.1 $P(n) \Rightarrow P(n+1)$.

we can think of the induction step as a machine which turns proofs into proofs: see Figure 3.1. For example, if we give it a proof of $P(7)$, say, it will give us a proof of $P(8)$.

Starting at the proof of $P(0)$, using the machine we get a proof of $P(1)$. If we feed that proof into the machine again, we get a proof of $P(2)$, and in a similar way we get proofs of $P(3)$, $P(4)$, ... In other words, we get proofs of $P(n)$ for all possible values of n.

EXAMPLE: Factorial

Suppose we define

```
fac :: num -> num

fac 0     = 1
fac (n+1) = (n+1) * fac n
```

and suppose we want to prove that `fac` gives a positive result for all natural numbers. Formally, we want to prove

```
P(n):  fac n > 0
```

for all natural numbers n. To do this, we use mathematical induction, and so we have to give the two steps

- Prove $P(0)$: fac 0 > 0;
- Prove $P(n+1)$: fac (n+1) > 0, assuming that $P(n)$: fac n > 0 is already proven.

Proof: As we said above, the proof has two parts.
The *base case* requires a proof of fac 0 > 0. Now, fac 0 = 1, and since 1 is greater than 0 we have fac 0 > 0 as we require.

We then have to prove the *induction step*. In this we have to show

```
P(n+1): fac (n+1) > 0
```

on the assumption that P(n) holds. Now, we know from the definition of fac that

```
fac (n+1) = (n+1) * fac n
```

and if n is a natural number then (n+1) > 0. We have assumed that P(n) holds, so that fac n > 0. This means that fac (n+1) is a product of two positive numbers, and is therefore positive. In other words, fac (n+1) > 0, completing the proof of the induction step, and the proof itself.

■

We use the box, ■, to signify the end of a proof.

Induction and recursion

Taking the factorial example as a guide, we can see a strong resemblance between making a proof by induction, and a definition by recursion. The function definition has two cases: the value is given outright at zero:

```
fac 0 = 1
```
(†)

and at (n+1) the value, fac (n+1), is given in terms of fac n (and n):

```
fac (n+1) = (n+1) * fac n
```
(‡)

The equation (‡) acts like the machine of the induction proof, turning a value at n into a value at (n+1). Just as we explained how the two parts of an induction give proofs P(n) for each n, the two equations give a value to the function fac at each n. To start, (†) gives a value at 0; using (‡) on this gives a value at 1, repeating this gives values at 2, 3 and so forth.

Seeing this link can make induction seem less alien: if we think of an induction proof building proofs P(0), P(1) and so on just as a function definition builds the results fac 0, fac 1, ... the way in which P(n) is assumed while we are proving P(n+1) is no different from the way we use the value fac n whilst defining fac (n+1). In particular, it is no more 'circular' than a recursive definition of a function like factorial.

This relationship between induction and recursion is no accident, and each time we meet a way of defining functions over a data type we shall also find an induction principle which allows us to prove properties of these functions. We now continue with further examples of proofs built by induction over the natural numbers.

EXAMPLE: Powers

This section proves a relationship between two functions. The first calculates powers of two

```
power2 :: num -> num
power2 0     = 1                                                    (1)
power2 (n+1) = 2 * power2 n                                         (2)
```

and the second calculates sums of powers

```
sumPowers : num -> num
sumPowers 0     = 1                                                 (3)
sumPowers (n+1) = sumPowers n + power2 (n+1)                        (4)
```

We aim to prove that

```
P(n):  sumPowers n + 1 = power2 (n+1)
```

for all natural numbers n. Note here the binding power of function application means that the left-hand side means (sumPowers n)+1, *not* sumPowers (n+1). There are two stages in the proof:

- Prove P(0): sumPowers 0 + 1 = power2 (0+1);
- Prove P(n+1): sumPowers (n+1) + 1 = power2 (n+2), assuming that P(n): sumPowers n + 1 = power2 (n+1) is already proven.

Proof: We begin with the base case. We look at each half of P(0) separately:

```
sumPowers 0 + 1
  = 1 + 1                                                    by (3)
  = 2                                                        arithmetic
```

```
power2 1
  = 2                                                        by (1)
```

Each side simplifies to 2, and so they are equal. Note that we have added an explanation of each step of the proof. sumPowers 0 + 1 is equal to 1 + 1 by the definition of the function sumPowers; and 1+1 is equal to 2 by arithmetic.

Now, we look at P(n+1). The left-hand side is

```
sumPowers (n+1) + 1
  = sumPowers n + power2 (n+1) + 1                           by (4)
  = sumPowers n + 1 + power2 (n+1)                           arithmetic
```

```
          = power2 (n+1) + power2 (n+1)                    by P(n)
          = 2 * power2 (n+1)                               arithmetic
```

The right-hand side is

```
    power2 (n+2)
          = 2 * power2 (n+1)                               by (2)
```

This shows that the two sides are equal, and so that P(n+1) is true, assuming P(n) is. This proves the induction case, and completes the proof.

∎

The proof here relates the two functions power2 and sumPowers; instead of actually calculating the sum in sumPowers, we can use power2, thus:

```
    sumPower n = power2 (n+1) - 1
```

This process of replacing one definition by another is often called **program transformation** and it is a powerful technique for developing one (more efficient, for instance) program from another.

EXAMPLE: Sales analysis

This section looks at an example from the programs we have developed so far. We reintroduced the maxSales function in Section 3.1 above. From the same application area we have

```
    totalSales :: num -> num


    totalSales 0     = sales 0
    totalSales (n+1) = totalSales n + sales (n+1)
```

maxSales n is intended to give the maximum sales in the weeks 0 to n, whilst totalSales n gives the total sales for that (n+1)-week period. We would expect that for all n, the total sales for a period would be smaller than or equal to having made the maximum sales in each of the (n+1) weeks. Formally,

```
    P(n):  totalSales n ≤ (n+1) * maxSales n
```

To prove this by induction we have to:

- Prove P(0): `totalSales 0 ` $\leqslant$ ` (0+1) * maxSales 0`;
- Prove P(n+1): `totalSales (n+1)` $\leqslant$ `(n+2) * maxSales (n+1)`, assuming that P(n): `totalSales n` $\leqslant$ `(n+1) * maxSales n` is already proven.

Proof: First we have to prove the base case. We look at each side separately:

```
totalSales 0                        (0+1) * maxSales 0
  = sales 0                           = 1 * sales 0
                                      = sales 0
```

Since they are equal, this gives P(0). We then have to prove P(n+1). We start by looking at the left-hand side:

```
totalSales (n+1)
  = totalSales n + sales (n+1)              by def of totalSales
  ≤ (n+1) * maxSales n + sales (n+1)                    by P(n)
```

Again, after each step of the proof we have added an explanation. The first equality comes from the definition of `totalSales`; the inequality comes from P(n), which we assume whilst proving P(n+1).

How are `maxSales n` and `sales (n+1)` related to the right-hand side, `maxSales (n+1)`? The definition of `maxSales` says that it is the maximum of the two values. As we argued earlier, this means that

```
maxSales (n+1) ⩾ maxSales n                                   (†)
maxSales (n+1) ⩾ sales (n+1)                                  (‡)
```

and so

```
totalSales (n+1)
  ≤ (n+1) * maxSales n + sales (n+1)              see above
  ≤ (n+1) * maxSales (n+1) + maxSales (n+1)       by (†), (‡)
  = (n+2) * maxSales (n+1)                        by arithmetic
```

which is exactly what we wanted to prove. This completes the proof of the induction step, and therefore the whole proof.

■

3.3   Building induction proofs

Here we look at some details of how to build proofs using induction. As we said before, the structure of a proof is often very similar to the structure of the functions it involves. Induction proofs usually go with functions defined by primitive recursion; that is, functions fun defined thus:

- fun 0 is defined outright;
- fun (n+1) is defined using fun n.

This mirrors the induction proof, in which P(0) is proved outright and P(n+1) is proved using P(n).

Induction proofs all follow a similar pattern, and we first give a template which can be filled in to help build a proof.

A proof template

The template in Figure 3.2 gives the overall structure of the proof, and it is evident that we have used this structure in the examples given so far. It is sensible to write down the goal first, and especially to be clear about what are the sub-goals P(0) and P(n+1), obtained from P(n) by replacing n by 0 and (n+1), before trying to find the proofs themselves. The example of power2 and sumPowers from Section 3.2 can be put into the template, as in Figure 3.3.

Next we look at how to get the proofs of P(0) and P(n+1) themselves. Before that, we say something about the equations involved.

Stage 0   Write down the goal of the proof, in English

Stage 1   Write down the goal of the proof: proving,

- P(n), for all n

Stage 2   Write down the two sub-goals of the induction proof,

- P(0)
- P(n+1) assuming P(n)

Stage 3   Prove P(0)

Stage 4   Prove P(n+1), remembering that you can, and probably *should*, use P(n) somewhere in the proof.

Figure 3.2   Induction template.

Stage 0	To prove that the sum of powers of two up to n, plus 1, is equal to the (n+1)st power of two.
Stage 1	P(n): sumPowers n + 1 = power2 (n+1)
Stage 2	• sumPowers 0 + 1 = power2 (0+1)
	• sumPowers (n+1) + 1 = power2 (n+2) assuming sumPowers n + 1 = power2 (n+1)

Figure 3.3 Template for power2 example.

Equations

In all proofs involving functions, the resources we have are the *definitions* of the functions involved. The equations describe the effect of the functions on any value of the variables. Here we have the functions power2 and sumPowers, defined by

```
power2 0     = 1                                        (1)
power2 (r+1) = 2 * power2 r                             (2)

sumPowers 0     = 1                                     (3)
sumPowers (r+1) = sumPowers r + power2 (r+1)            (4)
```

We have changed the name of the variables in the definitions to r from n; this does not change the meaning of the definitions.

We make the change so that the variables in the definitions do not get confused with the variables in the proof. We can apply these definitions for *any* value of r. For example, if we replace r with (n+1) in the second equation for power2 we get

```
power2 (n+2) = 2 * power2 (n+1)
```

As a general piece of advice, it is best to keep variables distinct, and to change the variables in definitions if necessary.

Finding proofs

Here we look at how to find proofs of P(0) and P(n+1). In proving the former, we have the defining equations to use; in proving P(n+1), we can additionally use P(n). Indeed, we *expect* to use the induction hypothesis in proving P(n+1), and it is worth checking a proof which does not use it.

The main pieces of advice for constructing proofs of equalities are

- look separately at each side;
- use the definitions, and general facts (of, for example, arithmetic) to simplify each side;
- explain each step of the proof.

This is precisely what happens in

```
sumPowers 0 + 1
  = 1 + 1                                                  by (3)
  = 2                                                      arithmetic


power2 1
  = 2                                                      by (1),(2)
```

In the induction step, we start the same way, and get

```
sumPowers (n+1) + 1
  = sumPowers n + power2 (n+1) + 1                         by (4)


power2 (n+2)
  = 2 * power2 (n+1)                                       by (2)
```

Note that in the case of `power2`, we use the value of the power function at `(n+2)`; we replace `r` by `(n+1)` to do this. Now, to make any more progress we have to use the induction hypothesis, `P(n)`, which equates `sumPowers n + 1` and `power2 (n+1)`. Both of these are involved here, and continuing the proof on the left-hand side we get

```
sumPowers (n+1) + 1 = ...
  = sumPowers n + 1 + power2 (n+1)           arithmetic
  = power2 (n+1) + power2 (n+1)              by P(n)
  = 2 * power2 (n+1)                         arithmetic
```

which finally equates the two sides.

The general advice when proving general properties and not just equalities is similar: use the equations and induction hypothesis to simplify the property to something which can be proved. We can see this in the example of

```
totalSales n ≤ (n+1) * maxSales n
```

in Section 3.2.

EXERCISES

The first exercises here refer to the sales analysis examples introduced in Section 2.2 and further discussed in Section 3.1.

3.5 After defining the function

```
productSales :: num -> num
productSales 0     = sales 0
productSales (n+1) = sales (n+1) * productSales n
```

we can define

```
zeroInPeriod2 :: num -> bool
zeroInPeriod2 n = (productSales n = 0)
```

zeroInPeriod2 is intended to be a new way of defining 'zeroInPeriod'. Prove that it has the same behaviour by proving for all natural numbers n that

```
zeroInPeriod n = zeroInPeriod2 n
```

3.6 We can say that all sales in a period 0 to n are the same explicitly, thus:

```
equalSales1 :: num -> bool
equalSales1 0     = True
equalSales1 (n+1) = equalSales1 n & (sales n = sales (n+1))
```

We can also define the function this way:

```
equalSales2 :: num -> bool
equalSales2 n = (totalSales n = (n+1)*maxSales n)
```

Prove that the two functions have the same behaviour.

In the following exercises, you may assume that for all n, sales n $\geqslant$ 0.

3.7 Give a proof that for all natural numbers n, totalSales n $\geqslant$ 0.

3.8 Define a function minSales which returns the minimum sales value in the weeks 0 to n. Define the function

```
zeroInPeriod3 n = (minSales n = 0)
```

and give a proof that for all natural numbers n,

```
zeroInPeriod n = zeroInPeriod3 n
```

3.9 Define a function which checks whether all sales in a period are zero. Show that this has the same behaviour as a function which checks whether the total sales for the period are zero.

3.10 Prove that for all natural numbers n,

```
fac (n+1) ⩾ power2 n
```

3.11 Prove that for all natural numbers n,

```
fib (n+1) ⩾ power2 (n div 2)
```

You need to use a slightly strengthened version of induction here, in which we infer `P(n+1)` from `P(n)` and `P(n-1)`.

SUMMARY

This chapter has shown how we can prove that programs have properties. Such proofs cover all possible inputs, and so are more powerful than tests, which cover only a selection of representative cases.

The first proofs given use the defining equations to reason directly about function behaviour. If a function definition contains cases, given by guards, it is likely that the proof will break into cases also.

Many functions are defined by recursion; we use the method of *induction* to cover proofs involving these functions. To help with induction proofs, the chapter contains suggestions for

- a template for the overall structure of the proof, making clear what are the two sub-goals of the induction proof;
- changing the names of the variables used in definitions, to avoid confusion with the variables used in the induction proof;
- how to find proofs for the sub-goals `P(0)` and `P(n+1)`. In finding proofs of equations, it is suggested that the definitions are used to simplify the two sides of the equations as much as possible, before applying the induction hypothesis if this is appropriate.

As with earlier chapters, a full understanding of proofs can only come from looking at exercises.

---

4 Data structures: Lists

Collections of objects often occur in the situations we try to model in a program. For instance,

- A telephone directory is a collection of pairs of names and numbers.
- A book is a collection of chapters, each of which is a collection of sections. Sections, in turn, are made up of paragraphs, and so on.
- A bill from a shop is a collection of prices (numbers), or of pairs of names and prices.
- A simple picture is a collection of lines.

Lists in Miranda represent collections of objects of a particular type, and in this chapter we begin to write programs which handle lists.

4.1   Lists in Miranda

For any type `t`, there is a type of lists of items of type `t`, and this type is
written `[t]`. For instance,

```
[1,2.3,4,1,4] :: [num]
[True]        :: [bool]
```

We read these as '`[1,2.3,4,1,4]` is a list of num' and '`[True]` is a list of
bool'. `string` is taken to be a synonym for `[char]`, and the two lists which
follow are the same.

```
['a','a','b'] :: [char]
"aab"         :: [char]
```

We can build lists of items of any particular type, and so we can have lists of
functions and lists of lists of numbers, for instance.

```
[totalSales,totalSales]  :: [ num -> num ]
[ [12,2] , [2,12] , [] ] :: [ [num] ]
```

As can be seen, the list with elements e_1, e_2 to e_n is written by enclosing the
elements in square brackets, thus

$$[e_1, e_2, \ldots, e_n]$$

As a special case the empty list, `[]`, which contains no items, is an element of
every list type.

```
[] :: [num]
[] :: [[bool]]
[] :: [ num -> num ]
...
```

Lists are collections in which the *order* of the items is significant. `[1,2]` and
`[2,1]` are different lists, because although they contain the same items, their
ordering is different. The first element of `[1,2]` is 1, whilst of `[2,1]` it is 2.
The *number of occurrences* of an item also matters: `[True]` contains one
item, `[True,True]` contains two, which happen to be the same.

There are some other ways of writing down lists of numbers:

- `[n..m]` is the list `[n,n+1,...,m]`; if n exceeds m, the list is empty.

```
[2..7]   = [2,3,4,5,6,7]
[3.1..7] = [3.1,4.1,5.1,6.1]
```

- [n,p..m] is the list of numbers from n to m in steps of p-n. For example,

    [7,6..3]   = [7,6,5,4,3]
    [0,0.3..1] = [0,0.3,0.6,0.9]

- In both cases, it can be seen that if the step size does not allow us to reach m exactly, the last item of the list is the largest in the sequence which is less than m.

EXERCISES

4.1 Give Miranda type definitions, using ==, for the examples of the telephone directory, book and shop bill given at the start of the chapter.

4.2 How many items does the list [2,3] contain? How many does [[2,3]] contain? What is the type of [[2,3]]?

4.3 What is the result of evaluating [2..2]? What about [2,7..4]?

4.2 Defining functions over lists

Suppose we want to define the function

    sumList :: [num] -> num

which sums a list of numbers. Our definition will have to cover lists of length 0, 1, 2 and so on. How can the definition work for all cases? We can divide up the type of lists as follows: every list is either

- the empty list, [], or
- non-empty. In this case it will have a first element, or *head*, and a remainder, or *tail*. For instance, [2,3,4,5] has head 2 and tail [3,4,5]. A list with head a and tail x is written (a:x).

We can now look at the definition of sumList. It will divide into the two cases suggested above:

- The sum of the empty list is 0.
- The sum of a non-empty list, (a:x), is given by adding a to the sum of x.

For example, in the case of [2, 3, 4, 5]

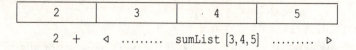

The Miranda definition will be

```
sumList []    = 0                          (1)
sumList (a:x) = a + sumList x              (2)
```

As we did earlier, in making a calculation we use the first equation whose patterns match the corresponding arguments, so that in the case of sumList,

```
sumList [2,3,4,5]
= 2 + sumList [3,4,5]                       by (2)
= 2 + (3 + sumList [4,5])                   by (2)
= 2 + (3 + (4 + sumList [5]))               by (2)
= 2 + (3 + (4 + (5 + sumList [])))          by (2)
= 2 + (3 + (4 + (5 + 0)))                   by (1)
= ... = 14                                  arithmetic
```

The list constructor

The last section introduced the operator ':', which is sometimes called 'cons'. This operator or **constructor** (hence the name 'cons') builds a list from an item and a list, and we can see every non-empty list as being built this way. For instance,

```
[5]    = 5:[]
[4,5] = 4:[5] = 4:(5:[])
[2,3,4,5] = 2:3:4:5:[]
```

In the final expression, we have used the fact that ':' associates to the right – this means that

```
a:b:c = a:(b:c)
a:b:c ≠ (a:b):c
```

All the notation for lists given so far can be defined using ':'. Lists can be of any type, so

```
(:) :: num -> [num] -> [num]
(:) :: bool -> [bool] -> [bool]
...
```

These types express the fact that the elements of a list must all be of the same type: you cannot put a number onto the front of a Boolean list, for instance. In fact we can express the type of (:) in a single expression

```
(:) :: * -> [*] -> [*]
```

where * is a type variable, which stands for any type (such as num or bool). We look at the details of this in Chapter 6.

To illustrate another function on lists, suppose we want to double every element of a numerical list.

2	3	4	2

We can double the first element, or head, simply by multiplying it by two. The final result is built by putting this on the front of the doubled tail, using ':':

4 :
6	8	4

This is the list

4	6	8	4

as required. The Miranda definition will be

```
double :: [num] -> [num]

double []    = []
double (a:x) = (2*a) : double x
```

and the calculation of an example gives

```
double [2,3]
= (2*2) : double [3]
= 4 : double [3]
= 4 : ( (2*3) : double [])
= 4 : ( 6 : double [] )
= 4 : ( 6 : [] )
= 4 : [6]
= [4,6]
```

List operators

The length of a list is given by #, which is built into the system. It can be defined in this way:

```
#[]     = 0
#(a:x) = 1 + #x
```

The empty list has length zero; a non-empty list, a:x, is one item longer than its tail, x.

When we introduced strings as lists of char, we saw that ++ could be used to join two strings. This is true for lists of any type, so that

```
[2] ++ [3,4,5] = [2,3,4,5]
[] ++ [2,3] ++ [] ++ [4,5] = [2,3,4,5]
```

Only lists of the same type can be joined, so the type of ++ will be

```
(++) :: [num] -> [num] -> [num]
(++) :: [bool] -> [bool] -> [bool]
...
```

How is ++ defined? Joining [] and any list y will give the result y

```
[] ++ y = y
```

but now we should look at the case of joining a:x to y. In pictures, we have

Taking off the head, a, we can combine x and y

and then put a at the front, using ':', thus

The full definition of append in Miranda is then

```
[] ++ y     = y
(a:x) ++ y = a : (x++y)
```

The associativity and binding powers of the full collection of list operators are given in Appendix E.

Pitfalls: Cons and append

++ and ':' do similar but different things!

- ++ takes two lists and returns a list, so for instance

    ```
    [2] ++ [3,4,5] = [2,3,4,5]
    ```

    but 2 ++ [3,4,5] gives an error:

    ```
    type error in expression
    cannot unify num with [*]
    ```

    since the first argument of ++ is expected to be a list, of some type *, rather than a number.

- ':' takes an element and a list, giving a list

    ```
    2 : [3,4,5] = [2,3,4,5]
    ```

    whilst [2] : [3,4,5] gives the error:

    ```
    type error in expression
    cannot cons [num] to [num]
    ```

    as there is an attempt to use ':' to 'cons' a [num], rather than a num, as an item onto a list of num.

The simplest way to remember the behaviour is by the equations

```
item :  list = list
list ++ list = list
```

Other problems can come from the binding power of : and ++. As can be seen from Appendix E, the comparison operators = and so on bind more tightly than : and ++, making the expressions

```
2:[3]=x                 [2]++[3]=[2,3]
```

badly formed. Parentheses need to be added

```
(2:[3])=x               ([2]++[3])=[2,3]
```

to have the intended effect.

EXERCISES

4.4   Write out [True, True, False] and [2] using ':' and [].

4.5   Give calculations of

```
sumList [34,2,0,1]
double [0]
"tea"++"cup"
```

4.6   Design test data for the functions sumList and double.

4.7   Define a function

```
productList :: [num] -> num
```

which returns the product of a list of numbers. You should take the product of an empty list to be 1. Why is 1 a better choice than 0?

4.8   Define a function

```
and :: [bool] -> bool
```

which returns the conjunction of a list. Informally,

$$\text{and } [e_1, e_2, \ldots, e_i] = e_1 \ \& \ e_2 \ \& \ \ldots \ \& \ e_i$$

The conjunction of an empty list should be True.

4.9   Define a function

```
flatten :: [[num]] -> [num]
```

which 'flattens' a list of lists of numbers into a single list of numbers. For example,

```
flatten [[3,4],[],[31,3]] = [3,4,31,3]
```

An informal definition is given by

$$\text{flatten } [e_1, e_2, \ldots, e_i] = e_1 \ \texttt{++} \ e_2 \ \texttt{++} \ \ldots \ \texttt{++} \ e_i$$

4.3 Designing functions over lists

Previous sections have introduced the list types, and given some elementary definitions of functions over lists. Here we go into more detail about how more complex list manipulating functions can be designed in Miranda. We begin by looking at a sequence of examples.

EXAMPLE: Sorting

The task here is to write a function which will sort a list of numbers into ascending order. A list like

7	3	9	2

is sorted by taking the tail [3,9,2] and sorting it to give

2	3	9

It is then a matter of inserting the head, 7, in the right place in this list, giving

2	3	7	9

In Miranda, we have the definition of iSort – the 'i' is for *insertion* sort:

```
iSort :: [num] -> [num]

iSort []    = []                        (1)
iSort (a:x) = insert a (iSort x)        (2)
```

This is a typical example of top-down definition. We have defined iSort assuming we can define insert. The development of the program has been in two separate parts, since we have a definition of the function iSort using a simpler function insert, together with a definition of the function insert itself. Solving each sub-problem is simpler than solving the original problem itself.

Now we have to define the function

```
insert :: num -> [num] -> [num]
```

To get some guidance about how insert should behave, we look at some examples. Inserting 7 into [2,3,9] was given above, whilst inserting 1 gives

1	2	3	9

Looking at these two examples we see that:

- In the case of 1, if the item to be inserted is smaller than (or equal to) the head of the list, we add it to the front of the list.

- In the case of 7, if the item is greater than the head, we insert it in the tail of the list, and add the head to the result, thus:

		3	7	9
2	:			

The function can now be defined, including the case that the list is empty.

```
insert a []    = [a]                              (3)
insert a (b:y) = a:(b:y)       , if a <= b        (4)
               = b : insert a y , otherwise       (5)
```

We now show the functions in action, in the calculation of iSort [3,9,2].

```
iSort [3,9,2]
= insert 3 (iSort [9,2])                    by (2)
= insert 3 (insert 9 (iSort [2]))           by (2)
= insert 3 (insert 9 (insert 2 (iSort []))) by (2)
= insert 3 (insert 9 (insert 2 []))         by (1)
= insert 3 (insert 9 [2])                   by (3)
= insert 3 (2 : insert 9 [])                by (5)
= insert 3 [2,9]                            by (3)
= 2 : insert 3 [9]                          by (5)
= 2 : [3,9] = [2,3,9]                       by (4)
```

Developing this function has shown the advantage of looking at examples while trying to define a function; the examples can give a guide about how the definition might break into cases, or the pattern of the recursion. We also saw how using top-down design can break a larger problem into smaller problems which are easier to solve.

EXERCISES

4.10 Can you use the iSort function to find the minimum and maximum elements of a list of numbers? How would you find these elements without using iSort?

4.11 Design test data for the `insert` function. Your data should address different possible points of insertion, and also look at any exceptional cases.

4.12 By modifying the definition of the `insert` function we can change the behaviour of the sort, `iSort`. Re-define `insert` so that

- the list is sorted in descending order;
- duplicates are removed from the list. For example,

      iSort [2,1,4,1,2] = [1,2,4]

  under this definition.

4.13 Design test data for the duplicate-removing version of `iSort`, explaining your choices.

EXAMPLES: Membership and selection ——————————————

Given a list, how can we decide whether a particular item belongs in it? We define the function

      memberList :: [num] -> num -> bool

whose result is a Boolean value, signalling whether the second argument appears in the first. An item b can appear in a list (a:x) in two ways:

- it can be equal to a, or,
- it can appear in the tail x.

The function definition reflects this

      memberList []   b = False
      memberList (a:x) b = (a=b) \/ memberList x b

Often the function receives the definition

      mem []   b = False
      mem (a:x) b = True   , if (a=b)
                  = mem x b   , otherwise

This has the same effect as the definition of `memberList`, but it is less clear. The 'or' which appeared in the informal definition has been replaced with a guard. It is clearer in general to use the Boolean operations \/, & and ~ to combine Boolean values, rather than to use the guards.

Given a string, how can we *select* or *filter* the digits from it, so that

```
digits :: string -> string
digits "the34reIs32w" = "3432"
```

There are two cases, when the string is (first:rest):

- When first is a digit, it will be the first element of the output string;
- when it is not a digit, it will not appear in the output string.

In either case, the remainder of the output is given by finding the digits in rest. As a Miranda definition, we have

```
digits [] = []
digits (first:rest)
    = first : digits rest    , if digit first
    =           digits rest    , otherwise
```

in which we use the function digit :: char -> bool to test whether a character is a digit. An example calculation gives

```
digits "s32w"
    ?? digit 's' = False
= digits "32w"
    ?? digit '3' = True
= '3' : digits "2w"
    ?? digit '2' = True
= '3' : ('2' : digits "w")
    ?? digit 'w' = False
= '3' : ('2' : digits "")
= '3' : ('2' : [])
= "32"
```

EXERCISES

4.14   Define a function

```
memberNum :: [num] -> num -> num
```

so that memberNum l s returns the *number* of times the item s appears in the list l; design test data for your function.

4.15   Give a definition of memberList which uses the function memberNum.

4.16 Define a function

```
unique :: [num] -> [num]
```

which filters out the numbers which occur exactly once in a list. For instance

```
unique [2,4,2,1,4] = [1]
```

You will probably find that the function memberNum is useful in your definition.

4.17 If you are allowed to assume that the list argument of memberList is sorted into ascending order, can you modify the definition so that it is not in general necessary to examine the whole list in order to be able to conclude that an item is *not* an element of the list? You may like to consider the example

```
memberList [2,4,6] 3
```

for guidance.

4.18 For the original definitions of memberList and mem give evaluations of

```
memberList [2,4,6] 4
mem [2,4,6] 4
```

The evaluation using memberList can be shortened if you notice that

```
True \/ e = True
```

whatever the value of e. This is an example of 'lazy' evaluation; we only evaluate the argument e if we need to.

Pattern matching

Patterns in Miranda are given by

- Constant integers, characters and Booleans: -2, '1', True.
- Variables: x, varNumber17.
- Tuples of patterns: for example $(p_1, p_2, \ldots, p_k)$, where $p_1, \ldots$ are patterns.
- Natural number patterns: for example (n+2).
- List patterns: $(p_1:p_2)$, where p_1 and p_2 are patterns, and
- Constructor patterns, which will be introduced in Chapter 9.

As can be seen from this, patterns can be **nested**: a tuple or list pattern can be built itself from patterns. Indeed, we saw this earlier with the definition of the shift function.

In this section we look at the example of the function to sum a list of pairs of numbers, and see that there is often more than one way to define a particular function using pattern matching. Obviously,

```
sumPairs :: [(num,num)] -> num
sumPairs [] = 0
```

but there are a number of possibilities for the case of the non-empty list. We can choose to use a simple list pattern, thus:

```
sumPairs (a:x) = fst a + snd a + sumPairs x              (1)
```

A non-empty list is matched by (a:x). The components of its first element, a, are accessed using the built-in functions fst and snd.

We also use a simple list pattern in the second definition, but use a where clause to define the first and second parts of the pair a.

```
sumPairs (a:x) = c + d + sumPairs x                      (2)
               where
               c = fst a
               d = snd a
```

Alternatively again, we can use a conformal pattern match to extract the components in a where clause

```
sumPairs (a:x) = c + d + sumPairs x                      (3)
               where
               (c,d) = a
```

The conformal pattern match (c,d) = a will only succeed if a is a pair; in this case, c is matched to its first element and d to its second.

As an alternative to definitions (1) to (3), we can give a nested pattern:

```
sumPairs ((c,d):x) = c + d + sumPairs x                 (4)
```

In this case a non-empty list of pairs is matched – to succeed the list must be non-empty, as it is built using ':', and have as its first element a pair (c,d). The three components c, d and x are then used on the right-hand side.

The final definition uses a different strategy, in which an auxiliary function to sum a pair of numbers is defined separately:

```
sumPairs (a:x) = sumPair a + sumPairs x                 (5)
sumPair  (c,d) = c+d
```

The pattern match over the pair is made in the definition of `sumPair`, whilst the match over the list is in the main function `sumPairs`.

Each of these forms of definition has its advantages. The first three use a simple top-level pattern, and extract the components of the pair in different ways; in the fourth, a nested pattern is used to extract the components at top level. The final definition separates the processing of the list from the processing of the items. This *separation* makes the function potentially easier to modify: we could change the function to sum a list of triples, or pairs of pairs of numbers without modifying the `sumPairs` function.

As was explained above, pattern matching in Miranda is *sequential*. Take the example of a function to *zip* together two lists into a list of pairs, so that

```
zip2 [2,3,4] [4,5,78] = [(2,4),(3,5),(4,78)]
zip2 [2,3] [1,2,3]    = [(2,1),(3,2)]
```

Note that in the second case, elements from the longer list are thrown away if there is no corresponding element in the other list. The function is defined by

```
zip2 (a:x) (b:y) = (a,b) : zip2 x y
zip2 x y         = []
```

The second equation will only be used if the arguments fail to match the first, which means that at least one of the lists is empty. It could be written with all the patterns disjoint, but the definition is correspondingly longer:

```
zip2 (a:x) (b:y) = (a,b) : zip2 x y
zip2 (a:x) []    = []
zip2 []    y     = []
```

EXERCISES

4.19 Modify definitions (2) and (4) of `sumPairs` to sum a list of triples of numbers, (c,d,e).

4.20 Modify definitions (3) and (5) of `sumPairs` to sum a list of pairs of pairs of numbers, ((c,d),(e,f)).

4.21 Do a calculation of

```
sumPairs [ (2,3), (6,-7) ]
```

for each of the definitions (1) to (5) of `sumPairs`.

4.22 Define a function `zip3` to zip together three lists of numbers. Can you modify your definition so that there is no overlap between the equations?

4.23 Define a function

    unZip2 :: [(num,num)] -> ([num], [num])

which takes a list of pairs into a pair of lists. You might find it helpful first to define two functions

    unZipLeft, unZipRight :: [(num,num)] -> [num]

which give the lists of first elements and second elements, respectively

    unZipLeft [(2,4),(3,5),(4,78)] = [2,3,4]
    unZipRight [(2,4),(3,5),(4,78)] = [4,5,78]

4.4   A library database

A library uses a database to keep a record of the books on loan to borrowers.

Types

In modelling this situation, we first look at the types of the objects involved. People and books are represented by strings

    string == [char]
    person == string
    book   == string

The database can be represented in a number of different ways. We choose to make it a list of (person,book) pairs. If the pair ("Alice", "Spot") is in the list, it means that "Alice" has borrowed the book called "Spot". We therefore define

    database == [(person, book)]

An example object of this type is

    exampleBase
    = [("Alice", "Postman Pat"), ("Anna", "All Alone"),
        ("Alice", "Spot"), ("Rory", "Postman Pat")]

After defining the types of the objects involved, we consider the functions which work over the database:

- Given a person, we want to find the book(s) they have borrowed, if any.

- Given a book, we want to find the borrower(s) of the book, if any. (It is assumed that there may be more than one copy of any book.)

- Given a book, we want to find out whether it is borrowed.

- Given a person, we may want to find out the number of books they have borrowed.

Each of these **lookup** functions will take a database, and a person or book, and return the result of the query. Their types will be

```
books        :: database -> person -> [book]
borrowers    :: database -> book -> [person]
borrowed     :: database -> book -> bool
numBorrowed  :: database -> person -> num
```

Note that borrowers and books return lists; these can contain zero, one or more items, and so in particular can signal that a book has no borrowers, or that a person has no books on loan.

Two other functions need to be defined. We need to be able to make a loan, of a book to a person, and also to return a loan. These functions will take a database, plus the loan information, and return a *different* database, which is the original with the loan added or removed. These **update** functions will have type

```
makeLoan   :: database -> person -> book -> database
returnLoan :: database -> person -> book -> database
```

Defining the lookup functions

We start by looking at the function

```
books :: database -> person -> [book]
```

which forms a model for the other lookup functions borrowers, borrowed and numBorrowed. For the exampleBase, we have

```
books exampleBase "Alice" = [ "Postman Pat", "Spot" ]
books exampleBase "Rory"  = [ "Postman Pat" ]
```

How are these found? We have looked already at two functions whose design can help:

- The function `digits` of Section 4.3, shows how to *filter* certain items from a list. In this example we need to find the pairs whose first halves are equal to `"Alice"` and then to return the second halves of those pairs.

- The function `sumPairs` of the same section is defined over a list of pairs, and the discussion of pattern matching there is relevant here.

To design a function it is often helpful first to think of the left-hand side. In checking through the database we will need to check each pair one-by-one, and so we will pattern match over the first argument.

The `sumPairs` function gives guidance about the exact form of the left-hand sides when dealing with a list of pairs. If we take our guidance from definition (4) of `sumPairs` we will use a nested pattern like `((c,d):x)` to match a non-empty list of pairs. The left-hand sides will be

```
books []               borrower =
books ((pers,bk):rest) borrower =
```

No books can be borrowed by `borrower` in an empty database, as no books are borrowed by anybody

```
books [] borrower = []
```

Now, informally, given a list `((pers,bk):rest)`, the book `bk` will be included in the output if `pers` is `borrower`; otherwise it will not be included, much like the definition of `digits`. This completes the definition.

```
books :: database -> person -> [book]
books [] borrower = []
books ((pers,bk):rest) borrower
  = bk : books rest borrower   , if pers = borrower
  =      books rest borrower   , otherwise
```

As we said at the start, `books` forms a model for the other lookup functions, which we leave as an exercise.

Defining the update functions

The database is modified, or updated by the functions

```
makeLoan   :: database -> person -> book -> database
returnLoan :: database -> person -> book -> database
```

Making a loan is done by adding a pair to the database, which can be done simply by adding it to the front of the list of pairs:

```
makeLoan dBase pers bk = (pers,bk) : dBase
```

Note that there is no pattern match over the database here – the same operation is used whether the database is empty or not. Also, the function is not recursive.

To return a loan, we need to check through the database, and to remove the first pair (pers,bk)

```
returnLoan ((p,b):rest) pers bk
  = rest                           , if p=pers & b=bk
  = (p,b) : returnLoan rest pers bk  , otherwise
returnLoan [] pers bk
  = error ("returnLoan failed on " ++ pers ++ " " ++ bk)
```

The function signals an error when called on a database which does not contain the pair (pers,bk). An alternative would be to return the database unchanged when a pair is not present.

There is some ambiguity in the way that the function is described: should all loans of bk to pers be cancelled by returnLoan, or just the first? To remove them all, we can modify the definition to

```
returnLoan2 ((p,b):rest) pers bk
  =           returnLoan2 rest pers bk  , if p=pers & b=bk
  = (p,b) : returnLoan2 rest pers bk  , otherwise
returnLoan2 [] pers bk
  = []
```

This function will not signal an error when the pair to be removed is not present.

Testing

Miranda acts like a calculator, and this is useful when we wish to test functions like those in the library database. Any function can be tested by typing expressions to the Miranda prompt. For example,

```
makeLoan [] "Alice" "Fireman Sam"
```

To test more substantial examples, it is sensible to put test data into a script, so we might include the definition of exampleBase as well as various tests

```
test1 = borrowed exampleBase "Spot"
test2 = makeLoan exampleBase "Alice" "Fireman Sam"
```

and so on. Adding them to the script means that we can repeatedly do them without having to type them out in full each time. Another device which can help is to use $$, which is short for 'the last expression evaluated'. The following sequence makes a loan, then another, then returns the first:

```
makeLoan exampleBase "Alice" "Fireman Sam"
makeLoan $$ "Rory" "Gorilla"
returnLoan $$ "Alice" "Fireman Sam"
```

EXERCISES

4.24   Go through the calculation of

```
books exampleBase "Alice"
books exampleBase "Rory"
```

4.25   Define the functions borrowers, borrowed and numBorrowed.

4.26   Criticise the following suggested definition of books:

```
books [] borrower = []
books ((pers,bk):rest) borrower
  = [ bk ]                 , if pers = borrower
  = books rest borrower    , otherwise
```

4.27   Give calculations of

```
returnLoan exampleBase "Alice" "Spot"
returnLoan exampleBase "Alice" "All Alone"
```

4.28   Modify the definition of returnLoan to return the database unchanged when a pair is not present.

4.29   What is wrong with the following attempted definition of returnLoan?

```
returnLoan ((p,b):rest) pers bk
  = rest                      , if p=pers & b=bk
  = returnLoan rest pers bk   , otherwise
  ... as above ...
```

4.30   Why has the [] case of returnLoan been changed in returnLoan2? You might find it helpful to run through an example calculation.

4.31   Define a function `layout`

```
layout :: [book] -> string
```

which takes a list of books, and which returns a `string` that displays the books one per line. Your function should join the strings together, placing newline characters between the strings.

4.32   How could you combine `layout` and `books` to give a function

```
booksLayout :: database -> person -> [char]
```

which displays the books on loan to a person one per line?

4.33   [*Harder*] How would you modify your database and access functions so that

- There was a maximum number of books which could be loaned to a particular person?
- There is a list of keywords associated with each book, so that books could be found by the keywords associated with them?
- Dates are associated with loans, so that overdue books could be found if necessary, and the list of books borrowed by a borrower could be sorted by order of the date due? [To achieve this, you will need to think about how dates can be represented, and how ordering of dates is implemented.]

4.5   List comprehensions

This section introduces **list comprehensions** which provide an alternative way of writing down some lists and list-manipulating functions. Specifically, they are useful for writing down lists built on the basis of others.

A SERIES OF EXAMPLES _____

For example, if the list ex is [2,4,7] then

```
[ 2*a | a<-ex]
```
(1)

will be

```
[4,8,14]
```

as it contains each of the elements a of the list ex, doubled: $2*a$. We can read (1) as saying

Take all $2*a$ so that a comes from ex.

In a similar way,

```
[ isEven n | n<-ex ] = [True,True,False]
```

if the isEven :: num -> bool function has the obvious definition.

In list comprehensions a<-ex is called a **generator** because it generates the data from which the results are built. On the left-hand side of the '<-' there is a variable, a, whilst on the right-hand side we put a list, in this case ex.

We can combine a generator with one or more **tests**, which are Boolean expressions, thus:

```
[ 2*a | a <- ex ; isEven a ; a>3 ]                              (2)
```

(2) is paraphrased as

Take all $2*a$ so that a comes from ex, a is even and a is greater than 3.

The result of (2) will therefore be the list [8], as 4 is the only even element of [2,4,7] which is greater than 3.

As well as placing a variable to the left of the arrow '<-', we can put any pattern. For instance,

```
sumPairs :: [(num,num)] -> [num]
```

```
sumPairs pairList = [ a+b | (a,b) <- pairList ]
```

Here we choose all the pairs in the list pairList, and add their components to give a single number in the result list. For example,

```
sumPairs [(2,3),(2,1),(7,8)] = [5,3,15]
```

We can add tests in such a situation, too.

```
newSumPairs :: [(num,num)] -> [num]
```

```
newSumPairs pairList = [ a+b | (a,b) <- pairList ; a<b ]
```

and in the example,

```
newAddPairs [(2,3),(2,1),(7,8)] = [5,15]
```

since the second pair in the list, (2,1), fails the test.

It is possible to put multiple generators into a list comprehension, and to combine generators and tests. These topics, as well as rules which govern how list comprehensions are evaluated together with a sequence of larger examples, are examined when we revisit the subject in Section 12.3. Readers who are interested are encouraged to look forward to the material, which should make sense without reading the intervening chapters.

Revisiting some earlier definitions

Here we look back at some of the examples given earlier in this chapter, and see how list comprehensions can be used to give alternative definitions. To double every element of a list, we can say

```
double :: [num] -> [num]
double l = [ 2*a | a<-l ]
```

In comparison to the original definition in Section 4.2, there is no pattern matching in the definition; whether l is empty or not, we simply take all the elements a and double them.

To find all the digits in a string – another example from Section 4.2 – we can say

```
digits :: string -> string
digits st = [ ch | ch<-st ; digit ch ]
```

The notation is most useful when we combine performing some transformation, as is done in double, and select elements, as in digits. A perfect case of this is given by the database functions of the preceding section.

Suppose we have to find all the books borrowed in the database db by the borrower borrower. We should run through all pairs (per,bk) in the database, and return the bk part when the per part is the borrower. Precisely this is given by

```
books :: database -> person -> [book]

books db borrower
   = [ bk | (per,bk) <- db ; per=borrower ]
```
(3)

A number of other examples are covered in the exercises.

A pitfall

This section addresses an important pitfall to do with the behaviour of variables: the definition (3) of books above might appear to be over-complicated. We imagine that we can say

```
books db borrower
    = [ bk | (borrower,bk) <- db ]                    (4)
```

The effect of this is to return all the books borrowed by *all* borrowers, not just the particular borrower borrower.

The reason for this is that the borrower in (borrower,bk) is a *new* variable, and not the variable on the left-hand side of the definition, so in fact (4) has the same effect as

```
books db borrower = [ bk | (new,bk) <- db ]
```

where it is clear that there is no constraint on the value of new to be equal to borrower.

EXERCISES

4.34 For the single generator examples of list comprehensions given in this section, show that it is never necessary to have more than one test.

4.35 How can the function

```
memberList :: [num] -> num -> bool
```

be defined using a list comprehension and an equality test?

4.36 Re-implement the database manipulating functions of the previous section using list comprehensions rather than the explicit recursive definitions given there.

4.6　Extended exercise: Supermarket billing

This collection of exercises looks at supermarket billing.[†] A scanner at a checkout will produce a list of bar codes, like

---

[†] I am grateful to Peter Lindsay *et al.* of the Department of Computer Science at the University of New South Wales, Australia for the inspiration for this example, which was suggested by their lecture notes.

```
[1234,4719,3814,1112,1113,1234]
```

which has to be converted to a bill

```
        Miranda Stores

Dry Sherry, 1lt...........5.40
Fish Fingers..............1.21
Orange Jelly..............0.56
Hula Hoops (Giant)........1.33
Unknown Item..............0.00
Dry Sherry, 1lt...........5.40


Total...................13.90
```

We have to decide first how to model the objects involved. Bar codes and prices (in pence) can be modelled by integers; names of goods by strings. We therefore say that

```
name    == string
price   == num
barCode == num
```

The conversion will be based on a *database* which links bar codes, names and prices. As in the library, we use a list to model the relationship.

```
database == [ (barCode,name,price) ]
```

The example database we use is

```
codeIndex :: database
codeIndex = [ (4719, "Fish Fingers", 121),
              (5643, "Nappies", 1010),
              (3814, "Orange Jelly", 56),
              (1111, "Hula Hoops", 21),
              (1112, "Hula Hoops (Giant)", 133),
              (1234, "Dry Sherry, 1lt", 540)]
```

The object of the script will be to convert a list of bar codes into a list of (name,price) pairs; this then has to be converted into a string for printing as above. We make the type definitions

```
tillType == [barCode]
billType == [(name,price)]
```

and then we can say that the functions we wish to define are

```
makeBill    :: tillType -> billType
formatBill  :: billType -> string
printBill   :: tillType -> string
```

The `printBill` function will combine the effects of `makeBill` and `formatBill`,

```
printBill tt = formatBill (makeBill tt)
```

The length of a line in the bill is decided to be 30. This is made a constant, thus:

```
lineLength :: num
lineLength = 30
```

Making `lineLength` a constant in this way means that to change the length of lines in the bill, only one definition needs to be altered; if 30 were used in each of the formatting functions, then each would have to be modified on changing the line length.

The rest of the script is developed through the sequences of exercises which follow.

First we develop the `formatBill` function from the bottom up: we design functions to format prices, lines and the total, and using these we finally build the `formatBill` function itself.

EXERCISES

4.37   Given a number of pence, 1023 say, the pounds and pence parts are given by 1023 div 100 and 1023 mod 100. Using this fact, and the `shownum` function, define a function

```
formatPence :: num -> string
```

so that, for example, `formatPence 1023 = "10.23"`.

4.38   Using the `formatPence` function, define a function

```
formatLine  :: (name,price) -> string
```

which formats a line of a bill, thus:

```
formatLine ("Dry Sherry, 1lt",540)
            = "Dry Sherry, 1lt..........5.40\n"
```

Recall that ' \n' is the newline character, that ++ can be used to join two strings together, and that # will give the length of a string.

The built-in function rep will build a list by repeating an item. For example,

```
rep 4 'n' = "nnnn"
```

4.39 Using the formatLine function, define

```
formatLines :: [ (name,price) ] -> string
```

which applies formatLine to each (name,price) pair, and joins the results together.

4.40 Define a function

```
makeTotal :: billType -> num
```

which takes a list of (name,price) pairs, and gives the total of the prices. For instance,

```
makeTotal [(" ... ",540),(" ... ",121)] = 661
```

4.41 Define the function

```
formatTotal :: num -> string
```

so that, for example,

```
formatTotal 661 = "\nTotal...................6.61"
```

4.42 Using the functions formatLines, makeTotal and formatTotal, define

```
formatBill :: billType -> string
```

so that on the input

```
[("Dry Sherry, 1lt",540),("Fish Fingers",121),
("Orange Jelly",56),("Hula Hoops (Giant)",133),
("Unknown Item",0),("Dry Sherry, 1lt",540)]
```

the example bill at the start of the section is produced.

This completes the definition of the formatting functions; now we have to look at the database functions which accomplish the conversion of bar codes into names and prices.

4.43 Define a function

```
look :: database -> barCode -> (name,price)
```

which returns the (name,price) pair corresponding to the barCode in the database. If the barCode does not appear in the database, then the pair ("Unknown Item", 0) should be the result. (You can assume that each bar code occurs only once in the database, so you do not have to worry about returning multiple results.)

4.44 Define a function

```
lookup :: barCode -> (name,price)
```

which uses look to look up an item in the particular database codeIndex.

4.45 Define the function

```
makeBill   :: tillType -> billType
```

which applies lookup to every item in the input list. For instance, when applied to [1234,4719,3814,1112,1113,1234] the result will be the list of (name,price) pairs given in Exercise 4.42. Note that 1113 does not appear in codeIndex and so is converted to ("Unknown Item",0).

This completes the definition of makeBill and, together with formatBill, gives the conversion program. We conclude with some further exercises.

4.46 Modify your script so that the bill is printed with the items sorted – this can be done using the built-in function sort in the appropriate place. Why are supermarket bills not printed in this form?

4.47 You are asked in addition to add a discount for multiple buys of sherry: for every two bottles bought, there is a 1.00 discount. From the example list of bar codes [1234,4719,3814,1112,1113,1234] the bill should resemble:

```
            Miranda Stores

    Dry Sherry, 1lt...........5.40
    Dry Sherry, 1lt...........5.40
    Fish Fingers..............1.21
    Hula Hoops (Giant)........1.33
    Orange Jelly..............0.56
    Unknown Item..............0.00

    Discount..................1.00

    Total....................12.90
```

You will probably find it helpful to define functions

```
    makeDiscount :: billType -> num
    formatDiscount :: num -> string
```

which you can use in a redefined

```
    formatBill :: billType -> string
```

4.48 Design functions which update the database of bar codes. You will need a function to add a `barCode` and a `(name,price)` pair to the `database`, while at the same time removing any other reference to the bar code already present in the database.

4.49 Re-design your system so that bar codes which do not appear in the database give no entry in the final bill. There are (at least) two ways of doing this:

- keep the function `makeBill` as it is, and modify the formatting functions, or
- modify the `makeBill` function to remove the 'unknown item' pairs.

4.50 [*Project*] Design a script of functions to analyse collections of sales. Given a list of `tillType`, produce a table showing the total sales of each item. You might also analyse the bills to see which *pairs* of items are bought together; this could assist with placing items in the supermarket.

4.7 Example: Text processing

In word-processing systems it is customary for lines to be filled and broken automatically, to enhance the appearance of the text. This book is no exception. Input of the form

```
The heat bloomed      in December as the
    carnival  season
              kicked into  gear.
Nearly helpless with sun and glare, I avoided Rio's
brilliant sidewalks
   and glittering beaches,
panting in dark   corners
and waiting out the inverted southern summer.
```

would be transformed by **filling** to

```
The heat bloomed in December as the
carnival season kicked into gear.
Nearly helpless with sun and glare,
I avoided Rio's brilliant sidewalks
and glittering beaches, panting in
dark corners and waiting out the
inverted southern summer.
```

To align the right-hand margin, the text is *justified* by adding extra inter-word spaces on all lines but the last.

```
The heat bloomed in December as the
carnival  season  kicked into gear.
Nearly helpless with sun and glare,
I avoided Rio's brilliant sidewalks
and glittering beaches, panting  in
dark  corners  and  waiting out the
inverted southern summer.
```

An input file in Miranda is treated as a string of characters, so programs to handle files or to work interactively will be string-manipulating operations.

The first step in processing text will be to split an input string into **words**, discarding any white space. The words are then re-arranged into lines of the required length. These lines can then have spaces added so as to justify the text. We therefore start by looking at how text is split into words. We first ask, given a string of characters, how should we define a function to take the first word from the front of a string?

A word is any sequence which does not contain the *whitespace* characters space, tab and newline:

```
whitespace = ['\n','\t',' ']
```

To guide the definition, consider two examples:

- `getWord " boo"` should be `""` as the first character is whitespace;
- `getWord "cat dog"` is `"cat"`. We get this by putting `'c'` on the front of `"at"`, which is `getWord "at dog"`.

```
getWord :: string -> string
getWord []    = []                                    (1)
getWord (a:x)
   = []                    , if member whitespace a    (2)
   = a : getWord x  , otherwise                        (3)
```

Consider an example:

```
getWord "cat dog"
= 'c' : getWord "at dog"                          by (3)
= 'c' : 'a' : getWord "t dog"                     by (3)
= 'c' : 'a' : 't' : getWord " dog"                by (3)
= 'c' : 'a' : 't' : []                            by (2)
= "cat"
```

In a similar way, the first word of a string can be dropped.

```
dropWord :: string -> string
dropWord []    = []
dropWord (a:x)
   = (a:x)          , if member whitespace a
   = dropWord x     , otherwise
```

It is easy to check that `dropWord "cat dog" = " dog"`. We aim to use the functions `getWord` and `dropWord` to split a string into its constituent words. Note that before we take a word from the string `" dog"`, we should remove the whitespace character(s) from the front. The function `dropSpace` will do this:

```
dropSpace :: string -> string
dropSpace []    = []
dropSpace (a:x)
   = dropSpace x    , if member whitespace a
   = (a:x)          , otherwise
```

How is a string `st` to be split into words? Assuming `st` has no whitespace at the start,

- the first word in the output will be given by applying `getWord` to `st`;
- the remainder will be given by splitting what remains after removing the first word, and the space that follows it; that is, by splitting the string `dropSpace (dropWord st)`.

The top-level function `splitWords` calls `split` after removing any white-space at the start of the string:

```
word == string

splitWords :: string -> [word]
splitWords x = split (dropSpace x)

split :: string -> [word]
split [] = []
split x
    = (getWord x) : split (dropSpace (dropWord x))
```

Consider a short example.

```
splitWords "  dog cat"
= split "dog cat"
= (getWord "dog cat")
            : split (dropSpace (dropWord "dog cat"))
= "dog" : split (dropSpace " cat")
= "dog" : split "cat"
= "dog" : (getWord "cat")
            : split (dropSpace (dropWord "cat"))
= "dog" : "cat" : split (dropSpace [])
= "dog" : "cat" : split []
= "dog" : "cat" : []
= [ "dog", "cat" ]
```

Now we have to consider how to break a list of words into lines. As before, we look how we can take the first line from a list of words:

```
line == [word]
getLine :: num -> [word] -> line
```

`getLine` takes two parameters. The first is the length of the line to be formed, and the second the list from which the words are taken. The definition uses # to give the length of a list. The definition will have three cases:

- In the case that no words are available, the line formed is empty.

- If the first word available is w, then this goes on the line if there is room for it: its length, #w, has to be no greater than the length of the line, len. The remainder of the line is built from the words that remain by taking a line of length len-(#w+1).

- If the first word does not fit, the line has to be empty.

```
getLine len []     = []
getLine len (w:ws)
   = w : restOfLine  , if #w <= len
   = []              , otherwise
     where
     newlen     = len - (#w + 1)
     restOfLine = getLine newlen ws
```

Why is the rest of the line of length len-(#w+1)? Space must be allocated for the word w *and* the inter-word space needed to separate it from the word which follows. How does the function work in an example?

```
getLine 20 ["Mary","Poppins","looks","like",...
= "Mary" : getLine 15 ["Poppins","looks","like",...
= "Mary" : "Poppins" : getLine 7 ["looks","like",...
= "Mary" : "Poppins" : "looks" : getLine 1 ["like",...
= "Mary" : "Poppins" : "looks" : []
= [ "Mary", "Poppins", "looks" ]
```

A companion function,

```
dropLine :: num -> [word] -> [word]
```

removes a line from the front of a list of words, just as dropWord is a companion to getWord. The function to split a list of words into lines of length at most lineLen can now be defined:

```
splitLines :: [word] -> [line]
splitLines [] = []
splitLines x
   = getLine lineLen x
           : splitLines (dropLine lineLen x)
```

This concludes the definition of the function to fill lines. To fill a string into lines, we write

```
fill :: string -> [line]
fill st = splitLines (splitWords st)
```

To print the results, we need to write a function

```
printLines :: [line] -> string
```

This is left as an exercise, as is justification of lines.

EXERCISES

4.51 Give a definition of the function

```
printLine :: line -> string
```

which turns a line into printable form. For example,

```
printLine [ "dog", "cat" ] = "dog cat"
```

4.52 Using the function `printLine`, or otherwise, define the function

```
printLines :: [line] -> string
```

which joins together the lines, separated by newlines.

4.53 [*Harder*] Modify the function `printLine` so that it justifies the line to length `lineLen` by adding the appropriate number of spaces between the words.

4.54 Design a function

```
wc :: string -> (num,num,num)
```

which, when given a text string, returns the number of characters, words and lines in the string. The end of a line in the string is signalled by the newline character, `'\n'`. Define a similar function

```
wcFormat :: string -> (num,num,num)
```

which returns the same statistics for the text *after* it has been filled.

4.55 Define a function

```
isPalin :: string -> bool
```

which tests whether a string is a palindrome – that is, whether it reads the same both backwards and forwards. An example is the string

```
Madam I'm Adam
```

Note that punctuation and white space are ignored in the test, and that no distinction is made between capital and small letters. You might first like to develop a test which simply tests whether the string is exactly the same backwards and forwards, and only afterwards take account of punctuation and capital letters.

4.56 [*Harder*] Design a function

```
subst :: string -> string -> string -> string
```

so that subst oldSub newSub st is the result of replacing the first occurrence in st of the substring oldSub by the substring newSub. For instance,

```
subst "much  " "tall " "How much  is that?"
   = "How tall is that?"
```

If the substring oldSub does not occur in st, the result should be st.

4.8 Definition forms

Many of the definitions of list-processing functions fall into a small number of different sorts. In this section we look back over the chapter and discuss the patterns which emerge.

Combining the items – folding

The first example of the chapter, sumList (Section 4.2), shows the total of a list of numbers being computed. The total of the list is given by **folding** plus into the list, thus:

```
sumList [2,3,71] = 2+3+71
```

In a similar way,

- ++ can be folded into a list of lists to flatten it;
- & can be folded into a list of Booleans to take their conjunction; and,
- maxi can be folded into a list of numbers to give their maximum.

Applying to all – mapping

Many functions call for all the elements of a list to be transformed in some way – this we call **mapping**. The first example, given in Section 4.2, is of doubling every element of a list of numbers:

```
double [2,3,71] = [4,6,142]
```

Other examples include

- taking the second element of each pair in a list of pairs;
- converting every item in a list of bar codes to the corresponding (name,price) pair;
- formatting each (name,price) pair in a list.

Selecting elements – filtering

Selecting all the elements of a list with a given property is also common. Section 4.2 has the example of the function which selects the digits from a string

```
digits "29 February 1996" = "291996"
```

Among the other cases are

- select each pair which has a particular person as its first element;
- select each pair which is *not* equal to the loan pair being returned.

Breaking up lists

A common pattern in the text-processing example is to take or drop items, such as characters, from a list while they have some property. The first example is getWord,

```
getWord "cat dog" = "cat"
```

but others include dropWord, dropSpace and getLine, where the condition depends upon the part selected so far as well as the item in question.

Combinations

These patterns of definition are often used together. In defining books for the library database, which returns all the books on loan to a given person, we filter out all pairs involving the person, and then take all second components of the results. Combinations of mapping and filtering are often most effectively given by a list comprehension, as indeed we saw for the books example in Section 4.5.

Other combinations of functions are also common:

- Definition (5) of sumPairs can be seen applying sumPair to each pair (mapping) followed by adding the results (folding +).

- Formatting the item part of a supermarket bill involves processing each item in some way, then combining the results, using ++.

Primitive recursion and folding

The form of many definitions is **primitive recursive**. The definition at [] is given outright; at (a:x), the value at x may be used. Sorting by insertion is a classic example:

```
iSort []    = []
iSort (a:x) = insert a (iSort x)
```

Miranda provides a mechanism to turn a prefix function, like insert, into an infix version. The name is preceded by $, so

```
iSort (a:x) = a $insert (iSort x)
```

and, in a given example, we have

```
iSort [4,2,3] = 4 $insert 2 $insert 3 $insert []
```

Looked at this way, the definition looks like $insert folded into the list [4,2,3]. We shall look at this again in more detail in Chapter 14.

The last 10%

The different kinds of definition discussed so far have all been primitive recursive: we were able to define the result for (a:x) in terms of the result for x. It has been said that at least 90% of all definitions of list processing functions are primitive recursive. Some are not, however; in this chapter a notable example is splitLines:

```
splitLines [] = []
splitLines x
  = getLine lineLen x
        : splitLines (dropLine lineLen x)
```

For a non-empty list x, the result splitLines x is defined using splitLines not on x but on (dropLine lineLen x).

This works because (dropLine lineLen x) will always be shorter than x itself, at least in sensible cases where no word in the text is longer than the line length lineLen!

4.9   Program design

Section 2.13 contains advice about program design which is equally applicable to list-processing programs. In the supermarket billing example, for instance, we worked bottom-up to build the formatting functions; and in defining sumPairs we saw the importance of thinking about the kind of pattern matching to be used.

Change is unavoidable

This section builds on the earlier advice and the experience of the last chapter. As we construct larger systems, one fact will confront us: however well we think of our designs in advance, we will be forced to make modifications as we proceed; two scenarios follow:

- On seeing the prototype output of our billing system, it may be decided to make the lines of the bill a different length. If we have made the line length a constant, all we need to do is to modify one definition; if not, we have to look for each use of the length in the script.

- A function returns a result of type t; on design it is seen that in some cases the operation can *fail*. We therefore have to modify the result type to (t,bool), with a False value to signal failure, and change the script accordingly. In particular, a function processing lists of these items will have to be modified. We saw in definition (5) of sumPairs that processing the items separately in the function sumPair meant that only one definition had to be modified.

These two examples show how changes can be demanded during program development. To make change possible it is helpful to follow the design principles we have given, as well as those which follow:

- Each function should do one thing: if we have to, say, process some data and then format the results, these should be two separate functions. If we have to change the formatting, then we only have to modify one of them; if there was a single function doing both tasks, we would have to modify a more complex piece of program.

- Each part of the problem should be performed by an identifiable function. It is possible to write a collection of functions which perform formatting, say, and to use them to format a piece of text. For instance

```
top text = form1 (process text) ++ form2 (process text)
```

It is clearer to say

```
top text = form (process text)
form out = form1 out ++ form2 out
```

since in the second definition we can see that all the formatting is done by `form`, and that therefore it is this function which should be modified if we want a changed format.

Designing definitions

The advice on making definitions from Section 2.13 is still most relevant. We should know the type of the function we are designing, and we should be clear about its purpose. For lists, we have just seen a classification of the different kinds of definition which commonly occur; keeping these in mind can help to focus how we want a definition to work, especially when we remember that they can be combined.

If we try to write a direct recursive definition of a function, we can meet two kinds of problem:

- We might find that another function has to be defined. Suppose we want to write a function to decide whether one string is a substring of another:

  ```
  subString :: string -> string -> bool
  ```

  so that, for instance

  ```
  subString "cat" "scathing" = True
  subString "cat" "cart" = False
  ```

  We will have

  ```
  subString st (a:x) = subString st x \/ ...
  ```

  In the ... part, we have to write a function which decides whether `st` is a substring of `(a:x)` starting at the front. This itself will require a recursive definition.

- In finding a definition we may need to generalize our goal, making the original goal a particular case of the new function. For instance, in text processing, we had the function

  ```
  getLine :: [word] -> [word]
  ```

  which gets a line from the start of a list of words. This cannot be defined directly, but only by defining the generalization

  ```
  getLine :: num -> [word] -> [word]
  ```

where the extra parameter gives the length of line to be found. The recursion then uses `getLine` with *different* values of line length. Another example occurs when we try to find the definition of the list `[1..n]`. The natural definition says

```
[1..n] = 1:[2..n]
```

which is given by a two-argument recursion

```
[m..n] = []          , if m>n
       = m:[m+1..n] , otherwise
```

Error handling

Some functions can have cases where a result is not defined. In defining `returnLoan` for the library database, there is a case that we might try to return a loan which has not been made, for instance. Three options are possible:

● We return the database unchanged. The way the program behaves is not affected by the error case. We could check that a loan has been made before calling the `returnLoan` function if we are concerned about this case.

● We make the result

```
error "problem in returnLoan"
```

in this case. If this happens, evaluation stops and the error message is printed. The program is stopped by the error case.

● We change the type of the result to `(database,bool)` with the second value being `False` if the loan was not present. After calling the `returnLoan` function we can look at the second part of the result to see whether the loan was present or not. This neither ignores the error, nor halts the program; it allows the function calling `returnLoan` to acknowledge the error without stopping the program.

Different strategies will be used in different circumstances, depending upon what is needed in each case. We return to the topic in the final part of the book.

SUMMARY

This chapter has introduced the type of lists – for each type `t` there is a type `[t]` of lists of items of type `t`. After giving the syntax of list constants we have discussed a range of examples of list-based programs:

sorting, adding a list, selecting elements and a number of case studies which use lists to represent data objects such as books, supermarket bills, databases, text and so forth. The chapter is concluded by discussions of the forms taken by list definitions and of program design, which build both on earlier insights and on the present chapter.

5 Reasoning about lists

Now we have seen the introduction of lists, it is possible to show many more proofs of properties of functions, which we prove by **structural induction**, the list analogue of induction over the natural numbers. The form of proofs is similar, and we will again give guidelines for constructing proofs.

As with numbers earlier, some proofs can work directly or by case analysis. We shall see some examples of this as we look at induction proofs by means of a series of examples and exercises. We shall also look at more complicated examples where we need to generalize the induction hypothesis before a proof can be found successfully; the latter material can be omitted on first reading the chapter.

5.1 Structural induction

Structural induction gives a method of proof for statements P(x) for all *finite* lists x, where

- [] is a finite list;
- (a:x) is a finite list if x is a finite list.

Proof by structural induction

To prove the property P(x) for all finite lists x we have to do two things.

Base case   Prove P([]).
Induction step   Prove P(a:x) assuming that P(x) holds already.

Again we can picture the induction step as a machine, Figure 5.1, turning proofs into proofs – if we know that P(x) holds, then we can use the machine to tell us that P(a:x) holds.

Starting with a proof of P([]) we can get a proof of P(x) for any finite x. For instance, if x is [2,37], we have P([]), and from the induction step, we have P([37]), and from the induction step again, P([2,37]).

Again, as for the natural numbers, there is a relationship between definitions by recursion and proofs by structural induction over lists. The value of a function at [] is given outright, whilst at (a:x), the value at x is used.

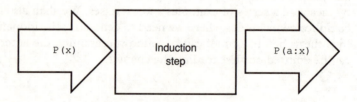

Figure 5.1   P(x) ⇒ P(a:x).

An induction template

To help construct proofs by structural induction, we supply a template to follow. The template is useful in forcing us to be clear about what are the specific goals of each part of the proof by induction:

Stage 0	Write down the goal of the proof, in English
Stage 1	Write down the goal of the proof: proving,

- P(x), for all finite lists x

Stage 2	Write down the two sub-goals of the induction proof,

- P([])
- P(a:x) assuming P(x)

Stage 3	Prove P([])
Stage 4	Prove P(a:x), remembering that you can, and probably *should*, use P(x) somewhere in the proof.

Finding proofs

The advice is similar to that we followed in Chapter 3.

In the remainder of this chapter we will always *change the names* of the variables used in definitions, to avoid confusion with the variables used in the induction proof. Remember that the equations can be used at *any* instance whatever.

In finding proofs of equations, we will aim to use the definitions to simplify the two sides of the equations as much as possible, before applying the induction hypothesis in the proof of P(a:x).

Next we look at a sequence of example proofs.

5.2   Proofs by structural induction

EXAMPLE: Sum and double

As we began to look at lists we wrote functions to give the total of a numerical list and to double each item in a numerical list:

```
sumList []     = 0                          (1)
sumList (b:y) = b + sumList y               (2)

double []     = []                          (3)
double (b:y) = (2*b) : double y             (4)
```

They are related – we can get the sum of a doubled list by doubling the sum of the list:

```
sumList (double x) = 2 * sumList x          (5)
```

which we aim to prove by structural induction. Following the template, our goals are

- Base case

$$\texttt{sumList (double [])} = 2 * \texttt{sumList []} \tag{6}$$

- Induction step

$$\texttt{sumList (double (a:x))} = 2 * \texttt{sumList (a:x)} \tag{7}$$

assuming

$$\texttt{sumList (double x)} = 2 * \texttt{sumList x} \tag{8}$$

Proof: We begin by looking at each side of (6), and simplifying it.

```
  sumList (double [])
= sumList []                                            by (3)
= 0                                                     by (1)
```

The right-hand side is

```
  2 * sumList []
= 2 * 0                                                 by (1)
= 0                                                     arithmetic
```

which shows that (6) holds. Next we have to prove (7), using the assumption (8). Simplifying the left-hand side we have

```
  sumList (double (a:x))
= sumList (2*a : double x)                              by (4)
= 2*a + sumList (double x)                              by (2)
```

and, by assumption (8), this is

```
= 2*a + 2 * sumList x                                   by (8)
= 2 * (a + sumList x)                                   arithmetic
```

Now, the right-hand side is

```
  2 * sumList (a:x)
= 2 * (a + sumList x)                                   by (2)
```

which shows the two sides are equal, and completes the proof.

■

Associativity of append

The operation to join or **append** two lists is defined by

$$[] \quad {+}{+} \ v = v \tag{1}$$
$$(c{:}u) \ {+}{+} \ v = c{:}(u{+}{+}v) \tag{2}$$

We say that it is associative because for all finite lists x, y and z,

$$x \ {+}{+} \ (y \ {+}{+} \ z) = (x \ {+}{+} \ y) \ {+}{+} \ z$$

We will show this by induction on x – this is a sensible choice because in the definition above we do recursion on the left-hand argument. In the proof y and z will be arbitrary, and so the result will hold for all choices of y and z. The result will therefore hold for all finite lists x, y and z.

Our goals in the proof will be

- Base case

$$[] \ {+}{+} \ (y \ {+}{+} \ z) = ([] \ {+}{+} \ y) \ {+}{+} \ z \tag{3}$$

- Induction step

$$(a{:}x) \ {+}{+} \ (y \ {+}{+} \ z) = ((a{:}x) \ {+}{+} \ y) \ {+}{+} \ z \tag{4}$$

assuming

$$x \ {+}{+} \ (y \ {+}{+} \ z) = (x \ {+}{+} \ y) \ {+}{+} \ z \tag{5}$$

At each stage we say which of the defining equations has been used to make the simplification. It can sometimes be helpful to show which part of an expression the simplification applies to – we do this by underlining in the proof which follows.

Proof: First we look at the base case, and examine the left-hand side

$$\underline{[] \ {+}{+} \ (y \ {+}{+} \ z)}$$
$$= (y \ {+}{+} \ z) \qquad \qquad \text{by (1)}$$

Note that here we have replaced v by (y ++ z) in (1). This is valid since we can replace v by *any* value. On the right-hand side

$$\underline{([] \ {+}{+} \ y)} \ {+}{+} \ z$$
$$= (y \ {+}{+} \ z) \qquad \qquad \text{by (1)}$$

which shows that (3) holds. In the induction case we again look at each side

$$\underline{(a{:}x) \ {+}{+} \ (y \ {+}{+} \ z)}$$
$$= a{:}(x \ {+}{+} \ (y \ {+}{+} \ z)) \qquad \qquad \text{by (2)}$$

$$
\begin{aligned}
&((a:x) \ ++ \ y) \ ++ \ z \\
&= \ \underline{(a:(x \ ++ \ y)) \ ++ \ z} && \text{by (2)} \\
&= \ a:((x \ ++ \ y) \ ++ \ z) && \text{by (2)}
\end{aligned}
$$

In the second sequence, we use two instances of (2). In the first x replaces u and y replaces v; in the second (x ++ y) replaces u and z replaces v. The two sides are equal given the induction hypothesis, (5).

■

EXAMPLE: Membership _____

The test for membership of a list is given by

```
member []    d = False                          (1)
member (c:z) d = (c=d) \/ member z d            (2)
```

which uses the 'or' operation

```
True  \/ w = True                               (3)
False \/ w = w                                  (4)
```

We claim that if we join two finite lists x and y,

```
member (x++y) b = member x b \/ member y b
```

We aim to prove this by induction on x. The goals will be

- Base case

  ```
  member ([]++y) b = member [] b \/ member y b      (3)
  ```

- Induction step

  ```
  member ((a:x)++y) b = member (a:x) b \/ member y b   (4)
  ```

  assuming

  ```
  member (x++y) b = member x b \/ member y b          (5)
  ```

Proof: Examining the base case first, we have

```
  member ([]++y) b
= member y b                              by (++ 1)
```

```
  member [] b \/ member y b
= False \/ member y b                     by (1)
= member y b                              by (4)
```

and so the base case holds. In the induction step, we first look at the left-hand side

```
  member ((a:x)++y) b
= member (a:(x++y)) b                          by (++ 2)
= (a=b) \/ member (x++y) b                      by (2)
= (a=b) \/ (member x b \/ member y b)           by (5)
```

On the right-hand side,

```
  member (a:x) b \/ member y b
= ((a=b) \/ member x b) \/ member y b           by (2)
```

These are equal, if we can show that '\/' is associative. This we do now.

∎

To prove a result for all Booleans, we need to prove it for `True` and `False`.[†]
Our aim is to show associativity of 'or':

```
x \/ (y \/ z) = (x \/ y) \/ z
```

In the case that x is `True`, each side reduces to `True`; in the `False` case they reduce to `(y \/ z)`, giving the result.

EXERCISES

5.1 Prove that for all finite lists x,

```
x ++ [] = x
```

5.2 Try to prove

```
x ++ (y ++ z) = (x ++ y) ++ z
```

by structural induction on z. What goes wrong with the proof?

[†] This establishes the result for all *defined* Booleans; we need to show that it also holds for an undefined value if it is to hold for all Booleans. This will be the case for the example of associativity given here.

5.3   Prove for all finite lists x and y that

```
sumList (x ++ y) = sumList x + sumList y
```

and therefore that

```
sumList (x ++ y) = sumList (y ++ x)
```

5.4   Show that for all finite lists x and y,

```
double (x ++ y) = double x ++ double y
#(x ++ y) = #x + #y
```

and that for all finite lists x,

```
#(double x) = #x
```

5.5   By induction on x prove that for all finite lists x and y,

```
sumList (x ++ (a:y)) = a + sumList (x ++ y)
```

5.6   Using the previous exercise or otherwise, prove that for all finite lists x,

```
sumList (double x) = sumList (x ++ x)
```

5.7   We can flatten a list of lists using

```
flatten []    = []
flatten (c:z) = c ++ flatten z
```

Prove that for all w

```
flatten [w] = w
```

and that for all finite lists x and y

```
flatten (x ++ y) = flatten x ++ flatten y
```

5.8   Complete the sketch proof of the associativity of 'or'.

5.3   Case studies

The examples examined so far are for small-scale definitions; the same methods apply to larger-scale examples equally well. In this section we give a sequence of exercises coming from the case studies.

EXERCISES

5.9 Show that for all finite databases db and all people per

```
numBorrowed db per = #(books db per)
```

5.10 Show that for all finite databases db and all books bk

```
borrowed db bk = (borrowers db bk ~= [])
```

5.11 If pers is not equal to per show that for all finite databases db,

```
books (makeLoan db per bk) pers = books db pers
```

On the other hand, show that

```
books (makeLoan db per bk) per = bk : books db per
```

5.12 Using the function

```
sorted :: [num] -> bool

sorted []      = True
sorted [a]     = True
sorted (a:b:x) = (a<=b) & sorted (b:x)
```

show that iSort satisfies

```
sorted (iSort x) = True
```

for all finite lists of defined numbers, x. You need the numbers to be defined to make sure that any comparisons a<=b will give a result.

5.13 Show that for all finite tt of tillType,

```
#(makeBill tt) = #tt
```

5.14 Under suitable assumptions show that the length of a line in the supermarket bill is lineLength.

5.15 Show that, assuming the characters in st are defined,

```
member (getWord st) ' ' = False
```

5.16 Formulate and prove a result which says that getLine will only give lines of the appropriate length, at most. You will probably need to define a function which gives the length of a list of words, counting one for each space between words as well as the lengths of the words themselves.

5.4 Generalizing the proof goal

It is not always easy to build a proof in a straightforward way; that is, by induction over a goal we set ourselves. In this section we explore an example in which only after two false starts are we able to build a proof of the property we seek. The section is more technical than the rest of the chapter and can be omitted on first reading.

The shunting function

The shunt function moves the elements from one list onto another, thus:

```
shunt :: [num] -> [num] -> [num]
```

```
shunt []     y = y                               (1)
shunt (a:x)  y = shunt x (a:y)                    (2)
```

Starting with an empty second argument, we have

```
shunt [2,3,1] []
= shunt [3,1] [2]
= shunt [1] [3,2]
= shunt [] [1,3,2]
= [1,3,2]
```

and so we can reverse lists using this function:

```
rev :: [num] -> [num]
rev l = shunt l []                               (3)
```

Now we turn to looking at properties of the rev function.

First proof attempt

Reversing a list twice should give us back the list we started with, and so we aim to prove that rev (rev x) = x (call this property $Q(x)$) for all finite lists x. The base case is easily established, but when we look at the induction step, we meet our first problem:

```
rev (rev (a:x))
= shunt (shunt (a:x) []) []          by (3)
= shunt (shunt x [a]) []             by (2)
```

This has no direct relationship to rev and to the induction hypothesis, talking as it does of (shunt x [a]). A clue to the problem is that rev is not the function defined by recursion – it is simply a specialization of shunt. Can we find a *generalization* of Q(x) which talks explicitly about shunt and which is to be proved by induction?

Now, rev specializes shunt by replacing y with []. If we replace this by y, we have

```
shunt (shunt x y) []
```

and this should be equal to shunt y x. When y is replaced by [], we get Q(x). We therefore aim to prove this generalization.

Second proof attempt

Our aim is to show

```
shunt (shunt x y) [] = shunt y x
```

for all finite lists x and y. In the case that x is [], the proof is simple. Now we look at the induction step:

```
  shunt (shunt (a:x) y) []
= shunt (shunt x (a:y)) []                                    by (2)
```

We would now like to claim by induction that this is equal to shunt (a:y) x, but to do this we need the induction hypothesis to give the result that

```
shunt (shunt x (a:y)) [] = shunt (a:y) x
```

rather than

```
shunt (shunt x y) [] = shunt y x
```

To get around this, we strengthen the induction hypothesis to become

```
shunt (shunt x z) [] = shunt z x    for all z
```

so that in particular it will hold when (a:y) replaces z. We now try again.

The successful proof attempt

In logical notation, our induction formula P(x) is

$$\forall z. \text{ shunt (shunt x z) [] = shunt z x}$$

Now we can state what is required. The goals will be

- Base case

$$\forall \ z. \ \text{shunt (shunt [] z) []} = \text{shunt z []} \tag{4}$$

- Induction step

$$\forall \ z. \ \text{shunt (shunt (a:x) z) []} = \text{shunt z (a:x)} \tag{5}$$

assuming

$$\forall \ z. \ \text{shunt (shunt x z) []} = \text{shunt z x} \tag{6}$$

Proof: In the base case we prove

$$\forall \ z. \ \text{shunt (shunt [] z) []} = \text{shunt z []} \tag{4}$$

by proving it for an arbitrary y in place of z.

The left-hand side simplifies to the right-hand side in one step:

```
shunt (shunt [] y) []
= shunt y []                                          by (1)
```

In a similar way we prove

$$\forall \ z. \ \text{shunt (shunt (a:x) z) []} = \text{shunt z (a:x)} \tag{5}$$

by proving it for an arbitrary y. Simplifying the left-hand side, we have

```
shunt (shunt (a:x) y) []
= shunt (shunt x (a:y)) []                            by (2)
```

Now, by (6), at the particular value (a:y) for z,

```
= shunt (a:y) x                                       by (6)
= shunt y (a:x)                                       by (2)
```

This is the right-hand side, and so the proof is complete for an arbitrary y, giving a proof of (5), and completing the induction proof.

■

This example shows that we may have to generalize what has to be proved in order for induction proofs to work. This seems paradoxical: we are making it harder for ourselves, apparently. We are in one way, but at the same time we make the induction hypothesis *stronger*, so that we have *more* resources to use when proving the induction step.

EXERCISES

5.17 Prove for all finite lists x and y that

```
rev (x ++ y) = rev y ++ rev x
```

5.18 Given the definition

```
rev2 []    = []
rev2 (a:x) = rev2 x ++ [a]
```

prove that for all finite lists x,

```
rev x = rev2 x
```

5.19 Using the function

```
facAux :: num -> num -> num
facAux 0     p = p
facAux (n+1) p = facAux n ((n+1)*p)
```

we can define

```
fac2 n = facAux n 1
```

Prove that for all natural numbers n,

```
fac n = fac2 n
```

SUMMARY

This chapter has shown that in most cases a straightforward attempt will yield a proof that a recursively-defined function has certain properties, with the induction proof following the pattern of the recursive definition.

The base case, for the empty list [], is proved outright, whilst the case of the non-empty list (a:x) is proved from the induction hypothesis for the list x.

In cases where the straightforward approach fails, as examined in the optional Section 5.4, there might well need to be a search for the appropriate generalization of the property before it can be proved by an induction. The example given there illustrated how the failed proof attempts can be used to guide the re-formulation of the problem before a proof is tried again.

Part II

Abstraction

The first part of the book introduced the basics of functional programming in Miranda. Definitions over lists, numbers, Booleans and so forth are written using pattern-matching equations. The equations themselves have multiple right-hand sides, guarded by Boolean expressions, and local definitions in where clauses. In this part we introduce two important new ideas:

- Functions themselves are data objects. In particular, they can be the arguments or results of other functions.
- Function definitions can apply to whole classes of types, rather than to a single type.

Putting these two ideas together gives us a very powerful way of building general functions, which can be re-used in different ways at different types.

This part is entitled **abstraction** because the usual way of forming these general functions is to abstract from a particular function – like a function to double every number in a list of numbers – to form something more general – in this case the **higher-order** function which applies a function like double to every item in a list.

The concluding chapter of this part discusses how the types of Miranda expressions and definitions are checked, first using the simple types of the first part, and then using the **polymorphic** types introduced here.

Generalization

In this chapter it is shown that functions may take functions as arguments; as a result, many definitions become polymorphic: they may be used over whole collections of types rather than over a single type.

6.1 Functions as arguments

This section introduces the idea that functions (just as much as numbers, tuples and so on) can be arguments of other functions, which for this reason are called **higher-order** functions. We do this in the context of an example, and in the light of what was said about general forms of definition in Section 4.8.

EXAMPLE: Double and treble

One of the first functions we defined over lists of numbers was

```
double :: [num] -> [num]
double []    = []
double (a:x) = (2*a) : double x
```

which doubles each element of a list; similarly,

```
treble :: [num] -> [num]
treble []    = []
treble (a:x) = (3*a) : treble x
```

which trebles each element of a list. In the terminology of Section 4.8 both are mapping functions, in which every element of a list is changed in some way. The pattern of the definitions is the same; what differs is the way in which the elements of the lists are changed, or **transformed**, in each case.

Each transformation of the elements can be written down as a function:

```
times2,times3 :: num -> num

times2 n = 2*n
times3 n = 3*n
```

Any function from numbers to numbers can be used in mapping – we could therefore make a function from numbers to numbers an **argument** of a general mapping function. double and treble can then be seen as two examples of a general mapping function *applied* to times2 and times3.

The general mapping function between lists of numbers will have to take *two* arguments:

- the transformation to be applied to each element: a function, and
- the list input.

```
mapNum f []    = []
mapNum f (a:x) = f a : mapNum f x
```

The definition has two cases:

- when the input is empty, so is the result;
- on input (a:x), the head of the result is given by f applied to a, and the tail by applying f to every element in the tail – by mapNum f x, in other words.

As we said earlier, particular mapping functions are given by applying mapNum to the appropriate arguments, thus:

```
double l = mapNum times2 l
treble l = mapNum times3 l
```

An example calculation gives

```
mapNum times2 [2,3]
= times2 2 : mapNum times2 [3]
= 4 : mapNum times2 [3]
= 4 : ( times2 3 : mapNum times2 [] )
= 4 : ( 6 : mapNum times2 [] )
= 4 : ( 6 : [] )
= 4 : [6]
= [4,6]
```

which mirrors exactly the example calculation in Chapter 4. As we saw in that chapter, a list comprehension can also be used to define the operation of applying to every member of a list, thus:

```
mapNum f l = [ f a | a <-l ]
```

What is the type of mapNum? It has two arguments, and so its type will be

```
t₁ -> t₂ -> t
```

where t_1 is the type of the first argument, t_2 the type of the second and t the type of the result.

The first argument is a transformation or function from num to num, and so t_1 is (num -> num); the second argument and result are lists of numbers, so t_2 and t are [num]. Putting this together, we have

```
mapNum :: (num -> num) -> [num] -> [num]
```

Why higher-order functions?

What is the advantage of defining the mapNum function, and using it in the definition of double and treble? There are three separate reasons for using mapNum:

- It becomes easier to *understand* the definition, since it makes clear that it is a mapping by using the mapNum function. To understand the function we simply therefore have to understand the function mapped along the list.

- It becomes easier to *modify* the definition of double if that is necessary. If we want to change the transformation of the elements, all we need to do is to change the function which gives the transformation, times2; we leave the top level definition unchanged.

- It becomes easier to *re-use* definitions – once mapNum is defined it can be used in a variety of circumstances, which were perhaps not originally intended. We could, for instance, use it to convert a list of prices in pence to prices in pounds, prior to printing.

If we define higher-order functions to reflect the sorts of definition we are accustomed to seeing, such as those in Section 4.8, then we are likely to be able to use them again and again, in differing circumstances.

EXAMPLES: Sales analysis revisited ───────────────────────────

Here we examine the sales analysis functions introduced in Section 2.2. These functions were all defined to analyse a *fixed* function sales; we can instead define functions which take a function as an argument, so that the sales analysis examples are particular *applications* of the new functions.

We first look at a function to give the sum f 0 + ... + f n, where f is of type (num -> num):

```
total :: (num -> num) -> num -> num
total f n
  = f 0                    , if n=0
  = total f (n-1) + f n    , otherwise
```

Now totalSales is given by

```
totalSales n = total sales n
```

but once we have total it can be used to define many other functions as well. For example, we can sum the squares of numbers 0 to n:

```
sumSquares :: num -> num
sumSquares n = total sq n


sq :: num -> num
sq x = x*x
```

Other functions inspired by the sales analysis study are

```
maxFun :: (num -> num) -> num -> num
maxFun f n
   = f 0                            , if n=0
   = maxi (maxFun f (n-1)) (f n)    , otherwise
```

which gives the maximum of the values f 0 to f n, and,

```
zeroInRange :: (num -> num) -> num -> bool
zeroInRange f 0     = (f 0 = 0)
zeroInRange f (n+1) = zeroInRange f n \/ (f (n+1) = 0)
```

which decides whether there is a zero value for f on inputs 0 to n. Both these functions have many uses beyond the sales analysis example.

EXAMPLE: Folding

Another definition form over lists identified in Section 4.8 was folding: we give higher-order functions implementing this now.

The sum and maximum of a list are given by folding in the functions + and maxi, which have type (num -> num -> num), thus:

$$e_1 + e_2 + \ldots + e_n$$
$$e_1 \; \$maxi \; e_2 \; \$maxi \; \ldots \; \$maxi \; e_n$$

(recall that $maxi is the infix form of the prefix function maxi). For the one-element list [e] the result is e; the result for a general list is suggested by bracketing thus:

$$e_1 \; \$maxi \; (e_2 \; \$maxi \; \ldots \; \$maxi \; e_n)$$

and rearranging,

$$maxi \; e_1 \; (maxList \; [e_2 \; \ldots \; e_n])$$

Guided by this, in general we should have

```
foldNum :: (num -> num -> num) -> [num] -> num

foldNum f [a]     = a
foldNum f (a:b:x) = f a (foldNum f (b:x))
```

The type declaration for `foldNum` states that `f` is a function taking two numbers and returning a number; the second argument is a list of numbers, and the result is a number, as should be expected.

The functions to find the sum and maximum are given by

```
sumList l = foldNum (+) l
maxList l = foldNum maxi l
```

where (+) is used for the *prefix* form of the infix operator '+'.

EXAMPLE: Filtering lists

Often programs require certain items to be selected or *filtered* from a list. For example, we might want to pick out the digits or the letters in a string of characters, so that

```
digits  "29 February 1996" = "291996"
letters "29 February 1996" = "February"
```

Each character has to be tested to see whether it has the property we want, such as being a digit. The test takes a character, and returns an answer, which will be a Boolean value. We can therefore think of a **property** of characters as a function of type

```
char -> bool
```

Examples of these are

```
isDigit, isLetter :: char -> bool

isDigit  ch = ('0'<=ch & ch<='9')
isLetter ch = ('a'<=ch & ch<='z') \/ ('A'<=ch & ch<='Z')
```

The type of our function to filter elements from strings will be

```
filterString :: (char -> bool) -> [char] -> [char]
```

The first argument is the property for which we are testing, the second is the string to be filtered. Now we can define the function

```
filterString p [] = []
filterString p (a:x)
  = a : filterString p x    , if p a
  =     filterString p x    , otherwise
```

For a non-empty string, (a:x), there are two cases. We test whether a has the property by applying p; this gives a Boolean.

- In case p a is True, a is the first element of the result, with the remainder coming from filtering x;
- In case p a is False, the result comes from filtering x.

The functions digits and letters are now defined from filterString:

```
digits  st = filterString isDigit st
letters st = filterString isLetter st
```

An alternative definition of filterString is provided by

```
filterString p x = [ a | a<-x ; p a ]
```

Just as before, the advantages of using a higher-order function are re-usability (of the function filterString) and the ease with which we can modify one of the functions, such as letters, so that it picks out only the small letters. This can be done simply by modifying the property passed to filterString.

EXERCISES

6.1 Give definitions of functions to take a list of numbers, l, and

- return the list consisting of the squares of the numbers in l;
- return the sum of squares of items in l;
- check whether all items of the list are greater than zero.

6.2 Write definitions of functions to

- give the minimum value of a function on inputs 0 to n;
- test whether the values of f on inputs 0 to n are all equal;

- test if all values of f on inputs 0 to n are greater than zero, and
- check whether the values f 0, f 1 to f n are in increasing order.

6.3   State the type of and define a function `twice` which takes a function from numbers to numbers and an input number, and whose output is the function applied to the input twice. For instance, with the `times2` function and 7 as input, the result is 28.

6.4   Give the type of and define a function `iter` so that

```
iter n f x = f (f (f ... (f x)...))
```

where f occurs n times on the right-hand side of the equation. For instance, we should have

```
iter 3 f x = f (f (f x))
```

and `iter 0 f x` should return x unchanged.

6.5   Using `iter` and `times2`, define a function which on input n returns 2^n; remember that 2^n means one multiplied by two n times.

6.2   Polymorphism

The second concept which gives functional programming its power is explored in this section. As an illustration we examine how to find the length of a list, a topic first discussed in Section 4.2.

```
#[]    = 0
#(a:x) = 1 + #x
```

The length function takes a list as argument – the patterns used on the left-hand side of the equations are [] and (a:x) – but there is no constraint on the type of elements of the list in the definition. The definition will therefore be applicable to lists of any type, returning a number in each case.

The length function has a **polymorphic** type. Before we explain these types, we look again at the role of variables in equations. We then give a sequence of examples of polymorphic functions, and see that many functions we have seen already are in fact polymorphic.

Variables

When we write an equation like

```
square x = x*x
```

we use the variable x to mean that the equation holds for *all* values x (of type num). Given an equation involving a variable, any *instance* of it will also be valid; an instance is given by replacing the variable by an expression; so, for example,

```
square 2     = 2*2
square (3+4) = (3+4)*(3+4)
square (x+1) = (x+1)*(x+1)
```

In the first instance, x was replaced by the value 2; in the second by the expression (3+4); and in the third by the expression (x+1), which itself contains a variable. Note that in each case, all three x's are replaced with the *same* expression.

Equations and formulas can contain more than one variable:

```
sumSq n m = n*n + m*m
```

In taking an instance, different variables can take different values,

```
sumSq 3 4 = 3*3 + 4*4
```

but all occurrences of each variable, such as n, are replaced by the same value: 3 in this case.

Type variables

How can we express that [] is of type [num], [[bool]] and so forth? By saying that it has type

```
[] :: [*]                                                    (1)
```

where * is a **type variable**. Type variables in Miranda are written *, **, *** and so on. How is (1) interpreted? Just as for ordinary variables, any instance of it will hold, so

```
[] :: [num]
[] :: [[bool]]
[] :: [num -> num]
[] :: [[**]]
```

where in the four cases * is replaced by the types num, [bool], num -> num and [**].

When a function or object has a type involving one or more type variables, it has a *polymorphic* type – polymorphic means that it has 'many forms', or types. Often we call the function itself polymorphic, too.

An important polymorphic function is the list constructor 'cons' or ':' which can now be given its proper type. It takes an object and a list of items *of the same type* and gives a list of that type. If we call the arbitrary type '*', then

```
(:) :: * -> [*] -> [*]
```

which has as instances the types we listed in Section 4.2.

Polymorphic definitions

When do definitions give rise to polymorphic functions? The length function

```
#[]    = 0
#(a:x) = 1 + #x
```

has the type

```
# :: [*] -> num
```

because the argument is an arbitrary list, and the result a number. Another example is the function to join two lists, ++. It must join lists of the same type, since a list must consist of elements of the same type, but that type is arbitrary, so

```
(++) :: [*] -> [*] -> [*]
```

To reverse a list (a:x), we attach a to the end of x reversed

```
rev []    = []
rev (a:x) = rev x ++ [a]
```

In this definition there is no constraint on the type of elements, so

```
rev :: [*] -> [*]
```

A particularly simple example is the **identity** function which returns its argument unchanged: the type of the output is the same as that of the input, so

```
id :: * -> *

id x = x
```

Zipping two lists together results in a list of pairs:

```
zip2 (a:x) (b:y) = (a,b) : zip2 x y
zip2 x y         = []
```

There is no constraint on the type of the two argument lists, and *no relation between their types*. Because there is no relationship, we make the type of the first [*], and the second [**]. The type will then be

```
zip2 :: [*] -> [**] -> [ (*,**) ]
```

Instances of this type include

```
[num] -> [bool] -> [(num,bool)]
[num] -> [num]  -> [(num,num)]
```

We can see from this that multiple type variables behave just like multiple ordinary variables: different variables can be replaced by different values (and by the same, of course, as in the second example).

The polymorphic types given in the section are the most general types for the functions. A type t for f is the *most general type* of f if all types of f are instances of t. As we said, the type of zip2 given above is most general, however the type [*]->[*]->[(*,*)], whilst a type for the function, is *not* the most general, since, for example, [num] -> [bool] -> [(num,bool)] is not an instance of it.

REVISITING EXAMPLES

Many of the functions we have defined already are in fact polymorphic. We can use the Miranda system to deduce the most general type of a function, such as books, by commenting out its type declaration in the script, thus

```
|| books :: database -> person -> [book]
```

and then by typing

```
books ::
```

to the Miranda prompt. The result we get in that case is

```
books :: [ (*,**) ] -> * -> [**]
```

which is perhaps a surprise at first. This is less so if we rewrite the definition with books renamed `lookupFirst`, because it looks up all the pairs with a particular first part, and returns their corresponding second parts. Here it is with its variables renamed as well:

```
lookupFirst :: [ (*,**) ] -> * -> [**]
```

```
lookupFirst [] a = []
lookupFirst ((b,c):rest) a
   = c : lookupFirst rest a      , if b = a
   =       lookupFirst rest a      , otherwise
```

Clearly, from this definition there is nothing specific about books or people, and so it is polymorphic.

Other examples are more obviously polymorphic; from Section 2.9 we have

```
fst :: (*,**) -> *            snd :: (*,**) -> **

fst (x,y) = x                 snd (x,y) = y

shift :: ((*,**),***) -> (*,(**,***))
shift ((a,b),c) = (a,(b,c))
```

from Section 4.3:

```
member :: [*] -> * -> bool

member []    b = False
member (a:x) b = (a=b) \/ member x b
```

and finally, from Section 4.4, as we saw for books,

```
borrowed    :: [ (*,**) ] -> ** -> bool
numBorrowed :: [ (*,**) ] -> *  -> num
```

Why polymorphism?

What are the advantages of Miranda allowing definitions to be polymorphic? The main advantage is that by making definitions more general, there is a much greater chance of their being re-used. We originally wrote the functions books etc. to work on a particular library database, but in their polymorphic form we can see them as general database functions, usable over arbitrary types of entry.

Many list-processing functions are polymorphic: we have seen a number here and will see more when polymorphism and higher-order functions are combined. We can write a library of list-processing functions once and for all, and re-use them on each new type of list. In a non-polymorphic language, they need to be re-defined for each new type. This is both inefficient and unsafe: if we have more than one copy of a function definition in our system, we run the risk of these versions becoming different or inconsistent.

EXERCISES

6.6 Define the function `numEqual` which takes a list of items x, say, and an item a, say, and returns the number of times a occurs in x. What is the type of your function? How could you use `numEqual` to define `member`?

6.7 Define the 'flatten' function, `concat` so that

$$\text{concat } [e_1, \ldots, e_k] = e_1 \mathbin{++} \ldots \mathbin{++} e_k$$

What is the type of `concat`?

6.8 Give a function `unZip2` which turns a list of pairs into a pair of lists. What is its type?

6.9 There are two ways that one list can be contained in another:

- One is a *sublist* of the other if all the elements of one are contained in the other, in the same order. For example, $[1,3]$ is a sublist of $[1,2,3,4]$, but not of $[4,3,2,1]$.

- One is a *subsequence* of the other if it is a sublist and the elements occur in a single block. For instance, $[1,3]$ is a subsequence of $[1,3,4]$, but not of $[1,2,3,4]$.

Define functions to test for sublist and subsequence. Specify the test data you would use for them and explain your choice. What are the types of the functions?

6.10 Define functions

```
lookupFirst1  :: [ (*,**) ] -> * -> **
lookupSecond1 :: [ (*,**) ] -> ** -> *
```

lookupFirst1 takes a list of pairs and an item, and returns the second part of the first pair whose first part equals the item. You should explain what your function does if there is no such pair. lookupSecond1 does a similar thing with the roles of first and second reversed.

6.3 Putting the two together

Now we can explain some of the most commonly used and important higher-order functions: they are polymorphic *and* higher order.

Mapping, filtering and folding

At the start of the chapter we defined functions

- to map a function from numbers to numbers along a list of numbers;
- to fold a binary function along a list of numbers; and
- to filter characters with given properties from a string, or list of characters.

If we examine the definitions given, we see nothing particular to do with numbers or strings:

- any function from one type to another can be mapped along a list of items of the first type;
- a binary function over any type can be folded into a list of that type; and
- a list of any type can be filtered according to an appropriate property.

The definitions of the general functions are exactly the same as their special cases – all that is changed are their types.

Map

To map f along the list (a:x),

- the head is given by f applied to a, and
- the tail is given by mapping f along x.

f mapped along [] gives []

```
map :: (* -> **) -> [*] -> [**]
map f []    = []
map f (a:x) = f a : map f x
```

Alternatively,

```
map f x = [ f a | a <- x ]
```

What does the type say? map is a function of two arguments; the first is a function, from one type (call it 'thing') to another ('item'), the second argument will be a list of things, to be transformed into the result. This result is a list of items, given by mapping the function along the list of things. (Calling * and ** 'thing' and 'item' may see silly, but it can help to emphasize that the type variables stand for arbitrary types.) Examples of the use of map abound:

```
map times2 [2,3,4] = [4,6,8]
map isEven [2,3,4] = [True,False,True]
map small "Bongo Fury" = "bongo fury"
map (#) ["Clear","Spot"] = [5,4]
```

(The definitions of isEven and small are left as an exercise.) Moreover, we can redefine many of the functions of Chapter 4 using map and other polymorphic higher-order functions. For example, in making a supermarket bill, we have to format a number of lines, and to join the result together; we can write

```
formatLines :: [line] -> string
formatLines ls = concat (map formatLine ls)
```

where concat is the (polymorphic) built-in function to join a list of lists together into a single list.

Fold

The definition of fold will have two cases. Folding f into the singleton list [a] gives a. Folding f into a longer list is given by

```
fold f [e₁,e₂,...,eₖ]
= e₁ $f (e₂ $f ( ... $f eₖ)...)
= f e₁ (fold f [e₂,...,eₖ])
```

The Miranda definition is therefore

```
fold :: (* -> * -> *) -> [*] -> *

fold f [a]     = a
fold f (a:b:x) = f a (fold f (b:x))
```

in which the operation to be folded in must be a binary function over the type *. Examples include

```
fold (\/) [False,True,False] = True
fold (++) ["Freak ", "Out" , "", "!"] = "Freak Out!"
fold min2 [6] = 6
fold (*) [1..6] = 720
```

The `fold` function, which is known as `foldr1` in the Miranda standard environment, is not defined on an empty list.

We can modify the definition to give an extra argument which is the value on the empty list, and write

```
foldr f s []    = s
foldr f s (a:x) = f a (foldr f s x)
```

The 'r' in the definition is for 'fold, bracketing to the right'. Using this slightly more general function, whose type we predict is

```
(* -> * -> *) -> * -> [*] -> *
```

we can now define some of the standard functions of Miranda:

```
concat :: [[*]] -> [*]
concat xs = foldr (++) [] xs

and :: [bool] -> bool
and bs = foldr (&) True bs
```

We shall see in fact that the most general type of `foldr` is more general than we predicted:

```
(* -> ** -> **) -> ** -> [*] -> **
```

and that `foldr` can be used to define another cohort of list functions. For instance, we can reverse a list thus:

```
rev :: [*] -> [*]
rev l = foldr stick [] l

stick :: * -> [*] -> [*]
stick a x = x ++ [a]
```

We see more of the fold functions below.

Filter

As we explained when we introduced `filterString`, a *property* of characters is expressed by a function of type `char -> bool`. For an arbitrary type `*`, a property will be given by a function of type

```
* -> bool
```

For instance, the function `isEven` defined by

```
isEven n = (n mod 2 = 0)
```

is a property of numbers, and

```
nonEmpty st = (st ~= "")
```

is a property of strings.

Filtering an empty list gives an empty list. On a non-empty list `(a:x)`, there are two cases in the definition of `filter p (a:x)`:

- If a has the property; that is, the guard `p a` is `True`, then a is the head of the result; the tail is given by filtering x.
- If the guard is `False`, a is not to be included, and so the result is given by filtering x.

The definition of `filter` is therefore given by

```
filter :: (* -> bool) -> [*] -> [*]

filter p [] = []
filter p (a:x)
  = a : filter p x   , if p a
  =     filter p x   , otherwise
```

and we have

```
filter isEven [2,3,4] = [2,4]
filter nonEmpty ["Freak ", "Out" , "", "!"]
             = ["Freak ", "Out" , "!"]
```

A list comprehension serves to provide an equivalent definition:

```
filter p x = [ a | a <- x ; p a ]
```

EXERCISES

6.11 How would you define the sum of squares of the natural numbers 1 to n using map and `foldr`?

6.12 Given a list of numbers, define a function to give the sum of squares of the integers in the list.

6.13 How would you define the function # using map and `sumList`?

6.14 Given the function

```
addUp l = filter greaterOne (map addOne l)
```

where

```
greaterOne n = n>1
addOne n     = n+1
```

you are asked to redefine it using `filter` before map, thus:

```
addUp l = map fun1 (filter fun2 l)
```

What are the functions `fun1` and `fun2`?

6.15 What is the effect of

```
map addOne (map addOne l)  ?
```

Can you conclude anything in general about

```
map f (map g l)
```

where f and g are arbitrary?

6.16 What is the effect of

```
filter greaterOne (filter lessTen l)
```

where `lessTen n = n<10`? Can you conclude anything in general about

```
filter p (filter q l)
```

where p and q are arbitrary?

6.17 How does the function

```
mystery l = foldr (++) [] (map sing l)
```

behave, where `sing a = [a]` for all a?

6.4 Using the higher-order functions

Here we look at the higher-order functions (HOFs) map, `filter` and the folds `fold` and `foldr` in some longer examples. We see in particular how they are used in combination.

EXAMPLE: Library database ──────────────────────

Section 4.4 contains an example library database, in which the functions were defined directly, using recursion. Here we consider how the HOFs can be used instead.

Recall that a `database` is a list of (person , book) pairs. The function

```
books :: database -> person -> [book]
```

takes a `database` and a person, `per`, and gives as a result the list of all books borrowed by `per`. The algorithm has two phases:

- All pairs whose first half is `per` have to be found – a filter;
- for each of these pairs, we take the second half – a map.

So we can say

```
books db per = map snd (filter isPer db)
                where
                isPer (p,b) = (p = per)
```

There are two things worth noting about this definition:

- The isPer function checks whether the first half of a pair is per. As it is defined in a where clause it can use per in its definition, since the variables on the left-hand side of an equation can be used in the where defined functions.

- There is no pattern matching in the definition, unlike the earlier definition, where we had to make cases for the database argument. Using map and filter means that the definition is itself higher level, and is substantially easier to read. (Of course, pattern matching has to happen somewhere; in fact, it takes place in the definitions of map and filter themselves.)

As a second example, consider the function

```
returnLoan :: database -> person -> book -> database
```

designed to return the loan of book b to person p. We can say

```
returnLoan db p b
  = filter notPB db
    where
    notPB pr = (pr ~= (p,b))
```

if we wish to remove *all* pairs (p,b). To remove the *first* pair (p,b) we could define a version of filter which removes a first occurrence only. This could be re-used as required later.

EXAMPLE: Supermarket billing ⎯⎯⎯⎯⎯⎯⎯⎯⎯⎯⎯⎯⎯⎯⎯⎯⎯⎯

In following this section you will need to refer to the supermarket billing exercise in Chapter 4. Many of the operations of this exercise can be written using the HOFs. For instance, we are asked to:

- Format each line (mapping) and then to join the results together (folding in the function (++)).
- Look up individual items in a database of bar codes (map and filter), and then to look up a list of such items (map again).
- Find the number of bottles of sherry bought (filter and other functions), and to calculate a discount from that.

EXERCISES

6.18 Define the functions `borrowers` and `numBorrowed` of the library database making use of higher-order functions rather than recursion and pattern matching.

6.19 Define a function

```
filterFirst :: (* -> bool) -> [*] -> [*]
```

so that `filterFirst p l` removes the first element of `l` which does not have the property `p`. Use this to give a version of `returnLoan` which only returns one copy of a book. What does your function do on a list all of whose elements have property `p`?

6.20 Can you define a function

```
filterLast :: (* -> bool) -> [*] -> [*]
```

which removes the last occurrence of an element of `l` without property `p`? How could you define it using `filterFirst`?

6.21 Using the HOFs described earlier, redefine the functions `formatLines`, `lookup` and `makeBill` of the supermarket billing example.

6.22 How can you define the `makeDiscount` operation without using recursion? How would you modify `makeBill` so that unknown items are not a part of the bill?

6.5   Generalizing: Splitting up lists

Many list-manipulating programs involve splitting up lists in some way, as a part of their processing. One way of doing this is to select some or all the elements with a particular property – this we have seen with `filter`. Other ways of processing include taking or dropping elements of the list from the front – this we saw in the text processing example. If we know the number of elements to be dropped, we can use

```
take, drop :: num -> [*] -> [*]
```

where `take n l` and `drop n l` are intended to take or drop n elements from the front of the list; if the list contains less than n elements, we drop as many as possible. So,

```
take n []       = []
take 0 l        = []
take (n+1) (a:x) = a : take n x
```

and drop is defined similarly.

In Chapter 4 we looked at an example of text processing, in which lists were split to yield words and sentences. The functions getWord and dropWord defined there were *not* polymorphic, as they were designed to split at whitespace characters.

It is a general principle of functional programming that programs can often be rewritten to use more general polymorphic and/or higher-order functions, and we illustrate that here.

The function getWord was originally defined so:

```
getWord :: string -> string
getWord []    = []
getWord (a:x)
    = []                  , if member whitespace a          (1)
    = a : getWord x   , otherwise
```

What forces this to work over strings is the test in (1), where a is checked for membership of whitespace. We could generalize the function to have the 'splitting set', splitSet as a **parameter**, thus:

```
getFront :: [*] -> [*] -> [*]
getFront splitSet []    = []
getFront splitSet (a:x)
    = []                          , if member splitSet a
    = a : getFront splitSet x   , otherwise
```

The type is now polymorphic – we check membership of the splitSet rather than whitespace; we have lost nothing in this generalization since we have

```
getWord st = getFront whitespace st
```

getFront will select the front of a list until a character is found in the splitSet. In other words, we take characters from the front until some property holds – can we generalize again, to take into account an *arbitrary* property?

A property over the type * is represented by a function of type (* -> bool), just as we saw in discussing filter. We can therefore write

```
getUntil :: (* -> bool) -> [*] -> [*]
getUntil p []     = []
getUntil p (a:x)
   = []                    , if p a
   = a : getUntil p x    , otherwise
```

in which the test member splitSet a has been replaced by the test p a, the arbitrary property p applied to a. We can of course recover getFront and getWord from this definition. For example,

```
getFront splitSet l = getUntil p l
                      where
                        p a = member splitSet a
```

Anticipating the next chapter a little, we can in fact write,

```
getFront splitSet = getUntil (member splitSet)
```

Built into Miranda are the functions takewhile and dropwhile, which are like getUntil and dropUntil, except that they take elements until the condition *fails* to be True. For instance,

```
takewhile :: (* -> bool) -> [*] -> [*]
takewhile p []     = []
takewhile p (a:x)
   = a : takewhile p x   , if p a
   = []                  , otherwise
```

getUntil can be defined using takewhile, and vice versa.

EXERCISES

6.23 Give the generalizations dropFront and dropUntil of the dropWord function.

6.24 How would you define the function dropSpace using dropUntil and dropFront?

6.25 How would you split a string into lines using getUntil and dropUntil?

6.26 The function getLine of Chapter 4 has a polymorphic type – what is it? How could you generalize the test in this function? If you do this, does the type of the function become more general? Explain your answer.

SUMMARY

This chapter has introduced two of the most fertile ideas in functional programming:

- We have seen that functions can be arguments to other functions, which are called higher-order. A function parameter can represent an operation to be mapped along a list, or a property used to filter the elements of a list, for example.

- We have also seen that definitions can be of polymorphic objects; a mapping operation can be applied to all types of list, for instance. Polymorphic definitions are found where definitions constrain the types only weakly; in defining the function to give the length of a list, all that is required of the argument is that it is a list; the type of the elements is irrelevant.

These two properties combined give us functions like `map`, `filter` and `fold`, all of which can be combined and used in diverse situations. Higher-order polymorphic functions are ideal candidates for libraries of re-usable functions.

We saw in the final section that in many situations where functions of a monomorphic type have been defined, it is possible to *generalize* them. This is done by supplying them with the appropriate parameters (which are often themselves functions), and makes them general polymorphic operations that are widely applicable. We looked at the particular example of generalizing the functions originally defined in the context of text processing.

7 Further generalization

As we saw in the previous chapter, functions can be arguments of other, *higher-order*, functions. Functions and operations can also give functions as *results*, another way of making them higher-order. This chapter shows how this is achieved, and re-examines some of our examples to see how the ideas fit into program development.

A longer example – building an index for a document – is used to show how these new ideas fit into program development. The chapter concludes with some examples of program verification involving higher-order polymorphic objects, where it is shown that the theorems proved about them are re-usable in exactly the same way as the functions themselves.

7.1 Function composition

Perhaps the simplest way of structuring a program is to do a number of things one after the other – each part can be defined separately. In a functional program this is achieved by **composing** a number of functions together: the output of one function becomes the input of another (Figure 7.1).

In Chapter 4 we gave the function `fill`, to take a text (that is, a `string`) and to split it into filled lines. It was written thus:

```
fill :: string -> [line]
fill st = splitLines (splitWords st)                          (1)
```

so that first the text is split into a list of words which is then split into lines. The component functions have types

```
splitWords :: string -> [word]
splitLines :: [word] -> [line]
```

Because composition is so frequently used, there is a Miranda notation for it, '`.`', an infix dot. The definition of `fill` can be rewritten

```
fill = splitLines . splitWords
```

This definition has exactly the same effect as the definition (1), but says directly that the function `fill` is a composition of the two, without the necessity of applying either side to an argument. It is easier to read, and makes explicit the fact that `fill` is a composition.

How is composition, '`.`', defined? For any functions f and g, the effect of f.g is given by the equation

```
(f.g) x = f (g x)
```

Not all pairs of functions can be composed. The output of g, g x, becomes the input of f, so that the output type of g must equal the input type of f.

In the example, the output type of `splitWords` and the input type of `splitLines` are both `[word]`.

The type constraint can be expressed by giving '`.`' the type

```
(.) :: (** -> ***) -> (* -> **) -> (* -> ***)
```

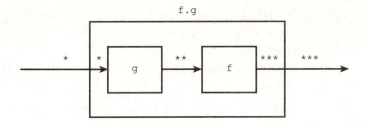

Figure 7.1   Function composition.

which shows that, if we call the first input f and the second g,

- The input of f and the output of g are the same type: **.
- The result f.g has the input type of g, *, and the output type of f, ***.

This is illustrated in Figure 7.1.

Composition is **associative**; that is, f.(g.h) is equal to (f.g).h for all f, g and h. We can therefore write f.g.h unambiguously to mean 'do h, then g, then f'.

Pitfalls of composition

There are a number of pitfalls associated with composition, which can trap the unwary:

- The order in f.g is significant, and can be confusing; f.g means 'first apply g and then apply f to the result', and *not* the other way round, even though f occurs to the left of g. The reason we write (f.g) for 'g then f' is that we write arguments to the right of functions. The argument is therefore closer to g than to f, and the order of the functions in (f.g) x is the same as in the repeated application, f (g x).

- There is an error caused by the binding power of function application. It is a common error to write f.g x thinking it means f.g applied to x. Because function application binds more tightly than anything else, it is parsed as f.(g x), which will in general lead to a type error. For, example, if succ is defined by succ x = x+1 then evaluating

  ```
  succ.succ 1
  ```

  gives the type error message

  ```
  cannot unify num with *->num
  ```

since there is an attempt to treat succ 1 as a function to be composed with succ. Such a function has to have a type whose output is num, hence the requirement of type *->num.

- Function application and composition can get confused. If, for example, f has type num -> bool, then

    - f.a means f composed with the *function* a; a therefore needs to be of type s -> num for some type s.
    - f a means f applied to the object a, which will be a number.

EXERCISES

7.1   Redefine the function printBill from the supermarket billing exercise in Chapter 4 so that composition is used.

7.2   If id is the polymorphic identity function, id x = x, explain the behaviour of the expressions id.f and id f. If f is of type num -> bool, at what type is id used in each case? What type does h have if h id is properly typed?

7.2   Functions as results

We have seen that functions can be combined together using the composition operator '.'; this can be done on the right-hand side of function definitions. The simplest example of this is

twice f = f.f   (1)

f is a function, and the result is f composed with itself. For this to work, it needs to have the same input and output type, so we have

twice :: (* -> *) -> (* -> *)

This states that twice takes one argument, a function of type (* -> *), and returns a result of the same type. For instance, if succ is the function to add one to a number, then

```
(twice succ) 12
= (succ.succ) 12                                                    by (1)
= succ (succ 12)                                                    by '.'
= 14
```

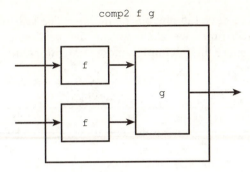

comp2 f g

Figure 7.2   Plumbing f and g together.

We can generalize `twice` so that we pass a parameter giving the number of times a function is to be composed with itself

```
iter :: num -> (* -> *) -> (* -> *)

iter 0 f     = id
iter (n+1) f = f . iter n f
```

As an example, we can define 2^n as `iter n double 1`, if double doubles its argument.

   We can return *any* function using a `where` clause to make its definition. For example, if given n we are to return the function which adds n, we can say

```
addNum :: num -> (num -> num)
addNum n = h
           where
           h m = n+m
```

The result is a function h, and h is itself defined by an equation in the `where` clause. Another example is given by the 'plumbing' illustrated in Figure 7.2:

```
comp2 f g = h
            where
            h x y = g (f x) (f y)
```

To add the squares of 3 and 4 we can write

```
comp2 sq add 3 4
```

where add and sq have the obvious definitions. The last two examples are somewhat cumbersome; we shall see in the next section that partial application will make their definition more straightforward.

7.3 Give calculations of

```
iter 3 double 1
(comp2 succ (*)) 3 4
comp2 sq add 3 4
```

7.4 Define a function `total`

```
total :: (num -> num) -> (num -> num)
```

so that `total f` is the function which at value n gives the total

```
f 0 + f 1 + ... + f n
```

7.5 [*Harder*] Define a function

```
slope :: (num -> num) -> (num -> num)
```

which takes a function `f` as argument, and returns (an approximation to) its derivative `f'` as result.

7.6 [*Harder*] Define a function

```
integrate :: (num -> num) -> (num -> num -> num)
```

which takes a function `f` as argument, and returns (an approximation to) the two-argument function which gives the area under its graph between two end points as its result.

7.3   Partial application

The function `multiply` multiplies together two arguments:

```
multiply :: num -> num -> num
multiply a b = a*b
```

so that `multiply` 2 3 equals 6. What happens if `multiply` is applied to *one* argument 2? The result is a *function*, which when given an argument b will return double the value, 2*b.

This is an example of a general phenomenon: any function taking two or more arguments can be *partially applied* to one or more arguments. This gives a very powerful way of forming functions as results.

As an example, suppose that every element of a list is to be doubled. The function can be defined thus:

```
doubleList :: [num] -> [num]
doubleList = map (multiply 2)
```

In this definition there are two partial applications:

- `multiply 2` is a function from numbers to numbers, given by applying `multiply` to one rather than two arguments;
- `map (multiply 2)` is a function from `[num]` to `[num]` given by partially applying `map`.

How is the type of a partial application determined? There is a simple rule which explains it.

Rule of Cancellation

If the type of a function `f` is

$$t_1 \rightarrow t_2 \rightarrow \ldots \rightarrow t_n \rightarrow t$$

and it is applied to arguments

$$e_1::t_1, \ e_2::t_2, \ \ldots, \ e_k::t_k$$

(where $k \leqslant n$), then the result type is given by **cancelling** the types t_1 to t_k

$$\cancel{t_1} \rightarrow \cancel{t_2} \rightarrow \ldots \rightarrow \cancel{t_k} \rightarrow t_{k+1} \rightarrow \ldots \rightarrow t_n \rightarrow t$$

which gives

$$t_{k+1} \rightarrow t_{k+2} \rightarrow \ldots \rightarrow t_n \rightarrow t$$

For example,

```
multiply 2        :: num -> num
multiply 2 3      :: num
doubleList        :: [num] -> [num]
doubleList [2,3] :: [num]
```

The idea of partial application is important. We have already seen that many functions can be defined as *specializations* of general operations like map, filter and so on. These specializations arise by us passing a function to the general operation – this function is often given by a partial application, as in the examples

```
map (multiply 2)
filter (not . member whitespace)
```

Syntax: Associativity

Function application is taken to be **left-associative**, so that

```
f a b = (f a) b
f a b ≠ f (a b)
```

The function space symbol '->' is **right-associative**, so that

```
t -> u -> v = t -> (u -> v)
t -> u -> v ≠ (t -> u) -> v
```

The arrow is *not* associative. If

```
f :: num -> num -> num
g :: (num -> num) -> num
```

then f will yield a function from num to num when given a num – an example is multiply. On the other hand, when given a function of type num -> num, g yields a num. An example is

```
g :: (num -> num) -> num
g h = (h 0) + (h 1)
```

The function g defined here takes a function h as argument and returns the sum of h's values at 0 and 1.

How many arguments do functions have?

Partial application can appear confusing: in some contexts functions appear to take one argument, and in others two. In fact, *every function in Miranda takes exactly one argument*. If this application yields a function, then this function may be applied to a further argument, and so on. Consider the multiplication function again:

```
multiply :: num -> num -> num
```

This is shorthand for

```
multiply :: num -> (num -> num)
```

and so it can therefore be applied to a number. Doing this gives (for example)

```
multiply 4 :: num -> num
```

This can itself be applied to give

```
(multiply 4) 5 :: num
```

which, since function application is left-associative, can be written

```
multiply 4 5 :: num
```

Our explanations earlier in the book are consistent with this full explanation of the system. We hid the fact that

```
f e₁ e₂ ... eₖ
t₁ -> t₂ -> ... tₙ -> t
```

were shorthand for

```
( ...((f e₁) e₂) ... eₖ)
t₁ -> (t₂ -> (...(tₙ -> t)...))
```

but this did no harm to our understanding of how to use the Miranda language.

Examples of partial applications will be seen throughout the material to come, and can be used to simplify and clarify many of the preceding examples. Three simple examples are the text-processing functions

```
dropSpace = dropwhile (member whitespace)
dropWord  = dropwhile ((~).member whitespace)
getWord   = takewhile ((~).member whitespace)
```

We look at further examples in the next section, after examining partially-applied operators.

Operator sections

The operators of the language can be partially applied, giving what are known as **operator sections**. Examples include

(+2)	The function which adds two to its argument.
(2+)	The function which adds two to its argument.
(>2)	The function which returns whether a number is greater than two.
(3:)	The function which puts the number 3 on the front of a list.
(++"\n")	The function which puts a newline at the end of a string.

The general rule here is that a section of the operator op will put its argument to the side which completes the application. That is,

```
(op a) b = b op a
(a op) b = a op b
```

When combined with higher-order functions like map and filter, the notation is both powerful and elegant. For example,

```
filter (0<) . map (+1)
```

is the function which adds one to each member of a list, and then removes those which are not positive.

EXERCISES

7.7 Use partial applications to define the functions addNum, comp2 and total given in the previous section.

7.8 How would you re-define the function filter (0<) . map (+1) thus:

```
map sec₁ . filter sec₂
```

where sec_1 and sec_2 are operator sections?

7.4   Examples

This section explores how partial applications and operator sections can be used to simplify and shorten definitions. Often it is possible to avoid giving an explicit function definition if we can use a partial application to return a function. Revisiting the examples of Chapter 6, we see that to double a list we can write

```
double = map (*2)
```

using an operator section (*2) to replace the times2 function, and giving the function definition directly by partially applying map.

To filter out the even elements in a numerical list, we have to check whether the remainder on dividing by two is equal to zero. As a function we can write

```
(=0).(mod 2)
```

This is the composition of two operator sections: first find the remainder, then check if it is equal to zero. (Why can we not write (mod 2 = 0)?) The filtering function can then be written

```
getEvens = filter ((=0).(mod 2))
```

In the library database example, when defining books we wrote

```
books db per = map snd (filter isPer db)
```

with the definition of isPer in a where clause. We can replace this with

```
books db per = map snd (filter ((=per).fst) db)
```

The function (=per).fst takes the first component of a pair, using fst, and then compares it with the person of interest, per. Our final example comes from the list-splitting study. We defined

```
getFront splitSet l = getUntil p l
                      where
                      p a = member splitSet a
```

The local definition is not now needed, as we can define the function p by a partial application

```
getFront splitSet l = getUntil (member splitSet) l
```

The function itself can be given a direct definition, by partial application also

```
getFront splitSet = getUntil (member splitSet)
```

7.5 Currying and uncurrying

Making a function of two or more arguments accept its arguments one at a time is called **currying** after Haskell B. Curry,[†] who was one of the pioneers of a mathematical version of functional programming called the λ-calculus. An **uncurried** version of a two-argument function can be given by bundling the arguments into a pair, thus:

```
multiplyUC :: (num,num) -> num
multiplyUC (a,b) = a*b
```

but it is most usual to present curried versions, as they can be partially applied.

There are two higher-order functions which convert between curried and uncurried functions;

```
curry :: ((*,**) -> ***) -> (* -> ** -> ***)
curry g a b = g (a,b)
```

curry multiplyUC will be exactly the same function as multiply;

```
uncurry :: (* -> ** -> ***) -> ((*,**) -> ***)
uncurry f (a,b) = f a b
```

uncurry multiply will be exactly the same function as multiplyUC. curry and uncurry are inverse functions.

Partial application of functions is done on the arguments from left to right, so a function cannot directly be applied to its second argument only. This effect is achieved indirectly by first transforming the order in which the function takes its arguments and then partially applying it:

```
converse :: (* -> ** -> ***) -> (** -> * -> ***)
converse f b a = f a b
```

[†] In fact, the first person to describe the idea was Schönfinkel, but 'Schönfinkeling' does not have the same elegance of expression!

converse map will takes as its first argument the list and as its second the function to be mapped; it can be applied to its first argument, having the effect of applying map to its second only.

7.6   Example: Creating an index

This section explores a different aspect of text processing to those we have looked at already. How can an index for a document be produced automatically? We use the example to illustrate how higher-order functions are used in many parts of the final program. Polymorphism allows their use at different types, and their function parameters mean that they can be used to different effect in different situations.

To make the example texts shorter, a scaled-down version of the indexing problem is investigated. This is only done for ease of presentation, as all the important aspects of the system are explored here.

We should first specify what the program is to do. The input is a text string, in which lines are separated by the newline character ' \n' . The index should give every line on which the word in question occurs. Only words of length at least five are to be indexed, and an alphabetical listing of the results produced. Within each entry, a line number should only occur once, if at all.

We can represent the index as a list, with each entry being an item. What will a single entry be? It has to associate a collection of line numbers with each word in the text; we can therefore represent each entry by a pair consisting of a list of numbers, of type [num], and a word, of type string. The top-level function will therefore be

```
makeIndex :: doc -> [ ([num],word) ]
```

where we use the type synonyms

```
doc  == string
line == string
word == string
```

to distinguish the different uses of the string type in the design which follows.

How can the program be designed? We focus on the **data structures** which the program will produce, and we can see the program as working by making a series of modifications to the data with which we begin. This **data-directed** design is common in Miranda functional program development.

At the top level, the solution will be a **composition** of functions. These perform the following operations, in turn:

- Split the text, a doc, into lines, giving an object of type [line].
- Pair each line with its line number, giving an object of type [(num, line)].
- Split the lines into words, associating each word with the number of the line on which it occurs. This gives a list of type [(num, word)].
- Sort this list according to the alphabetical ordering of words (strings), giving a list of the same type.
- Amalgamate entries for the same word into a list of numbers, giving a list of type [([num], word)].
- Shorten the list by removing all entries for words of less than five letters, giving a list of type [([num], word)].

The definition follows; note that we have used comments to give the type of each component function in the composition:

```
makeIndex
  = shorten .        ||  [([num],word)]  ->  [([num],word)]
    amalgamate .     ||  [([num],word)]  ->  [([num],word)]
    makeLists .      ||  [(num,word)]    ->  [([num],word)]
    sortLs .         ||  [(num,word)]    ->  [(num,word)]
    allNumWords .    ||  [(num,line)]    ->  [(num,word)]
    numLines .       ||  [line]          ->  [(num,line)]
    splitup          ||  doc             ->  [line]
```

Once the type of each of the functions is given, development of each can proceed independently. The only information necessary to use a function is its *type*, and these types are specified in the definition above. Each of the functions can now be given, in turn.

To split a string into a list of lines it must be split at each occurrence of the newline character, '\n'. How is this written as a function? One solution is to write functions analogous to getWord and dropWord, which together were used earlier in splitWords. Alternatively, we can use the functions getFront and dropFront from Chapter 6. The definition is left as an exercise.

```
splitup :: doc -> [line]
```

The next function should pair each line with its line number. If the list of lines is linels, then the list of line numbers is

```
[1..#linels]
```

Stepping back from the problem, it is apparent that the lists of lines and line numbers need to be combined into a list of pairs, by zipping the two lists together. The `zip2` function has already been defined to do exactly this, so the required function is written thus

```
numLines :: [line] -> [ ( num , line ) ]
numLines linels
   = zip2 [1..(#linels)] linels
```

Now the lines have to be split into words, and line numbers attached. We first consider the problem for a single line.

```
numWords :: ( num , line ) -> [ ( num , word ) ]
```

Splitting into words can be done by the function `splitWords` of Chapter 4. Each of these words is then to be paired with the (same) line number. Stepping back from the problem, we see that we have to perform an operation on every item of a list, the list of words making up the line. This is a job for `map`:

```
numWords (number , lin)
   = map addLineNo (splitWords lin)
     where
     addLineNo wd = (number,wd)
```

To apply this to the whole text, the function `numWords` has to be applied to every line. This is again done by `map`, and the individual results joined together or **concatenated**. We make a direct definition of the function, by composing its two parts. First we map the function `numWords`, then we concatenate the results, using `concat`:

```
allNumWords :: [ ( num , word ) ] -> [ ( num , word ) ]
allNumWords = concat . map numWords
```

What has been achieved so far? The text has been transformed into a list of line-number/word pairs, from which an index is to be built. For instance, the text

```
"cat dog\nbat dog\ncat"
```

will be converted to

```
[(1,"cat") , (1,"dog") , (2,"bat") , (2,"dog") , (3,"cat")]
```

The list must next be sorted by word order, and lists of lines on which a word appears be built. The ordering relation on pairs of numbers and words is given by

```
compare :: ( num , word ) -> ( num , word ) -> bool
compare ( n1 , w1 ) ( n2 , w2 )
    = w1 < w2 \/ ( w1 = w2 & n1 < n2 )
```

The words are compared for dictionary order. For pairs containing the same words, ordering is by page number.

Sorting a list is most easily done by a version of the **quicksort** algorithm. The list is split into parts smaller than and larger than a given element; each of these halves can be sorted separately, and then joined together to form the result.

```
sortLs :: [ ( num , word ) ] -> [ ( num , word ) ]

sortLs []    = []
sortLs (a:x) = sortLs smaller ++ [a] ++ sortLs larger
```

The lists `smaller` and `larger` are the lists of elements of x which are smaller (or larger) than the element a. Note that it is here that duplicate copies are removed – any other occurrence of the element a in the list x does not appear in either `smaller` or `larger`.

How are the two lists defined? They are given by selecting those elements of x with given properties: a job for `filter`, or a list comprehension. Going back to the definition of `sortLs`,

```
sortLs (a:x)
  = sortLs smaller ++ [a] ++ sortLs larger
    where
    smaller = [ b | b<-x ; compare b a ]
    larger  = [ b | b<-x ; compare a b ]
```

After sorting, the index may look something like

```
[(2,"bat") , (1,"cat") , (3,"cat") , (1,"dog") , (2,"dog")]
```

The entries for the same word need to be accumulated together. First each entry is converted to having a *list* of pages associated with it, thus

```
makeLists ::   [ (num,word) ] -> [ ([num],word) ]
makeLists
  = map mklis
    where
    mklis ( n , st ) = ( [n] , st )
```

For our example, this gives

```
[ ([2],"bat") , ([1],"cat") , ([3],"cat") ,
  ([1],"dog") , ([2],"dog") ]
```

After this, the lists associated with the same words are amalgamated:

```
amalgamate [] = []
amalgamate [a] = [a]
amalgamate ((l1,w1):(l2,w2):rest)
   = (l1,w1) : amalgamate ((l2,w2):rest)  , if w1 ~= w2   (1)
   = amalgamate ((l1++l2,w1):rest)        , otherwise     (2)
```

The first two cases are simple, with the third doing the work:

- If we have two adjacent entries with different words, case (1), then
  we know that there is nothing to add to the first entry – we therefore
  have to amalgamate entries in the *tail* only.
- If two adjacent entries have the same word associated, case (2), they
  are amalgamated and the function is called again on the result. This is
  because there may be other entries with the same word, also to be
  amalgamated into the leading entry.

Consider an example:

```
amalgamate [ ([2],"bat") , ([1],"cat") , ([3],"cat") ]
= ([2],"bat") : amalgamate [([1],"cat"),([3],"cat")]  by (1)
= ([2],"bat") : amalgamate [ ([1,3],"cat") ]          by (2)
= ([2],"bat") : [ ([1,3],"cat") ]
= [ ([2],"bat") , ([1,3],"cat") ]
```

To meet the requirements, one other operation needs to be performed.
'Small' words of less than five letters are to be removed:

```
shorten = filter sizer
           where
           sizer (nl,wd) = #wd > 4
```

Again, the `filter` function proves useful. The index function can now be
defined in full:

```
makeIndex :: doc -> [ ([num],word) ]
makeIndex
   = shorten . amalgamate . makeLists . sortLs .
         allNumWords . numLines .  splitup
```

As was said at the beginning of this section, function composition provides a powerful method for structuring designs: programs are written as a **pipeline** of operations, passing the appropriate data structures between them.

It is easy to see how designs like these can be modified. To take one example, the indexing program above filters out short words only as its final operation. There are a number of earlier points in the chain at which this could have been done, and it is a worthwhile exercise to consider these.

EXERCISES

7.9 Define the function `splitup` using the functions `getFront` and `dropFront` from Chapter 6, or the built-in functions `takeuntil` and `dropuntil`. You should be careful that your functions do not give an empty word when there are empty lines in the doc; this happens in the examples "cat\n\ndog" and "fish\n".

7.10 How would you re-define `sortLs` so that duplicate copies of an item are not removed? For the index, this means that if a word occurs twice on line 123, say, then 123 occurs twice in the index entry for that word.

7.11 How could the functions `getUntil` and `dropUntil` be used in the definition of `amalgamate`?

7.12 Explain how the function `sizer` can be defined as a composition of built-in functions and operator sections; the role of `sizer` is to pick the second half of a pair, find its length, and compare the result with 4.

7.13 How is the folowing definition of the last equation for `amalgamate` incorrect? Give an example calculation to justify your answer.

```
amalgamate ((l1,w1):(l2,w2):rest)
  = (l1,w1) : amalgamate ((l2,w2):rest)   , if w1 ~= w2
  = (l1++l2,w1) : amalgamate rest         , otherwise
```

7.14 Give a definition of

```
printIndex :: [ ([num],word) ] -> string
```

which gives a neatly laid-out printed version of an index.

7.15 Modify the program so that words of less than five letters are removed as a part of the definition of `allNumWords`.

7.16 Modify the `makeIndex` function so that instead of returning the list of line numbers on which a word occurs, you have to give the total number of times which the word occurs. You will need to make sure that you count multiple occurrences of a word in a single line. There are two ways of tackling the problem:

- Modify the program as little as is necessary – you could return the length of a list rather than the list itself, for instance.

- Take the program structure as a guide, and write a (simpler) program which calculates the number of occurrences directly.

7.17 Modify the program so that capitalized words like `"Dog"` are indexed under their uncapitalized equivalents (`"dog"`). This does not work well for proper names like `"Amelia"` – what could you do about that?

7.18 The function `sortLs` is limited to sorting lists of type `[(num,word)]` because it calls the `compare` function. Re-define the function so that it takes the comparison function as a *parameter*. What is its type after this re-definition?

7.7 Design revisited

We have already discussed the design of functions and scripts in Sections 2.13 and 4.9, where two fundamental points emerged:

- We can design a system before starting to write it, by thinking about it from the top down. In this way a complex task is broken into a number of smaller and simpler tasks. We can also think of the design of single functions in more than one stage: first looking at the left-hand side, then at the right, and finally at the `where` clause, if any.

- Top-down design, with separate parts of a program working independently, is important not least because nearly every practical system has to be modified during its lifetime.

We now have more facilities at our disposal. We can write functions which take functions as arguments and return functions as results; we are also able to write definitions which apply to whole classes of types at once; these definitions have polymorphic types.

This ability gives us greater freedom to separate different parts of a program. For instance, if we have to apply an operation to every element of a list we can

- write the particular operation as one function definition, op, say, and

●　　write a general function, map, which applies an arbitrary function to every element of a list. The particular operation becomes an *argument* of the general function.

Given this separation, we can modify the definition of op completely independently of map. The definitions we write also become easier to understand, and when they are polymorphic, they become candidates for **re-use**.

Chapter 7 showed how functions could be the results of other functions, particularly through partial application. This is useful in giving direct definitions of functions, as compositions for example, and also in allowing the parameters to HOFs (like map) to be defined directly (like multiply 2) rather than having to be defined in a where clause.

How do collections of higher-order functions arise? One way which we saw in Section 4.8 is to recognize patterns of definitions, and to build a **toolkit** of HOFs to reflect these patterns.

Once we have a toolkit of list-processing functions, we can build programs up using them. This toolkit approach was used in the indexing example, where some 80% of the work was done by toolkit functions. We had to define the functions amalgamate and sortLs to complete the work. Amalgamating entries in a list is particular to the indexing program, and it is no surprise that we will, in any sizable program, need to define some functions from scratch rather than by re-using other definitions.

The example of sortLs is more interesting; it is monomorphic, but we can change the definition so that it becomes a polymorphic higher-order function, ready for re-use. The function used compare, which was the ordering – we now make this a *parameter*, called comp, and obtain

```
sort :: (* -> * -> bool) -> [*] -> [*]
sort comp (a:x)
  = sort comp smaller ++ [a] ++ sort comp larger
    where
    smaller = [ b | b<-x ; comp b a ]
    larger  = [ b | b<-x ; comp a b ]
```

The original sortLs is given by sort compare.

This *generalization* is not isolated; another example is that of list splitting, seen in Chapter 6. In each case we have to recognize

●　　the general operation – this is the higher order function, which will often be polymorphic, and

●　　the particular case – this will be a function argument to the general higher-order function; this argument is monomorphic in many cases.

This split makes the definitions we make more modular, and also gives us HOFs which are candidates for re-use in a toolkit. With experience, we begin to be able to see when there are opportunities to generalize; often they can be seen during design and implementation itself, giving a modified design or implementation.

7.8　Verification

Verification can take on a different character when we look at higher-order polymorphic functions. We can start to prove equalities between functions, rather than between values of functions, and we shall also see that we are able to prove theorems which resemble their subjects in being general and re-usable; that is, being applicable in many contexts.

Function-level verification

We claimed in Section 7.2 that the function `iter` is a generalization of `twice`, since

```
iter 2 f
= f . iter 1 f
= f . (f . iter 0 f)
= f . (f . id)
= f . f                                               by (1)
```

In proving this we have used the equality between two functions:

```
f . id = f                                                (1)
```

How is this proved? We examine how each side behaves on an arbitrary argument a,

```
(f . id) a
= f (id a)
= f a
```

so that for any argument a the two functions have the same behaviour. As black boxes, they are therefore the same, because for no argument do they behave differently. As what interests us here is their behaviour, we say that they are equal. We call this concept of equality **extensional**, and say that

Principle of extensionality:

Two functions f and g are equal if they have the same value at every argument.

This is called extensionality in contrast to the idea of **intensionality** in which we say two functions are the same only if they have the same definitions – we no longer think of them as black boxes, as we are allowed to look inside them to see how the mechanisms work, as it were. If we are interested in the results of our programs, all that matters are the values given by functions, not how they are arrived at. We therefore use extensionality when we are reasoning about function behaviour in Miranda. If we are interested in *efficiency* or other performance aspects of programs, then the way in which a result is found *will* be significant, however. This is discussed further in the chapters to come.

EXERCISES

7.19 Show that function composition is associative; that is, for all f, g and h,

```
f.(g.h) = (f.g).h
```

7.20 Show that for all f,

```
id . f = f
```

7.21 Show that the function swap defined in Section 7.5 satisfies

```
swap.swap = id
```

Hint: to show this, you might want to prove that for any f,

```
swap (swap f) = f
```

7.22 Two functions f and g are *inverses* if it can be shown that

```
f.g = id           g.f = id
```

Prove that the functions curry and uncurry of Section 7.5 are inverses. Can you think of other pairs of inverse functions?

7.23 Prove that for all natural numbers n,

```
iter n id = id
```

7.24   A function f is called **idempotent** if

```
f.f = f
```

Show that the functions abs and entier are idempotent. Can you think of any other idempotent functions?

Higher-level proofs

Our verification thus far has concentrated on first-order, monomorphic functions. Just as map, filter and fold generalized patterns of definition, we shall find that proofs about these functions generalize results we have seen already. To give some examples, we saw in Chapter 5 that

```
double (x++y) = double x ++ double y
```

for finite lists x and y. When double is defined as map (*2) it becomes clear that we have an example of a general result,

```
map f (x++y) = map f x ++ map f y
```

which is valid for *any* function f. We also claimed that

```
sumList (x++y) = sumList x + sumList y                    (sumThm)
```

for all finite lists x, y. The function sumList is given by folding in (+),

```
sumList = foldr (+) 0
```

and we have, generally,

```
foldr f st (x++y)
  = f (foldr f st x) (foldr f st y)                       (foldThm)
```

if f is associative, and st is an identity for f; that is,

```
f a (f b c) = f (f a b) c
f a st = a = f st a
```

for all a, b, c. Obviously (+) is associative and has 0 as an identity, and so (sumThm) is a special case of (foldThm).

Now we give two full proofs of examples in the same vein.

EXAMPLE: Map and composition ——————————————————————

A first example concerns map and composition. Recall the definitions

```
map f []    = []                      (1)
map f (a:x) = f a : map f x           (2)
(f.g) x     = f (g x)                 (3)
```

It is not hard to see that

```
map (f.g) x = (map f . map g) x       (4)
```

for every finite list x. Applying (f.g) to every member of a list should be the same as applying g to every member and applying f to every member of the result. It is proved just as easily, by structural induction. The base case requires the identity to be proved for the empty list.

```
map (f.g) [] = []                              by (1)
```

```
(map f . map g) [] = map f (map g [])          by (3)
                   = map f []                   by (1)
                   = []                         by (1)
```

Assuming that map (f.g) x = (map f . map g) x is true, it is now necessary to prove that

```
map (f.g) (a:x) = (map f . map g) (a:x)
```

Again, it is enough to analyse each side of the equation:

```
map (f.g) (a:x) = (f.g) a : map (f.g) x        by (2)
                = f (g a) : map (f.g) x        by (3)
```

```
(map f . map g) (a:x)
  = map f (map g (a:x))                        by (3)
  = map f (g a : map g x)                      by (2)
  = f (g a) : map f (map g x)                  by (2)
  = f (g a) : (map f . map g) x                by (3)
```

The induction hypothesis is exactly what is needed to prove the two sides equal, completing the proof of the induction step and the proof itself.

■

The Miranda list type also contains infinite and partial lists. In a later part of the book these will be explained, and it will be shown that (4) is true for all lists x, and therefore that the functional equation

```
map (f.g) = (map f).(map g)
```

holds in general.

Map and filter

The last proof showed how properties of functional programs could be proved from the definitions of the functions in a straightforward way. The properties can state how the program behaves – that a sorting function returns an ordered list, for instance – or can relate one program to another. This latter idea underlies **program transformation** for functional languages. This section introduces an example called **filter promotion** which is one of the most useful of the basic functional transformations.

```
filter p . map f = map f . filter (p.f)
```

The equation says that a map followed by a filter can be replaced by a filter followed by a map. The right-hand side is potentially more efficient than the left, since the map operation will there be applied to a shorter list, consisting of just those elements with the property p. An example is given by the function first defined in Section 7.3.

```
filter (0<) . map (+1)
```

Instead of mapping first, the function can be replaced by

```
map (+1) . filter ((0<).(+1))
   = map (+1) . filter (0<=)
```

and it is clear that here the transformed version is more efficient, since the test (0<=) is no more costly than (0<). The proof that

```
(filter p . map f) x = (map f . filter (p.f)) x
```

for finite lists x is by structural induction and follows the reiteration of the definitions of map, filter and composition.

```
map f []    = []                                    (1)
map f (a:x) = f a : map f x                         (2)
```

```
filter p []    = []                        (3)
filter p (a:x) = a : filter p x   , if p a (4)
               =     filter p x   , otherwise (5)


(f.g) x     = f (g x)                       (6)
```

The base case consists of a proof of

```
(filter p . map f) [] = (map f . filter (p.f)) []    (7)
```

This is true since

```
(filter p . map f) []
  = filter p (map f [])                       by (6)
  = filter p []                               by (1)
  = []                                        by (3)
```

and

```
(map f . filter (p.f)) []
  = map f (filter (p.f) [])                    by (6)
  = map f []                                   by (3)
  = []                                         by (1)
```

In the induction step, a proof of

```
(filter p . map f) (a:x)
  = (map f . filter (p.f)) (a:x)               (8)
```

is required, using the induction hypothesis

```
(filter p . map f) x = (map f . filter (p.f)) x    (9)
```

The proof begins with an analysis of the left-hand side of (8).

```
(filter p . map f) (a:x)
  = filter p (map f (a:x))                     by (6)
  = filter p (f a : map f x)                   by (2)
```

There are two[†] cases to consider: whether p (f a) is True or False. In the first case,

---

[†] We should also think about what happens when p (f a) is undefined; in this case both sides will be undefined, and so equal.

```
= f a : filter p (map f x)                by (4)
= f a : (filter p . map f) x              by (6)
= f a : (map f . filter (p.f)) x          by (9)
= f a : map f (filter (p.f) x)            by (6)
= map f (a: (filter (p.f) x))             by (2)
= map f (filter (p.f) (a:x))              by (4)
= (map f . filter (p.f)) (a:x)            by (6)
```

A similar chain of reasoning gives the same result in case p (f a) is False. This establishes (8) assuming (9), and so together with (7) completes the proof of the filter promotion transformation in the case of finite lists; it holds, in fact, for all lists.   ■

EXERCISES

7.25 Prove that if f is associative, and st is an identity for f, the equation

> foldr f st (x++y) = f (foldr f st x) (foldr f st y)

which was called (foldThm) above, holds.

7.26 Argue that the result

> concat (x ++ y) = concat x ++ concat y

is a special case of (foldThm), using

> concat = foldr (++) []

as the definition of concat.

7.27 Prove that for all finite lists x, and functions f,

> concat (map (map f) x) = map f (concat x)

7.28 Prove that

> (0<) . (+1) = (0<=)

as is used in the theorem relating map and filter.

7.29 Prove for all finite lists l that

> filter p (filter q l) = filter (p & q) l

SUMMARY

The main point of this chapter has been to give the mechanism for returning functions as results of other functions. This is chiefly done by applying a function to fewer than its number of arguments, which we called **partial application**. We discussed how this fits into Miranda as we have already explained it, and discovered the formal justification to be that *all* Miranda functions take a single argument, and may return a function as result. This mechanism gives us the chance to define functions directly, rather than using a `where` clause, for instance.

We also looked at the effects of HOFs on design, and gave the example of document indexing where a toolkit of higher-order functions supported program development.

We concluded the chapter by examining the possibilities for re-using *theorems* about higher-order functions, and discovered that many results we have seen already are particular cases of theorems concerning `map`, `filter`, `fold` and so on.

Types in Miranda

In the first part of the book, we looked at the monomorphic part of Miranda, in which the type variables *, ** and so on do not appear. We begin this chapter by reviewing the type constraints of the monomorphic language, before looking at the full language itself. Crucial to this is an explanation of **unification** which gives the mechanism for finding the appropriate **instance** of a polymorphic type when a polymorphic function is applied.

8.1 Monomorphic types

Here we review the type constraints present in Miranda expressions. Expressions are written on the right-hand sides of definitions and as guards, and are given to the Miranda prompt to be evaluated. After this we look at the constraints on the various components of definitions.

Miranda expressions

Apart from some special expression syntax for tuples and lists, Miranda expressions are formed by applying functions or operators to arguments. We said at the start of this book that every function and operator was typed, and that it is only possible to apply a function to expressions of its argument type. The rule which follows expresses exactly this.

Application Rule

> **IF** f has type s->t **AND** e has type s
> **THEN** f can be applied to e, and the result, f e, has type t.

The force of the rule is to say that a function can only be applied to arguments of its argument type. The rule of cancellation is given by applying this rule k times,

Cancellation Rule

> **IF** f has type $t_1 \rightarrow t_2 \rightarrow \ldots \rightarrow t_n \rightarrow t$
> **AND** e_1 has type t_1, $\ldots$, e_k has type t_k, where $k \leqslant n$,
> **THEN** f can be applied to e_1, $\ldots$, e_k
> and the result f $e_1 \ldots e_k$
> has type $t_{k+1} \rightarrow t_{k+2} \rightarrow \ldots \rightarrow t_n \rightarrow t$.

As a special case of the cancellation rule, we have the rules for the operators, such as addition. For instance,

Addition Rule

> **IF** e_1 and e_2 have type num
> **THEN** $e_1 + e_2$ has type num.

A similar special case gives the rules for typing operator sections, such as (*2). The rule for tuples states that,

Tuple Rule

> **IF** e_1 has type t_1, ..., e_k has type t_k
> **THEN** $(e_1, ..., e_k)$ has type $(t_1, ..., t_k)$.

In other words, the type of a tuple of elements is the tuple of their respective types. There is no restriction here on the types of the elements, whilst there *is* on forming lists of elements:

List Rule

> **IF** e_1, ..., e_k have type t
> **THEN** $[e_1, ..., e_k]$ has type $[t]$.

The list rule says that a collection of elements can be made into a list $[e_1, ..., e_k]$ only if the elements are all of the same type, t.

With the exception of the rule for lists like [n..m], these are all the rules needed to express the types of Miranda expressions, and how they are type-checked in the monomorphic case. There are some more rules which come from definitions in scripts, and we look at those next.

Miranda definitions

Simple definitions in Miranda associate a name with an expression, thus:

```
con :: num
con = 32+e
```

This definition is type correct if the expression on the right-hand side has the type specified.

Definitions of functions in Miranda consist of a number of equations, each of which can have multiple clauses on the right-hand side, and have local definitions attached. The constraints which apply are:

Guard Rule

> Each guard must be an expression of type bool.

Right-hand side Rule

> The expressions in each clause on the right-hand side of an equation must have the same type, t, say.

> If the type of the function is declared, then t is given by the cancellation rule from the declared type. For instance, if f is

declared to have type `num -> bool -> num`, then the right-hand sides of the equation

```
f x True = ...
```

must have type `num`.

Pattern Rule

Each pattern must not conflict with the argument type(s) of the function. For example, we can use a variable `x` for an argument of type `[num]`, but we cannot use the pattern `(n+1)` over this type.

Local Definitions Rule

The definitions in a `where` clause must conform to the typing restrictions above, given the additional information about the local variables used in the definitions. For instance, suppose that

```
f :: num -> bool -> num
f x y = x+2      , if y
      = h x + 3 , otherwise
        where
        h p = ...
```

The variables `x` and `y` can be used in defining `h`, and therefore we should type-check `h` using the information that `x::num` and `y::bool`.

This completes the enumeration of the rules which govern the types of parts of definitions, in the monomorphic case.

Aside – Types for local definitions

It is an unfortunate feature of Miranda that locally-defined functions and objects cannot have their types declared. It is possible to do this by dint of some editing to take the definition to the top level. The stages for the function `f` above are these:

- we have to comment out the `where`, using `||`;
- we then have to signal the end of the definition of `f`, by typing '`;`'. A definition is usually ended by the offside rule, but the semi-colon provides an explicit way of ending a block;
- we need to add the type information about `x` and `y`, and finally,
- we need to assert the type of `h`.

This is illustrated now:

```
f :: num -> bool -> num
f x y = x+2      , if y
        = h x + 3 , otherwise ;
        || where
        x :: num
        y :: bool
        h :: num -> num
        h p = ...
```

The effect of this is to raise the definition of h to the top level, and to declare the types of objects x and y at the top level also. This will cause difficulties if the names x, y or h are already used at this level, but can be overcome by changing the names of one or more of them. Note also that x and y are specified but not defined now; this transformation is only useful for type-checking, not for actual evaluation.

EXERCISES

8.1 Predict the type errors you would obtain by defining the following functions:

```
f (n+1) = 37
f True  = 34

g 0     = 37
g (n+1) = True

h x = True   , if x>0
    = 37      , otherwise

k x = 34
k 0 = 35
```

Check your answers by typing each definition into a Miranda script.

8.2 Express the type rules for the expressions

```
[n..m]
[n,p..m]
```

which form lists of numbers.

8.3 Express the type rules for the operator sections of '*'.

8.2 Polymorphic types

In Section 6.2 we saw the introduction of polymorphic types, and the intuition that a polymorphic definition arises when the variables in a definition are not constrained to be of a particular monomorphic type. To explore this idea, consider the functions

```
f (a,n) = (a , [1..n])
g (m,l) = m + #l
```

In the definition of f, a is unconstrained, whilst n must be a number, as it appears in the [1..n]. In defining g, m must be a num (since it is an argument to '+') and l must be a list, since we take its length. There is no constraint on the type of elements of l. We can therefore say that a will have type *, and l will have type [**], giving

```
f :: (*,num) -> (*,[num])                             (1)
g :: (num,[**]) -> num
```

What happens now if we make the definition

```
h   = g.f          , or
h y = g (f y)      ?                                   (2)
```

For this to type-check using the rules given in the monomorphic setting requires the type of (f y)

```
(* , [num])
```

to be equal to the input type of g, which is

```
(num , [**])
```

but these are not equal! Here is the point where we should remember that the type variables can be thought of as a shorthand for f and g having a whole collection of types,

```
f :: ([bool],num) -> ([bool],[num])
f :: ([***],num) -> ([***],[num])
    ...
```

These types are all instances of the *most general* type for f given in (1), and they are given by *substituting* for the type variables. In the first case we substitute [bool] for *, in the second [***] is substituted.

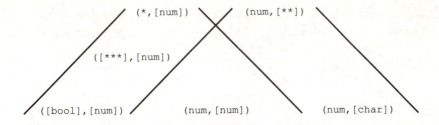

Figure 8.1   Unifying `(*,[num])` and `(num,[**])`.

What we have to do to type-check (2) is to look for *instances* of the types of f and g so that the input type of g is equal to the output type of f:

```
f :: (num,num) -> (num,[num])                                    (3)
g :: (num,[num]) -> num
```

and so we can give h the type `(num,num) -> num`.

How do we find these instances in general? We have to *unify* the types

```
(*,[num])                    (num,[**])
```

By this we mean that we have to find a way of substituting for the variables in the types so that we get the same result from each. In this case, we make the substitution of num for * and num for ** to give `(num,[num])`, and this gives the types for f and g in (3). This is illustrated in Figure 8.1, where the unification is shown as finding the overlap of the two cones beneath the types.

Now we are in a position to understand Miranda's type error messages, which we first met in the first chapter! A message like

```
type error in expression
cannot unify bool with num
```

results from typing `(True+4)`. For a function or operator application, there is an attempt to *unify* the type of the argument given, bool, with the type expected, num. It fails here because the two are different monomorphic types, and so no substitution can make them equal.

The unification in this case gives a monomorphic type, but it is possible for two types to have a polymorphic unifier, when we choose the *most general substitution* to unify the two. For instance, if we have

```
e :: (*,[*])
h :: (**,***) -> ***
```

and we want to form (h e), then we have to unify (*,[*]) with (**,***).
The most general unifier will replace ** by * and *** by [*], giving

```
e :: (*,[*])                                          (4)
h :: (*,[*]) -> [*]
```

and so (h e) :: [*]. The substitution we have given is the most general,
because any other unification of the two can be given by substituting into
(4).

Not every unification will succeed. We have seen the example of bool
and num already, but other cases can be more subtle. First consider the
example of unifying

```
[num] -> [num]               * -> [**]
```

We need to unify the argument and result types, simultaneously. This is
achieved by substituting [num] for the variable *, and num for the variable
**. Now we look at

```
[num] -> [num]               * -> [*]
```

We can unify [num] with *, by substituting [num] for *; similarly, we can
unify [num] with [*], by substituting num for *. We *cannot*, however,
simultaneously substitute both num and [num] for *, and so the unification
will fail.

EXERCISES

8.4   Do the following pairs of types unify? If so, give their most general unifier; if not,
explain why they fail to unify.

```
(num -> **)                (* -> bool)
(num,*,*)                  (*,*,[bool])
```

8.5   Show that we can unify (*,[*]) with (**,***) to give (bool,[bool]). Explain
how this can be given by a substitution from (4) above.

8.6   Can the function

```
f :: (*,[**]) -> **
```

be applied to the arguments (2,[3]), (2,[]) and (2,[True])? Explain your
answers.

8.7 Repeat the previous exercise for the function

```
f :: (*,[*]) -> *
```

Explain your answers.

8.8 Give the type of f [] [] if f has type

```
f :: [*] -> [**] -> * -> **
```

What is the type of the function h given by the definition

```
h x = f x x ?
```

8.9 [*Harder*] Give an *algorithm* which decides whether two type expressions are unifiable. If they are, your algorithm should return the most general unifying substitution; if not it should give some explanation of why the unification fails.

8.10 How can you use the Miranda system to check whether two type expressions are unifiable, and if so what is their unification? Hint: you can declare to the Miranda system the types of names without giving their definitions.

8.3 Polymorphic type-checking

Whilst the previous section gives an informal introduction to unification, this section goes into the process of unification and type-checking in a more technical way; the more technical part of it should be omitted on first reading.

An important example

Functions and constants can be used at different types in the same expression. A simple instance is

$$\#([]++[True,False]) + \#([]++[2,3,4]) \tag{1}$$

The first occurrence of [] is at [num], whilst the second is at [bool]. This is completely legitimate, and is one of the advantages of a polymorphic definition.

Now suppose we replace the [] by a variable, and define

$$funny\ x = \#(x++[True,False]) + \#(x++[2,3,4]) \tag{2}$$

The variable x is forced to have type [bool] *and* type [num]; it is *forced* to be polymorphic, in other words. This is not allowed in Miranda, as there is no way of expressing the type of funny. It might be thought that

```
funny :: [*] -> num
```

was the correct type, but this would mean that funny would have all the instance types

```
funny :: [num] -> num
funny :: [[char]] -> num
    ...
```

which it clearly does not. We conclude that constants and functions are treated differently: constants will very well appear at different incompatible types in the same expression, variables cannot.

The next section, which can be omitted on first reading by skipping to the section on Miranda expressions, explains how the distinction between (1) and (2) is maintained.

Technical consequences of the example

What is the significance of disallowing definition (2) but allowing definition (1)? Taking (1) first, we have a polymorphic definition of the form

```
[] :: [*]
```

and an expression #([]++[True,False]) + #([]++[2,3,4]) in which [] occurs twice; the first occurrence is at [bool], the second at [num]. To allow these completely independent uses to occur, we type-check each occurrence of a polymorphic value with *new* type variables. In this particular instance, we type-check []++[True,... with []::[**], say, and []++[2,... with []::[***].

Polymorphic Use Rule

Each instance of a polymorphic definition is type-checked *independently*, with a new instance of the type. That is, the variables in the type are replaced with hitherto unused type variables.

On the other hand, how is the definition of (2) disallowed? When we type-check the use of a *variable* we will not treat each instance as being of an independent type. Suppose we begin with no constraint on x, so x::*, say. The first occurrence of x forces x::[bool]. In the second, we use ++ to join lists of numbers and Booleans, which fails. In contrast, therefore, to the polymorphic use rule, we do not consider the variables to be independent, and so we implement the

Polymorphic Argument Rule

> The definition of a function is not permitted to *force* any of its arguments to be polymorphic. Variables are therefore *not* type-checked independently.

Miranda expressions

The two rules above summarize the distinction between variables and definitions. Given them, we are able to proceed with a revision of the rules of Section 8.1 for the full – polymorphic – language. The revisions involve us replacing tests for equality of types with tests for their being unifiable, which as we have seen is a more relaxed condition.

The most important rule explains what happens in application, where the type of the argument, and the argument type of the function have to be *unifiable*.

Polymorphic Application Rule

> **IF** f has type s->t, e has type u
> **AND** s and u can be unified, giving f :: s'->t' and e::s'
> **THEN** f can be applied to e, and the result, f e, has type t'.

The polymorphic cancellation rule is again given by applying the application rule k times. It is cumbersome to write down, but effectively each application is accompanied with a substitution to the result type, just as t is specialized to t' due to the unification of s and u in the polymorphic application rule.

The tuple rule is unchanged from Section 8.1, but the rule for lists is generalized. It is not necessary that the elements have the same type, but rather that their types are unifiable.

Polymorphic List Rule

> **IF** e_1 has type t_1, ..., e_k has type t_k
> **AND** t_1, ..., t_k unify to type t
> **THEN** $[e_1, ...,e_k]$ has type [t]

Miranda definitions

The type constraints from Section 8.1 carry over to the general case, except for the right-hand side rule, where an equality test is replaced by a unification.

Polymorphic Right-hand Side Rule

The expressions in each clause on the right-hand side of an equation must unify to some type, t, say.

There is an additional rule, which explains the type of a collection of equations. First we introduce some terminology: t_1 is *at least as general as* t_2 if t_2 can be obtained by substituting for variables in t_1.

Equation-set Rule

The types derived for each of a set of equations should unify to a type at least as general as the type declared for the function defined by the equations. In other words, the type given to each equation must be at least as general as the type declared for the function.

Two aspects of this rule require explanation: consider the example of map. The first equation is

```
map f [] = []
```

and from this is derived the type `* -> [**] -> [***]`, since the only constraints are that the second argument and the result are lists. This unifies with the type given by the second equation to give the familiar type for map.
Secondly, we might have asserted

```
map :: (num -> bool) -> [num] -> [bool]
```

which is more specific than the type which unifies the equation types – hence the constraint that the unifying type is at least as general as the declared type, rather than necessarily being *equal* to the declared type.
As discussed in the monomorphic case, local definitions are checked in the same way as top-level ones. Local definitions can be polymorphic, as in

```
odd = #(empty ++ id [True,False]) + #(empty ++ id [2,3,4])
      where
      empty = []
      id w  = w
```

and this makes apparent an important distinction between local definitions and variables.

EXERCISES

8.11 Explain the types of the functions defined in the `where` clause of

```
f x b l
  = appendL x ++ appendL []   , if tester l b
  = appendL l                 , otherwise
    where
    appendL x = x++l
    tester x b = b & (#l > #x)
```

8.12 Give the type of each of the individual equations which follow, and discuss the type of the function which together they define:

```
merge (a:x) (b:y) = a : merge x (b:y)   , if a<b
                  = a : merge x y       , if a=b
                  = b : merge (a:x) y   , otherwise
merge (a:x) []    = (a:x)
merge []    (b:y) = (b:y)
merge []    []    = []
```

8.13 Explain why the type of the standard function `foldr`

```
(* -> ** -> **) -> ** -> [*] -> **
```

involves two type variables rather than one. Discuss how the type of

```
foldr (+)
```

is determined.

8.14 Give the type of

```
exam1 = ([[]],[[]])
```

and discuss how this compares with the types of

```
exam2 = (empList,empList)
          where
          empList = [[]]
```

and

```
exam3 = double [[]]
          where
          double x = (x,x)
```

8.4 Special functions

Miranda contains some built-in functions which give equality, ordering and printing functions on many types. At first sight they appear to have the polymorphic types

```
(=)   :: * -> * -> bool
(<)   :: * -> * -> bool
show :: * -> string
```

but there are some important theoretical and practical caveats about this. Theoretically, the polymorphism of Miranda is **parametric** which means that the *same* definition, such as

```
#[]    = 0
#(a:x) = #x + 1
```

calculates the length of a list of any type. In contrast, the definitions of the comparison and show functions are **overloaded**. This means that there is a *different* definition at each type, which just happens to be called by the same name as functions with the same purpose at other types.

The practical restrictions are twofold. First, it is not possible to compare or print objects of an arbitrary type. In particular, we cannot compare or print functions, since to compare two functions of type num->num, say, requires us to look at their values at 0, 1, and so on – a test which potentially takes forever, if the functions are equal. Similarly, printing a function requires us to print an infinite collection of values. (The view we take of functions here is extensional, as discussed in Chapter 7.) The effect of these restrictions is as follows:

- The effect of trying to show an object of function type is to produce the string "<function>", so that, for example,

  ```
  show (id.id , 2 div 1) = "(<function>,2)"
  ```

- An attempt to compare functions results in the message

  ```
  program error: attempt to compare functions
  ```

  This is given by evaluating id=id and (2,id)=(2,id), but since equality is evaluated sequentially, we have

  ```
  (2,id)=(3,id) = False
  ```

The effect of equality is only *partial* on types with embedded functions, such as the type of (2,id), (num,*->*), and we advise strongly that equality is only used on types *without* embedded function types. These types are often called the *ground* types.

The second practical restriction is that the show function cannot be used in a definition in a polymorphic way, as in

```
print :: * -> string
print obj = show obj ++ "\n"
```

An acceptable definition would be

```
printNum :: num -> string
printNum obj = show obj ++ "\n"
```

where the type is restricted by the type declaration, since there is no constraint on the type of obj in the definition itself. The show in this case is restricted to the monomorphic type num -> string.

The reason for this restriction is system efficiency, rather than anything more fundamental. Since the definition for show is different at different types, in the polymorphic case there is an overhead in picking the correct implementation during expression evaluation; in the monomorphic case, the definition can be selected prior to evaluation.

EXERCISES

8.15 Investigate the Miranda definition of '<' on the types bool and $(t_1, t_2, \ldots, t_k)$.

8.16 Define a function

```
showBoolFun :: (bool -> bool) -> string
```

which displays a Boolean function as a table. Generalize this to

```
showBoolFunGen :: (* -> string) -> (bool -> *) -> string
```

whose first argument is a function to show elements of *. This argument is used in giving a table of the results of the function.

8.17 The Miranda system could check in the type-checker for potential uses of '=' over function types. Do you think this is preferable to having the system produce run-time errors? Justify your answer.

SUMMARY

The chapter explains the type constraints on expressions and definitions in Miranda. Central to these is function application, where the type of an argument to a function is required to be consistent with the argument type of that function. Technically, this is expressed as the ability to *unify* the two types: we aim to find a way of specializing the two types so that they become the same. The notion of unification is explored in an intuitive way, and then some more technical details of the polymorphism of definitions and variables are examined. After re-iterating the typing constraints for the polymorphic language, the chapter concludes with an examination of the 'special' functions of equality, ordering and show, which are, effectively, polymorphic only over the subclass of ground (non-functional) types.

Part III

Larger-scale Programming

The first part of the book introduced the main ideas of functional programming in the small. Building a bridge, the second part introduced the twin abstractions of higher-order functions and polymorphism. The third part examines programming at a larger scale.

Central to this part are ideas about data representation and design – we begin by showing how user-defined concrete or **algebraic** types can model many commonly occurring forms of data. One of the ideas we have emphasized in the second part of the book is the **separation** between program parts which allows both the independent development of separate parts, and the re-use of parts of programs. A similar separation between the data implementation and use is crucial to larger-scale development, and is supported by type abstraction, given by the Miranda `abstype` mechanism.

Our account of calculation has been deliberately vague about the exact order of evaluation used: are arguments evaluated before a function is applied to them, for instance? Underpinning this approach is the fact that a change in evaluation order cannot change the results produced; all it can do is to affect whether or not a result is produced. In looking at larger-scale systems, we need to be more explicit about evaluation.

We shall see that Miranda uses **lazy evaluation** to calculate results: arguments are only evaluated if it is necessary. Indeed, evaluation of a data structure like a list will only find the part of the list needed for the computation to continue. Lazy evaluation allows us to deal with traditional data structures in a different way: creating intermediate lists in a calculation may not be grossly inefficient, for instance. Moreover, new **infinite** data structures are possible. For example, taking the sum of the first two elements of an infinite list is quite possible, as it necessitates only that we evaluate the first two items, not the whole list. Infinite lists form a new way of structuring programs, as we can view them as **streams** or channels along which data can flow. In particular, input and output can be seen as lazy lists of this kind.

As programs become larger, the efficiency with which they can be evaluated becomes more important. We study both the time taken for programs to give results and the amount of space used during lazy evaluation of expressions.

All the ideas are backed up with examples as they are introduced, and with case studies putting them and earlier ideas together to build larger systems.

Algebraic types

Thus far we have been able to model types of data using

- the base types, num, bool and char, and
- composite types: tuples, $(t_1, t_2, \ldots, t_n)$; lists, $[t_1]$; and function types, $(t_1 \rightarrow t_2)$; where $t_1, \ldots, t_n$ are themselves types.

This gives a wide choice of types and we have seen quite complex structures, like an index for a document, represented by the appropriate combination of types – in the index example, [([num], [char])] was used.

However, there are other types we might choose to model which it is difficult to render using the constructs we have seen so far. Examples include:

- the type of months: January, ..., December;
- the type whose elements are either a number or a string: a house in a street will either have a number or a name, for instance;
- the tree data structure, like the example illustrated in Figure 9.1.

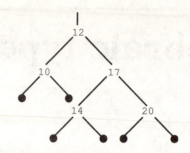

Figure 9.1 An example of a tree of numbers.

All these types can be modelled by Miranda **algebraic** types, which form the subject of this chapter.

9.1 Introduction

The definition of an algebraic type introduces the **constructors** of the type being defined, after the symbol ':: =', which itself follows the name of the type under definition. Names of constructors begin with a capital letter; all other identifiers start with a small letter. We give a sequence of examples of increasing complexity, before discussing the general form of these type definitions.

EXAMPLE: Enumerated types _____

The simplest sort of algebraic type consists of an enumeration of the elements of the type. For instance,

```
temp    ::= Cold | Hot
season  ::= Spring | Summer | Autumn | Winter
```

introduces two types. The type `temp` has two members, `Cold` and `Hot`, and `season` has four members.

To define functions over these types we use pattern matching: we can match against either a constant or a variable. To describe the (British!) weather we might say

```
weather :: season -> temp

weather Summer = Hot
weather x      = Cold
```

Pattern matching is sequential; the first pattern to match an argument will be used. This means that the British weather is only hot in the summer, and it is cold the rest of the year. The built-in Boolean type could be defined by

```
bool ::= False | True
```

The types carry an equality function, and the elements are ordered according to their order of definition, so that Cold is less than Hot, for instance.

In more formal terms, Cold and Hot are called the **constructors** of the type temp. The syntax of Miranda requires that constructors begin with capital letters, to distinguish them from functions and the like.

EXAMPLE: Product types ─────────────────────

Instead of using a tuple we can define a type with a number of components (often called a **product** type) as an algebraic type. An example might be

```
people ::= Person name age
```
(1)

where name is a synonym for string, and age for num, written thus:

```
name == string
age  == num
```

The definition of people should be read as saying

> To give an element of type people, you need to supply one object, n say, of type name, and another, a say, of type age. The element formed from them will be Person n a.

Example values of this type include

```
Person "Electric Aunt Jemima" 77
Person "Ronnie" 14
```

As before, functions are defined using pattern matching. A general element of type people has the form Person n a, and we can use this pattern on the left-hand side of a definition,

```
showPerson :: person -> string
showPerson (Person n a) = n ++ " -- " ++ shownum a
```

(recall that `shownum` gives a printable form of a num). For instance,

```
showPerson (Person "Electric Aunt Jemima" 77)
  = "Electric Aunt Jemima -- 77"
```

In this example, the type has a single constructor, `Person`, which is **binary** because it takes two elements to form a value of type `people`. For the enumerated types `temp` and `season` the constructors are called **nullary** (or **0-ary**) as they take no arguments.

The constructors introduced by algebraic type definitions can be used just like functions, so that `Person n a` is the result of applying the function `Person` to the arguments n and a; we can interpret (1) as giving the type of the constructor, here

```
Person :: name -> age -> people
```

An alternative definition of the type of people is given by the synonym

```
people == (name,age)
```

The advantages of using an algebraic type are threefold:

- Each object of the type carries an explicit *label* of the purpose of the element; in this case that it represents a person.
- It is not possible accidentally to treat an arbitrary pair consisting of a string and a number as a person; a person must be constructed using the `Person` constructor.
- The type will appear in any error messages due to mis-typing; a type synonym is expanded out (in the current version of Miranda) and so disappears from any type error messages.

There are also advantages of using a tuple, with a synonym declaration:

- The elements are more compact, and so definitions will be shorter.
- Using a tuple, especially a pair, allows us to re-use many polymorphic functions such as `fst`, `snd` and `zip2`.

In each system we model we will have to choose between these alternatives: our decisions will depend exactly on how we use the products, and on the complexity of the system.

Note that the approach here works equally well with unary constructors, so we might say

```
age ::= Years num
```

whose elements are `Years 45.3` and so on. It is clear from a definition like this that `45.3` is here being used as an age in years, rather than some unrelated numerical quantity. The disadvantage is that we cannot use functions defined over numbers directly over `age`.

The examples of types given here are a special case of what we look at next.

EXAMPLE: Alternatives

A shape in a simple geometrical program is either a circle or a rectangle. These alternatives are given by the type

```
shape ::= Circle num |
          Rectangle num num
```

which says that there are two ways of building an element of `shape`. One way is to supply the radius of a `Circle`; the other alternative is to give the sides of a `Rectangle`. Example objects of this type are

```
Circle 3
Rectangle 45.9 87.6
```

Pattern matching allows us to define functions by cases, as in

```
isRound :: shape -> bool
isRound (Circle r)     = True
isRound (Rectangle h w) = False
```

and also lets us use the components of the elements:

```
area :: shape -> num
area (Circle r)     = pi*r*r
area (Rectangle h w) = h*w
```

Extensions of this type, to accommodate the position of an object, are discussed in the exercises at the end of this section.

The general form

The general form of the algebraic type definitions which we have seen so far is

```
typename
    ::= Con₁ t₁₁ ... t₁ₖ₁ |
        Con₂ t₂₁ ... t₂ₖ₂ |
        ....
        Conₙ tₙ₁₁ ... tₙₖₙ
```

Each Con_i is a constructor, followed by k_i types, where k_i is a non-negative integer which may be zero. In the sections to come, we shall see two extensions of the definitions seen already:

- The types can be *recursive*; we can use the type we are defining, typename, as (part of) any of the types t_{ij}. This gives us lists, trees and many other data structures.

- The typename can be followed by one or more type variables which may be used on the right-hand side, making the definition *polymorphic*.

Recursive polymorphic types combine these two ideas, and this powerful mixture provides types which can be re-used in many different situations – the built-in type of lists is an example which we have already seen. Other examples are given in the sections which follow.

A synonym is simply a shorthand, and so a synonym type can always be expanded out (and therefore removed from the program). Synonyms cannot be recursive; so to define new recursive types, the algebraic type mechanism must be used.

EXERCISES

9.1 Re-define the function weather:: season -> temp so that a guard is used rather than pattern matching. Which of the definitions is preferable in your opinion?

9.2 Define the type of months as a Miranda algebraic type. Give a function which takes a month to its appropriate season – in doing this you might want to use the ordering on the type, which is defined automatically on each algebraic type.

9.3 What would be the `weather` function for New Zealand, which is on a similar latitude to Britain, but in the Southern Hemisphere? What would be the definition for Brazil, which is crossed by the Equator?

9.4 Define a function to give the length of the perimeter of a geometrical shape, of type `shape`.

9.5 Add an extra constructor to `shape` for triangles, and extend the functions `isRound`, `area` and `perimeter` to include triangles.

9.6 Define a function which decides whether a shape is regular: a circle is regular, a square is a regular rectangle and being equilateral makes a triangle regular.

9.7 The type `shape` takes no account of the position or orientation of a shape. After deciding how to represent points, how would you modify the original definition of `shape` to contain the centre of each object? You can assume that rectangles lie with their sides parallel to the axes, thus:

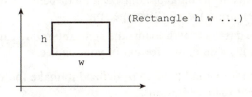

9.8 Calling the new shape type `newShape`, define a function

```
move :: num -> num -> newShape -> newShape
```

which moves a shape by the two offsets given:

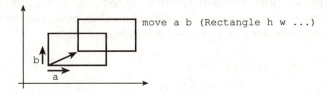

9.9 Define a function to test whether two `newShapes` overlap.

9.10 Some houses have a number; others have a name. How would you implement the type of 'strings or numbers' used as a part of an address? Write a function which prints one of these objects. Give a definition of a type of names and addresses using the type you have defined.

9.11 Re-implement the library database of Section 4.4 to use an algebraic type like `people` rather than a pair. Compare the two approaches to this example.

9.12 The library database of Section 4.4 is to be extended in the following ways:

- CDs and videos as well as books are available for loan.

- A record is kept of the authors of books as well as their titles. Similar information is kept about CDs, but not about videos.

- Each loan has a period: books one month, CDs one week and videos three days.

Explain how you would modify the types used to implement the database, and how the function types might be changed. The system should perform the following operations. For each case, given the types and definitions of the functions involved:

- give all items on loan to a given person;

- give all books, CDs or videos on loan to a particular person;

- give all items in the database due back on or before a particular day, and the same information for any given person;

- update the database with loans; the constant `today` can be assumed to contain today's date, in a format of your choice.

What other functions would have to be defined to make the system usable? Give their types, but not their definitions.

9.2 Recursive types

Types are often naturally described in terms of themselves. For instance, a (numeric) expression is either a **literal** number, or is given by combining two expressions using an operator such as plus or minus:

```
expr ::= Lit num |
         Add expr expr |
         Sub expr expr
```

Similarly, a tree is either nil or is given by combining a value and two sub-trees. For example, the number 12 and the trees in Figure 9.2 are assembled to give the tree in Figure 9.1. As a Miranda type we say

```
nTree::= NilT |
         Node num nTree nTree
```

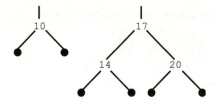

Figure 9.2   Two trees.

Finally, we have already used the type of lists: a list is either empty ([]) or is built from a head and a tail – another list – using the list constructor ':'. Lists will provide a good guide to using recursive (and polymorphic) definitions. In particular, they suggest how polymorphic higher-order functions over other algebraic types are defined, and how programs are verified. We now look at some examples in more detail.

Expressions

The type expr gives a model of the simple numerical expressions discussed above. These might be used in implementing a numerical calculator, for instance;

```
expr ::= Lit num |
         Add expr expr |
         Sub expr expr
```

Some examples are

```
2               Lit 2
2+3             Add (Lit 2) (Lit 3)
(3-1)+3         Add (Sub (Lit 3) (Lit 1)) (Lit 3)
```

where the informal expressions are listed in the left-hand column, and their expr forms in the right. Given an expression, we might want to

- evaluate it;
- print it;
- estimate its size – count the operators, say.

Each of these functions will be defined in the same way, using **primitive recursion**. As the type is itself recursive, it is not a surprise that the functions which handle the type will also be recursive. Also, the form of the recursive definitions follows the recursion in the type definition. For instance, to evaluate an operator expression we work out the values of the arguments and combine the results using the operator:

```
eval :: expr -> num

eval (Lit n)     = n
eval (Add e1 e2) = (eval e1) + (eval e2)
eval (Sub e1 e2) = (eval e1) - (eval e2)
```

Primitive recursive definitions have two parts:

- At the non-recursive, *base* cases – (Lit n) here – the value is given outright.
- At the recursive cases, the values of the function at the sub-expressions, eval e1 and eval e2 here, can be used in calculating the result.

The printing function has a similar form

```
showExpr :: expr -> num

showExpr (Lit n) = shownum n
showExpr (Add e1 e2)
    = "(" ++ showExpr e1 ++ "+" ++ showExpr e2 ++ ")"
showExpr (Sub e1 e2)
    = "(" ++ showExpr e1 ++ "-" ++ showExpr e2 ++ ")"
```

as does the function to calculate the number of operators in an expression; we leave this as an exercise. Other exercises at the end of the section look at a different representation of expressions for which a separate type is used to represent the different possible operators. Next, we look at another recursive algebraic type, but after that we return to expr and give an example of a non-primitive recursive definition of a function to re-arrange expressions in a particular way.

EXAMPLE: Trees of numbers ─────────────────────────────

Trees of numbers like that in Figure 9.1 can be modelled by the type

```
nTree::= NilT |
         Node num nTree nTree
```

The null tree is given by NilT, and the trees in Figure 9.2 by

```
Node 10 NilT NilT
Node 17 (Node 14 NilT NilT) (Node 20 NilT NilT)
```

Definitions of many functions are primitive recursive. For instance,

```
sumTree,depth :: nTree -> num
```

```
sumTree NilT           = 0
sumTree (Node n t t') = n + sumTree t + sumTree t'
```

```
depth NilT            = 0
depth (Node n t t')   = 1 + max2 (depth t) (depth t')
```

with

```
sumTree (Node 3 (Node 4 NilT NilT) NilT) = 7
depth   (Node 3 (Node 4 NilT NilT) NilT) = 2
```

As another example, take the problem of finding out how many times a number, p say, occurs in a tree. The primitive recursion suggests two cases, depending upon the tree:

- For a null tree, NilT, the answer must be zero.
- For a non-null tree (Node n t t'), we can find out how many times p occurs in the sub-trees t and t' by two recursive calls; we have to make a case split depending on whether p occurs at the particular node; that is, depending on whether or not p=n.

The final definition is

```
occurs :: nTree -> num -> num
```

```
occurs NilT p = 0
occurs (Node n t t') p
     = 1 + occurs t p + occurs t' p   , if n=p
     =     occurs t p + occurs t' p   , otherwise
```

The exercises at the end of the section give a number of other examples of functions defined over trees using primitive recursion. We next look at a particular example where a different form of recursion is used.

EXAMPLE: Rearranging expressions ─────────────────────────

The next example shows a definition which uses a more general recursion than we have seen so far. After showing why the generality is necessary, we argue that the function we have defined is total: it will give a result on all well-defined expressions.

The operation of addition is associative, so that the way in which an expression is bracketed is irrelevant to its value. We can, therefore, decide to bracket expressions involving '+' in any way we choose. The aim here is to write a program to turn expressions into right-bracketed form, as shown in the following table:

(2+3)+4	2+(3+4)
((2+3)+4)+5	2+(3+(4+5))
((2-((6+7)+8))+4)+5	(2-(6+(7+8)))+(4+5)

What is the program to do? The main aim is to spot occurrences of

```
Add (Add e1 e2) e3                                          (1)
```

and to transform them to

```
Add e1 (Add e2 e3)                                          (2)
```

so a first attempt at the program might say

```
try (Add (Add e1 e2) e3)
  = Add (try e1) (Add (try e2) (try e3))
try ...
```

which is primitive recursive: on the right-hand side of their definition the function try is only used on sub-expressions of the argument. This function will have the effect of transforming (1) to (2), but unfortunately (3) will be sent to (4):

```
((2+3)+4)+5)                                                (3)
(2+3)+(4+5)                                                 (4)
```

The problem is that in transforming (1) to (2) we may produce another pattern we are looking for at the top level: this is precisely what happens with (3) going to (4). We therefore have to call the function *again* on the result of the rearrangement

```
assoc :: expr -> expr

assoc (Add (Add e1 e2) e3)
  = assoc (Add e1 (Add e2 e3))                      (5)
```

The other cases in the definition make sure that the *parts* of an expression
are re-arranged as they should be:

```
assoc (Add e1 e2)
  = Add (assoc e1) (assoc e2)                        (6)
assoc (Sub e1 e2)
  = Sub (assoc e1) (assoc e2)
assoc (Lit n)
  = Lit n
```

Equation (6) will only be applied to the cases where (5) does not apply –
this is when e1 is either a Sub or a Lit expression. This is always the case in
pattern matching; the *first* applicable equation is used.

When we use primitive recursion we can be sure that the recursion will
terminate to give an answer: the recursive calls are only made on smaller
expressions, and so after a finite number of calls to the function, a base case
will be reached.

The assoc function is more complicated, and we need a more subtle
argument to see that the function will always give a result. Equation (5) is
the tricky one, but intuitively, we can see that some progress has been made –
some of the 'weight' of the tree has moved from left to right. In particular,
one addition symbol has swapped sides. None of the other equations moves
a plus in the other direction, so that after applying (5) a finite number of
times, there will be no more exposed addition symbols at the top level of the
left-hand side. This means that the recursion cannot go on indefinitely, and
so the function always leads to a result.

Mutual recursion

In describing one type, it is often useful to use others; these in turn may refer
back to the original type: this gives a pair of **mutually recursive** types. A
description of a person may refer to their biography, which itself might refer
to other people, for instance:

```
person ::= Adult name address biog |
           Child name
biog   ::= Parent string [person] |
           NonParent string
```

In the case of a parent, the biography contains some text, as well as a list of their children, as elements of the type `person`.

Suppose we want to define a function which prints a person's information, as a string. Printing this information will require us to print the biographical information, which itself contains information about a person. We have two mutually recursive functions:

```
showPerson (Adult nm ad bio)
  = showName nm ++ showAddress ad ++ showBiog bio
  ...
showBiog (Parent st perList)
  = st ++ concat (map showPerson perList)
  ...
```

EXERCISES

9.13 Give calculations of

```
eval (Lit 67)
eval (Add (Sub (Lit 3) (Lit 1)) (Lit 3))
showExpr (Add (Lit 67) (Lit (-34)))
```

9.14 Define the function

```
size :: expr -> num
```

which counts the number of operators in the expression.

9.15 Add the operations of multiplication and integer division to the type `expr`, and re-define the functions `eval`, `showExpr` and `size` to include these new cases. What does your definition of `eval` do when asked to perform a division by zero?

9.16 Instead of adding extra constructors to the `expr` type, as in the previous exercise, it is possible to factor the definition thus:

```
expr ::= Lit num |
         Op op expr expr

op ::= Add | Sub | Mul | Div
```

Show how the functions `eval`, `showExpr` and `size` are defined for this type, and discuss the changes you have to make to your definitions if you add the extra operation `Mod` for remainder on integer division.

9.17   Give calculations of

```
sumTree (Node 3 (Node 4 NilT NilT) NilT)
depth   (Node 3 (Node 4 NilT NilT) NilT)
```

9.18   Define functions to return the left- and right-hand sub-trees of an nTree.

9.19   Define a function to decide whether a number is an element of a tree.

9.20   Define functions to find the maximum and minimum values held in an nTree.

9.21   A tree is reflected by swapping left and right sub-trees, recursively. Write a function to reflect an nTree.

9.22   Define functions

```
collapse, sort :: nTree -> [num]
```

which turn a tree into a list. The function collapse should print the left sub-tree, then the value at the node and finally the right sub-tree; sort should sort the elements in ascending order. For instance,

```
collapse (Node 3 (Node 4 NilT NilT) NilT) = [4,3]
sort     (Node 3 (Node 4 NilT NilT) NilT) = [3,4]
```

9.23   Complete the definitions of showPerson and showBiog which were left incomplete in the text.

9.24   It is possible to extend the type expr so that it contains *conditional* expressions, If b e1 e2, where e1 and e2 are expressions, and b is a Boolean expression, a member of the type bExp.

```
expr ::= Lit num |
         Op op expr expr |
         If bExp expr expr
```

The expression If b e1 e2 has the value of e1 if b has the value True, otherwise it has the value of e2.

```
bExp ::= BoolLit bool |
         And bExp bExp |
         Not bExp |
         Equal expr expr |
         Greater expr expr
```

The five clauses here give:

- Boolean literals, `BoolLit True` and `BoolLit False`.
- The conjunction of two expressions; it is `True` if both halves have the value `True`.
- The negation of an expression. `Not be` has value `True` if `be` has the value `False`.
- `Equal e1 e2` is `True` when the two numerical expressions have equal values.
- `Greater e1 e2` is `True` when the numerical expression `e1` has a larger value then `e2`.

Define the functions

```
eval  :: expr -> num
bEval :: bExpr -> bool
```

by mutual recursion, and extend the function `showExpr` to print the redefined type of expressions.

9.3 Polymorphic algebraic types

Algebraic type definitions can contain the type variables `*`, `**` and so on, defining polymorphic types. The definitions are as before, the type variables used in the definition appearing after the type name on the left-hand side of the definition. A simple example is

```
pair * ::= Pair * *
```

and example elements of the type are

```
Pair 2 3   :: pair num
Pair [] [3] :: pair [num]
Pair [] []  :: pair [*]
```

A function to test the equality of the two halves of a pair is given by

```
equalPair :: pair * -> bool
equalPair (Pair x y) = (x=y)
```

The remainder of this section explores a sequence of further examples.

EXAMPLE: Lists ───────────────────────

The built-in type of lists can be given by a definition like

```
list * ::= NilList | Cons * (list *)
```

where the syntax [*], [] and ':' is used for list *, NilList and $Cons. Because of this, lists form a useful paradigm for recursive polymorphic types. In particular, we can see the possibility of defining useful families of functions over such types, and the way in which program verification can proceed by induction over the structure of a type.

EXAMPLE: Binary trees ───────────────────

The trees of Section 9.2 carry numbers at each node; there is nothing special about numbers, and we can equally well say that they have elements of an arbitrary type at the nodes:

```
tree * ::= Nil | Node * (tree *) (tree *)
```

The definitions of depth and occurs carry over unchanged:

```
depth :: tree * -> num
depth Nil            = 0
depth (Node n t t') = 1 + max2 (depth t) (depth t')
```

as do many of the functions defined in the exercises at the end of Section 9.2. One of these is the function collapsing a tree into a list. This is done by visiting the elements of the tree 'inorder', that is visiting first the left sub-tree, then the node itself, then the right sub-tree, thus:

```
collapse :: tree * -> [*]
collapse Nil = []
collapse (Node v t t')
  = collapse t ++ [v] ++ collapse t'
```

For example,

```
collapse (Node 12
              (Node 34 Nil Nil)
              (Node 3 (Node 17 Nil Nil) Nil))
    = [34,12,17,3]
```

Various higher-order functions are definable, also,

```
mapTree :: (* -> **) -> tree * -> tree **
mapTree f Nil = Nil
mapTree f (Node v t t')
    = Node (f v) (mapTree f t) (mapTree f t')
```

We shall return to trees in Section 11.7, where particular 'search' trees form a case study.

EXAMPLE: Union type ────────────────

Type definitions can take more than one parameter. We saw earlier the example of the type whose elements were either a name or a number. In general we can form a type whose elements come either from * or from **:

```
union * ** ::= One * | Two **
```

Members of the union type are either (One a), with a::*, or (Two b) with b::**. The 'name or number' type is given by union string num and

```
One "Duke of Prunes" :: union string num
Two 333.12345        :: union string num
```

We can tell whether an element is in the first half of the union by

```
isOne :: union * ** -> bool
isOne (One x) = True
isOne (Two x) = False
```

To define a function from union * ** to num, say, we have to deal with two cases,

```
fun :: union * ** -> num
fun (One x) = ... x ...
fun (Two y) = ... y ...
```

In the first case, the right-hand side takes x to a num, so gives a function from * to num; in the second case y is taken to num, a function from ** to num.

Guided by this, we can give a higher-order function which *joins together* two functions defined on * and ** to a function on union * **. The definition follows, and is illustrated in Figure 9.3:

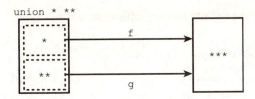

Figure 9.3 Joining together functions.

```
joinFuns :: (* -> ***) -> (** -> ***) -> union * ** -> ***

joinFuns f g (One v) = f v
joinFuns f g (Two v) = g v
```

If we have a function f :: * -> *** and we wish to apply it to an element of type union * **, there is a problem: what do we do if the element is in the second half of the union? A simple answer is to raise an error;

```
applyOne :: (* -> ***) -> union * ** -> ***
applyOne f (One x) = f x
applyOne f (Two y) = error "applyOne applied to Two!"
```

but in the next section we shall explore other ways of handling errors in more detail.

EXERCISES

9.25 Investigate which of the functions over trees discussed in the exercises of Section 9.2 can be made polymorphic.

9.26 Define a function twist which swaps the order of a union

```
twist :: union * ** -> union ** *
```

What is the effect of (twist.twist)?

9.27 Show that any function of type * -> ** can be transformed into functions of type

```
* -> union ** ***
* -> union *** **
```

9.28   How could you generalize `joinFuns` to `jFuns` so that it has type

```
jFuns :: (* -> ***) -> (** -> ****) ->
         union * ** -> union *** ****
```

You might find the answer to the previous exercise useful here, if you want to define `jFuns` using `joinFuns`.

The trees defined in the text are *binary*: each tree has exactly two sub-trees. We can instead define trees with an arbitrary list of sub-trees, thus:

```
gTree * ::= Leaf * | Gnode [gTree *]
```

The exercises which follow concern these trees.

9.29   Define functions

- to count the number of leaves in a `gTree`;
- to find the depth of a `gTree`;
- to sum a numeric `gTree num`;
- to find whether an element appears in a `gTree`;
- to map a function over the elements at the leaves of a `gTree`; and
- to flatten a `gTree` to a list.

9.30   How is the completely empty tree represented as a `gTree`?

9.4   Case study: Program errors

How should a program deal with a situation which ought not to occur? Examples of such situations include

- attempts to divide by zero, to take the square root of a negative number, and other arithmetical transgressions;
- attempts to take the head of an empty list – this is a special case of a definition over an algebraic type from which one case (here the empty list) is absent.

This section examines the problem, giving three approaches of increasing sophistication. The simplest method is to stop computation, and to report the source of the problem. This is indeed what the Miranda system does in the cases listed above, and we can do this in functions we define ourselves using the `error` function

```
error :: [char] -> *
```

An attempt to evaluate

```
error "Circle with negative radius"
```

results in the message `"Circle with negative radius"` being printed after computation stops.

The problem with this approach is that all the useful information in the computation is lost; instead of this, the error can be dealt with in some way *without* stopping computation completely. Two approaches suggest themselves, and we look at them in turn now.

Dummy values

The function `tl` is supposed to give the tail of a list, and it gives an error message on an empty list:

```
tl :: [*] -> [*]
tl (a:x) = x
tl []    = error "tl of []"
```

We could re-define it to say

```
tail :: [*] -> [*]
tail (a:x) = x
tail []    = []
```

Now, an attempt to take the tail of *any* list will succeed. In a similar way, we could say

```
divide :: num -> num -> num
divide n m = n/m   , if m ~= 0
           = 0     , otherwise
```

so that division by zero gives some answer. For `tail` and `divide` there have been obvious choices about what the value in the 'error' case should be; for `head` there is not, and instead we supply an extra parameter to `head`, which is to be used in the case of the list being empty:

```
head :: * -> [*] -> *
head b (a:x) = a
head b []    = b
```

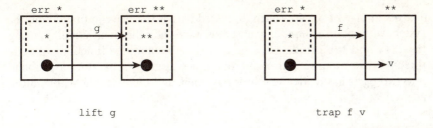

Figure 9.4 Error-handling functions.

In trapping an error, we aim to return a result of type **, from an input of type err *; we have two cases to deal with:

- in the OK case, we apply a function from * to **;
- in the Error case, we have to give the value of type ** which is to be returned. (This is rather like the value we supplied to head earlier.)

The higher-order function which achieves this is trap, whose arguments f and v are used in the OK and Error cases, respectively:

```
trap::(*->**)->**->err *->**

trap f v (OK x) = f x
trap f v Error   = v
```

We can see the functions lift and trap in action in the examples which follow. In the first, a division by zero leads to an Error which passes through the lifting to be trapped – 56 is therefore returned:

```
  trap (1+) 56 (lift (*3) (errDiv 9 0))
= trap (1+) 56 (lift (*3) Error)
= trap (1+) 56 Error
= 56
```

In the second, a normal division returns an OK 9. This is multiplied by three, and the trap at the outer level adds one and removes the OK:

```
  trap (1+) 56 (lift (*3) (errDiv 9 1))
= trap (1+) 56 (lift (*3) (OK 9))
= trap (1+) 56 (OK 27)
= 1 + 27
= 28
```

The advantage of the approach discussed here is that we can first define the system without error handling, and afterwards add the error handling, using the `lift` and `trap` functions together with the modified functions to *raise* the error. As we have seen numerous times already, separating a problem into two parts has made the solution of each, and therefore the whole, more accessible.

EXERCISES

9.31 Using the functions `lift` and `trap`, or otherwise, define a function

```
process :: [num] -> num -> num -> num
```

so that `process l n m` takes the nth and mth items of the list of numbers `l`, and returns their sum. Your function should return 0 if either (or both) of the numbers is (are) not one of the indices of the list: for a list of length p, the indices are 0, ..., p-1 inclusive.

9.32 Discuss the advantages and disadvantages of the three approaches to error handling discussed here.

9.33 What are the values of type `err (err *)`? Define a function

```
squash :: err (err *) -> err *
```

which will 'squash' `OK (OK a)` to `OK a` and all other values to `Error`.

9.34 In a similar way to `lift`, define the function

```
composeErr :: (* -> err **) ->
              (** -> err ***) ->
              (* -> err ***)
```

which composes two error-raising functions. How could you use ordinary function composition and the `squash` function to define `composeErr`?

9.35 The error type could be generalized to allow messages to be carried in the `Error` part, thus:

```
err * ::= OK * | Error string
```

How do the definitions of `lift`, `trap` and `composeErr` have to be modified to accommodate this new definition?

9.5   Design with algebraic data types

Algebraic data types provide us with a powerful mechanism for modelling types which occur both in problems themselves, and internally to the programs designed to solve them. In this section we suggest a three-stage method for finding the appropriate algebraic type definitions. We apply it in two examples: finding the 'edit distance' between two words; and a simulation problem.

An important moral of the discussion here is that we can start to design data *independently* of the program itself. For a system of any size, we should do this, as we will be more likely to succeed if we can think about separate parts of the system separately.

We shall have more to say about design of data types in the next chapter.

Edit distance

In discussing the stages of design, we follow the example of finding the **edit distance** between two strings. This is the shortest sequence of simple editing operations which can take us from one string to the other.

The example is a version of a practical problem: in keeping a display (of windows or simple text) up-to-date, the speed with which updates can be done is crucial. It is therefore desirable to be able to make the updates from as few elementary operations as possible; this is what the edit distance program achieves.

We suppose that there are five basic editing operations on a string. We can change one character into another, copy a character without modifying it, delete or insert a character and delete (kill) to the end of the string. We also assume that each operation has the same cost, except a copy which is free.

To turn the string "fish" into "chips", we could kill the whole string, then insert the characters one-by-one, at a total cost of six. An optimal solution will copy as much of the string as possible, and is given by

- inserting the character 'c',
- changing 'f' to 'h',
- copying 'i',
- inserting 'p',
- copying 's', and finally
- deleting the remainder of the string, "h".

In the remainder of this section we design a type to represent the editing steps, and after looking at another example of data type design, define a function to give an optimal sequence of editing steps from one string to another.

The analysis here can also be used to describe the difference between two lists of arbitrary type. If each item is a line of a file, its behaviour is similar to the Unix `diff` utility.

Design stages

Now we look at the three stages of algebraic type definition in detail:

- First we have to identify the *types* of data involved. In the example, we have to define

  ```
  edit :: = ...
  ```

  which represents the editing operations.

- Next, we have to identify the different sorts of data in each of the types. Each sort of data is given by a *constructor*. In the example, we can change, copy, delete or insert a character and delete (kill) to the end of the string. Our type definition is therefore

  ```
  edit :: = Change ... |
            Copy ... |
            Delete ... |
            Insert ... |
            Kill ...
  ```

  The '...' show that we have not yet said anything about the types of the constructors.

- Finally, for each of the constructors, we need to decide what its *components* or arguments are. Some of the constructors – `Copy`, `Delete` and `Kill` – require no information; the others need to indicate the new character to be inserted, so

  ```
  edit :: = Change char |
            Copy |
            Delete |
            Insert char |
            Kill
  ```

  This completes the definition.

We now illustrate how other type definitions work in a similar way.

EXAMPLE: Simulation _____

Suppose we want to model, or **simulate**, how the queues in a bank or post office behave; perhaps we want to decide how many bank clerks need to be working at particular times of the day. Our system will take as input the arrivals of customers, and give as output their departures. Each of these can be modelled as a type:

- `inmess` is the type of input messages. At a given time, there are two possibilities:

    - no-one arrives, represented by the 0-ary constructor `No`;
    - someone arrives, represented by the constructor `Yes`. This will have components giving the arrival time of the customer, and the amount of time that will be needed to serve them.

    Hence we have

    ```
    inmess ::= No | Yes arrival service

    arrival == num
    service == num
    ```

- Similarly, we have `outmess`, the type of output messages. Either no-one leaves (`None`), or a person is discharged (`Discharge`). The relevant information they carry is the time they have waited, together with when they arrived and their service time. We therefore define

    ```
    outmess ::= None | Discharge arrival wait service

    wait == num
    ```

_____

We return to the simulation example in Chapter 11.

Implementation of edit distance

The problem is to find the lowest-cost sequence of edits to take us from one string to another. We can begin the definition thus:

```
transform :: string -> string -> [edit]

transform [] [] = []
```

To transform the non-empty string `st` to `[]`, we simply have to `Kill` it, whilst to transform `[]` to `st`, we have to `Insert` each of the characters in turn:

```
          transform st [] = [Kill]
          transform [] st = map Insert st
```

In the general case, we have a choice: should we first use `Copy`, `Delete`, `Insert` or `Change`? If the first characters of the strings are equal we should copy; but if not, there is no obvious choice. We therefore try *all* possibilities and choose the best of them:

```
transform (a:x) (b:y)
  = Copy : transform x y                        , if a=b
  = best [ Delete   : transform x (b:y) ,
           Insert b : transform (a:x) y ,
           Change b : transform x y     ]  , otherwise
```

How do we choose the `best` sequence? We choose the one with the lowest cost:

```
best :: [[edit]] -> [edit]
best [a]   = a
best (a:x) = a     , if cost a <= cost b
           = b     , otherwise
             where
             b = best x
```

The `cost` is given by charging one for every operation except copy, which is equivalent to 'leave unchanged':

```
cost :: [edit] -> num
cost = (#) . filter (~=Copy)
```

EXERCISES

The first four exercises are designed to make you think about how data types are designed. *There are no right answers for them*, rather you should satisfy yourself that you have represented adequately the types you have in your informal picture of the problem.

9.36 It is decided to keep a record of vehicles which will use a particular car park. Design an algebraic data type to represent them.

9.37 If you knew that the records of vehicles were to be used for comparative tests of fuel efficiency, how would you modify your answer to the last exercise?

9.38 Discuss the data types you might use in a database of students' marks for classes and the like. Explain the design of any algebraic data types that you use.

9.39 What data types might be used to represent the objects which can be drawn using an interactive drawing program? To give yourself more of a challenge, you might like to think about grouping of objects, multiple copies of objects, and scaling.

9.40 How would you modify the edit distance program to accommodate a Swap operation, which can be used to transform "abxyz" to "baxyz" in a single step?

9.41 Define a function which, when given a list of edits and a string st, prints the sequence of strings given by applying the edits to st in sequence.

9.42 Give a calculation of transform "cat" "am". What do you conclude about the efficiency of the transform function?

9.6 Reasoning about algebraic types

Verification for algebraic types follows the example of lists, as first discussed in Chapter 5. The general pattern of structural induction over an algebraic type states that the result has to be proved for each constructor; when a constructor is recursive, we are allowed to use the corresponding induction hypotheses in making the proof. We first give some representative examples in this section, and conclude with a rather more sophisticated proof.

EXAMPLE: Trees ────────────────────────────

Structural induction over the type of trees is stated as follows:

Structural induction over trees   To prove the property P(t) for all finite t of type tree * we have to do two things.

> Nil **case**   Prove P(Nil).
>
> Node **case**   Prove P(Node v t t') assuming that P(t) and P(t')
> hold already.

We can, if we wish, follow the advice of Chapter 5 in specifying a template and in finding proofs.

Now we give a representative example of a proof. We aim to prove for all finite trees t that

```
map f (collapse t) = collapse (mapTree f t)
```

which states that if we map a function over a tree, and then collapse the result, we get the same result as collapsing before mapping over the list. The functions we use are defined as follows:

```
map f []    = []                                            (1)
map f (a:x) = f a : map f x                                 (2)

mapTree f Nil = Nil                                         (3)
mapTree f (Node v t t')
   = Node (f v) (mapTree f t) (mapTree f t')               (4)

collapse Nil = []                                          (5)
collapse (Node v t t')
   = collapse t ++ [v] ++ collapse t'                      (6)
```

Proof: In the Nil case, we simplify each side, giving

```
map f (collapse Nil)
= map f []                                            by (5)
= []                                                  by (1)

collapse (mapTree f Nil)
= collapse Nil                                        by (3)
= []                                                  by (5)
```

This shows that the base case holds. In the Node case, we have to prove

```
map f (collapse (Node v t t'))
    = collapse (mapTree f (Node v t t'))
```

assuming that

```
map f (collapse t)  = collapse (mapTree f t)               (7)
map f (collapse t') = collapse (mapTree f t')              (8)
```

hold. Looking at the goal, we can simplify the left-hand side thus:

```
map f (collapse (Node v t t'))
= map f (collapse t ++ [v] ++ collapse t')            by (6)
= map f (collapse t) ++ [f v] ++
    map f (collapse t')                               by (9)
= collapse (mapTree f t) ++ [f v] ++
    collapse (mapTree f t')                           by (7,8)
```

The final step is given by the two induction hypotheses, that the result holds for the two sub-trees t and t'. The result (9) is the equation

$$\text{map g (x++y) = map g x ++ map g y} \tag{9}$$

discussed earlier. Examining the right-hand side now, we have

```
collapse (mapTree f (Node v t t'))
= collapse (Node (f v) (mapTree f t) (mapTree f t'))  by (4)
= collapse (mapTree f t) ++ [f v] ++
    collapse (mapTree f t')                            by (6)
```

and this finishes the proof in the Node case. As this is the final case of the two for trees, the proof is complete. ∎

EXAMPLE: Errors

Structural induction for the type err * becomes proof by cases – because the type is not recursive, in none of the cases is there an appeal to an induction hypothesis. The rule is:

Structural induction over the error type   To prove the property P(x) for all defined[†] x of type err * we have to do two things:

> Error **case**   Prove P(Error).
>
> OK **case**   Prove P(OK v) for all defined v.

Our example proof is that, for all defined values v of type err num,

$$\text{trap abs 2 v} \geqslant 0$$

Proof: The proof has two cases. In the first v is replaced by Error:

```
trap abs 2 Error
= 2 ⩾ 0
```

In the second, v is replaced by OK n for a defined n:

[†] When the type is not recursive, the induction principle gives a proof for all defined objects. An object of this type is defined if it is Error, or OK v for a defined v.

```
trap abs 2 (OK n)
= abs n ⩾ 0
```

In both cases the result holds, and so the result is valid in general.

∎

Other forms of proof

We have seen that not all functions are defined by primitive recursion. The example we saw in Section 9.2 was of the function `assoc` which is used to re-arrange arithmetic expressions. Recall that

```
assoc (Add (Add e1 e2) e3)
  = assoc (Add e1 (Add e2 e3))                         (1)
assoc (Add e1 e2) = Add (assoc e1) (assoc e2)          (2)
assoc (Sub e1 e2) = Sub (assoc e1) (assoc e2)          (3)
assoc (Lit n)     = Lit n                              (4)
```

with (1) being the non-primitive recursive case. We would like to prove that the re-arrangement does not affect the value of the expression:

```
eval (assoc ex) = eval ex                              (5)
```

for all finite expressions ex. The induction principle for `expr` has three cases:

Lit **case**	Prove `P(Lit n)`.
Add **case**	Prove `P(Add e1 e2)`, assuming `P(e1)` and `P(e2)`.
Sub **case**	Prove `P(Sub e1 e2)`, assuming `P(e1)` and `P(e2)`.

To prove (5) for all finite expressions, we have the three cases given above. The `Lit` and `Sub` cases are given, respectively, by (4) and (3), but the `Add` case is more subtle. For this we will prove

```
eval (assoc (Add e1 e2)) = eval (Add e1 e2)            (6)
```

by induction on the number of `Add`s which are left-nested at the top level of the expression e1 – recall that it was by counting these that we proved the function would always terminate. Now, if there are no `Add`s at the top-level of e1, equation (2) gives (6). Otherwise we re-arrange thus:

```
eval (assoc (Add (Add f1 f2) e2)))
= eval (assoc (Add f1 (Add f2 e2)))
```

and since f1 contains fewer Adds at the top level,

```
= eval (Add f1 (Add f2 e2))
= eval (Add (Add f1 f2) e2)              by associativity of +
```

which gives the induction step, and therefore completes the proof.   ∎

This result shows that verification is possible for functions defined in a more general way than primitive recursion, and indeed, that the pattern of the proof for these often follows their pattern of definition.

EXERCISES

9.43   Prove that the function `weather` from Section 9.1 has the same behaviour as

    newWeather = makeHot . isSummer

when

    makeHot True = Hot
    makeHot False = Cold
    isSummer = (=Summer)

where recall that `(=Summer)` is an operator section whose effect is to test its argument for equality with `Summer`.

9.44   Is it the case that the `area` of each shape from Section 9.1 is non-negative? If so, give a proof; if not, give an example which shows it is not valid.

9.45   If we define the `size` of an `nTree` thus:

    size NilT   = 0
    size (Node v t t') = 1 + size t + size t'

then prove that for all finite `nTrees`, t,

    size t < 2^(depth t)

9.46   Show for all finite `nTrees` t that

    occurs t a = # (filter (=a) (collapse t))

The next two exercises refer back to the exercises of Section 9.3.

9.47   Prove that the function `twist` has the property that

    twist.twist = id

9.48 Explain the principle of structural induction for the type gTree. Formulate and prove the equivalent of the theorem relating map, mapTree and collapse for this type of trees.

SUMMARY

Algebraic types sharpen our ability to model types in our programs: we have seen in this chapter how simple, finite types like temp can be defined, as well as the more complex union and recursive types. Many of these recursive types are varieties of tree: we looked at numerical trees; elements of the type expr can also be thought of as trees representing the grammatical forms of expressions.

The type of lists gives a guiding example for various aspects of algebraic types:

- They are recursive and polymorphic, and many polymorphic higher-order functions can be defined over them – this carries over to the various types of tree and the error type, err, for example.
- There is a simple principle for reasoning over lists, structural induction, which is the model for structural induction over algebraic types.

The chapter also gives guidelines for defining algebraic types: the definition can be given in three parts: first the type name is identified; then the constructors are named; and finally, their component types are specified. As in other aspects of program development, this separation of concerns assists the system developer to produce simple and correct solutions.

In the chapters to come, algebraic types will be an integral part of the systems we develop, and indeed in the next case study we exhibit various aspects of these types. We shall also explore a different approach to types, abstract data types, and see how this approach complements and contrasts with the use of algebraic data types.

10 Case study: Huffman codes

We use the case study in this chapter as a vehicle to illustrate many of the features of the previous chapters – polymorphism, algebraic types and program design – and to illustrate the **module system** of Miranda, which is introduced first.

10.1 Modules in Miranda

So far, each of the Miranda scripts that we have seen is housed in a single file. If a program is of any size, we should **structure** the script, so that it is split between a number of files, or **modules**. The Miranda module system allows us to put together files to give working programs, as well as to re-use collections of definitions in different programs. The mechanics of the **directives** available are explained in this section; how the module system is used is the subject of the following section.

Inclusion

The basic directive is to include in one file the definitions given in another. If the file bat.m contains the line

```
%include "ant.m"
```

then all the definitions in file ant.m can be used in bat.m. These include directives which can occur anywhere in a Miranda file, but we recommend strongly that all compiler directives appear at the *start* of the file, after any introductory comments.

If the file cow.m contains the line

```
%include "bat.m"
```

then the definitions in bat.m will be visible in cow.m. What about the definitions of ant.m, which are themselves included in bat.m? In the default case, they are *not* visible in cow.m. The simple way of making these visible in cow.m is for that file to contain the two inclusions

```
%include "ant.m"
%include "bat.m"
```

which makes it clear that cow.m uses the definitions from both ant.m and bat.m.

As we saw earlier, the Miranda system maintains the '.x' files, containing information from the processing of the definitions in the corresponding '.m' files. Suppose we have at some point modified the file ant.m, and we then re-examine cow.m. The Miranda system will detect that file(s) upon which cow.m depends have been changed, and these will be re-processed *automatically*.

There are two ways of modifying the effect of a %include directive, at either side of the 'border' between the files:

- In the included file, we can give a %export directive, which controls exactly which of the definitions are exported.
- We can qualify the %include directive itself, to control exactly which definitions are 'imported'.

We look at these two forms of 'border control' in turn now.

Export controls

It often happens that a script contains definitions of some main functions, which themselves use auxiliary functions. We might have, for example,

```
reverse :: [*] -> [*]
reverse = shunt []

shunt :: [*] -> [*] -> [*]
shunt y []    = y
shunt y (a:x) = shunt (a:y) x
```

from which we only want the reverse function to be available. This is achieved by adding the directive

```
%export reverse
```

The general %export directive will be followed by a list of items for export, separated by spaces. For instance, we can say

```
%include "ant.m"
%export  "ant.m" reverse
```

which has the effect of exporting all definitions exported from the included file ant.m, as well as the definition of reverse. We might also say

```
%include "ant.m"
%export  "ant.m" + -shunt -ant1
```

This has the effect of exporting all definitions in ant.m, and all the definitions in the file itself, except for the definitions of shunt and ant1 (presumably this is in ant.m). The export of the definitions in the file itself is the effect of the '+'; if a %export directive is present, the default that all definitions in the file are exported no longer holds, and there has to be an explicit plus to make them visible.

Import controls

The script importing a file can control the definitions it imports in two ways. These are seen in the example

```
%include "ant.m" -ant2 process/ant3 -ant4
```

The definitions of ant2 and ant4 are *hidden* by this directive, and ant3 is *renamed* to process by this inclusion. One purpose of re-naming is to avoid name clashes, which would happen in this example if the including file also contained a definition of ant3.

In the example which follows we add as comments a further form of documentation. We show the source of the names used in the file thus:

```
%include "ant.m"        ||      antelope anteater
%include "bat.m"        ||      battery  bachelor
```

It may well be that the included files contain %export statements which restrict export to exactly these names – whatever the case, it helps us to find their definitions. The Miranda system can help with this also; typing ?name to the Miranda prompt will show the ultimate source of the definition of name.

Further details

There are some subtleties about the inclusion mechanism which need not be apparent to the beginner. Section 27 of the on-line Miranda manual contains a comprehensive account of the module system, where these points are covered.

EXERCISES

10.1 How is the %export directive used to solve the problem of including ant.m in both bat.m and the file which includes bat.m, cow.m? Compare this solution with that given in the text.

10.2 Can you get the effect of %export using %include? Can you get the effect of the qualifications of %include using %export? Discuss why both directives are included in the language.

10.3 Explain why you think it is the default that %included definitions are not themselves exported.

10.4 It is proposed to add the following option to the %export and %include directives. If the item -"file.m" appears, then none of the definitions in the file file.m is exported or included. Discuss the advantages and disadvantages of this proposal. How would you achieve the effect of this feature in the existing Miranda module system?

10.2 Modular design

Any computer system which is used seriously will be modified during its lifetime, either by the person or team who wrote it, or more likely by others. For this reason, all systems should be designed with *change* in mind.

We mentioned this earlier when we said that systems should be documented, with types given to all top-level definitions, and comments accompanying each script and substantial definition. Another useful form of description is to link each definition with proofs which concern it; if we know some of the logical properties of a function, we have a more solid conception of its purpose.

Documentation makes a script easier to understand, and therefore change, but we can give *structure* to a collection of definitions if they are split amongst modules or scripts, each script concerning a separate *part* of the overall system. The directives which link the files tell us how the parts of the system fit together. If we want to modify a particular part of a system, we should therefore be able to modify a single module (at least initially), rather than starting by modifying the whole of the system as a single unit.

How should we begin to design a system as a collection of modules? The pieces of advice which follow are aimed to make modification as straightforward as possible:

- Each module should have a clearly identified role.

- Each module should do one thing *only*. If a module has two separate purposes, these should be split between two separate modules. The chance of a change to one affecting the other is thereby reduced.

- Each part of the system should be performed by one module: each module should do one thing *completely*; it should be self-contained, in other words. If the code performing one part of the whole is split between two modules, then either their code should be merged, or there should be a module defined with the single purpose of bringing the two components together.

- Each module should %export only what is necessary. It is then clearer what the effect of a %import directive is: precisely the functions which are needed are imported. This process is often called **information hiding** in software engineering, which is itself the general study of principles for programming in the large.

- Modules should be *small*. As a rule of thumb, no module should be larger than can be printed on one side of a sheet of paper.

We have also mentioned design for re-use, particularly in the context of polymorphic types and higher-order functions. The module will be the unit of re-use, and a library will be accessed by means of a %include directive. Similar principles apply to the design of libraries. Each library should have a clearly defined purpose, like implementing a type together with basic operations over the type. In addition, we can say that:

- On including a general-purpose module, it is possible to suppress the definitions which are not used.

- Renaming at the %include can be used to avoid the name-clashes which can often occur: despite the (infinite) choice of names for functions, in practice we tend to choose from a very small subset!

The advice here might seem dry (or obvious) – we hope to illuminate what has been said in the case study which follows. In the next chapter we will return to the idea of information hiding when we meet abstract data types. In the remainder of this chapter we examine the case study of Huffman coding, whose foundations we explore now.

10.3 Coding and decoding

Electronic messages of various kinds are sent between machines and people by the billions each day. Such messages are usually sent as sequences of binary *bits*. For the transmission to be swift, the messages need to be coded as efficiently as possible. The area we explore here is how to build codes – translations of characters into sequences of bits – which produce messages as compact as possible.

Trees can be used to code and decode messages. Consider as an example the tree

We can see this as giving codes for the letters a, b and t by looking at the **routes** taken to reach the letters. For example, to get to b, we go *right* at the top node, and *left* at the next:

which gives b the code RL. Similarly, L codes a, and RR the letter t.

The codes given by trees are **prefix codes**; in these codes no code for a letter is the start (or prefix) of the code for another. This is because no route to a leaf of the tree can be the start of the route to another leaf.[†]

A message is also **decoded** using the tree. Consider the message RLLRRRRLRR. To decode we follow the route through the tree given, moving right then left, to give the letter b,

RLLRR...   LLRR...   LRR...

where we have shown under each tree the sequence of bits remaining to be decoded. Continuing again from the top, we have the codes for a then t,

RR...   R...   ...

so the decoded message begins with the letters bat.

In full, the message is battat, and the coded message is ten 'bits' long. The codes for individual characters are of different lengths; a is coded

---

[†] For more information about these Huffman codes, and a wealth of material on algorithms in general, see *Introduction to Algorithms*, T.H. Cormen *et al.*, MIT Press, 1990.

in one bit, and the other characters in two. Is this a wise choice of code in view of a message in which the letter t predominates? Using the tree

the coded message becomes RRRLLLRLL, a nine-bit coding. A Huffman code is built so that the most frequent letters have the shortest sequences of code bits, and the less frequent have more 'expensive' code sequences, justified by the rarity of their occurrence; Morse code is one of these 'efficient' codes.

The remainder of the chapter explores the implementation of Huffman coding, illustrating the module system of Miranda.

EXERCISES

10.5 What is the coding of the message battat using the tree below?

Compare the length of the coding with the others given earlier.

10.6 Using the first coding tree, decode the message RLLRLRLLRR. Which tree would you expect to give the best coding of the message? Check your answer by trying the three possibilities.

10.4 Implementation – I

We now begin to implement the Huffman coding and decoding, in a series of Miranda modules. The overall structure of the system we develop is illustrated at the end of the chapter, Figure 10.4.

As earlier, we first develop the types used in the system.

The types – types.m

The codes are sequences of bits, so we define

```
bit   ::=  L|R
hCode == [bit]
```

and in the translation, we will convert the Huffman tree to a table, for ease of coding:

```
table == [ (char,hCode) ]
```

The Huffman trees themselves carry characters at the leaves. We shall see presently that during their formation we also use information about the frequency with which each character appears; hence the inclusion of a number at the leaves and at the internal nodes:

```
tree ::= Leaf char num |
         Node num tree tree
```

A typical file containing the information is illustrated in Figure 10.1. The name of the file, with an indication of its purpose, is listed in the first comment; the definitions themselves are also commented.

Coding and decoding – coding.m

This module uses the types in types.m, and so begins with

```
%include "types.m"
```

The purpose of the module is to define functions to code and decode messages: we only export these, and not the auxiliary function(s) which may be used in their definition.

```
%export codeMessage decodeMessage
```

To code a message according to a table of codes, we look up each character in the table, and concatenate the results:

```
codeMessage :: table -> [char] -> hCode

codeMessage tbl = concat . map (lookupTable tbl)
```

```
||----------------------------------------------------------||
||                                                          ||
|| types.m                                                  ||
||                                                          ||
|| The types used in the Huffman coding example.            ||
||                                                          ||
|| August 1994                                              ||
||                                                          ||
||----------------------------------------------------------||


||----------------------------------------------------------||
|| Trees to represent the relative frequencies and          ||
|| therefore the Huffman codes.                             ||
||----------------------------------------------------------||

tree ::= Leaf char num | Node num tree tree

||----------------------------------------------------------||
|| The types of bits, Huffman codes and                     ||
|| tables of Huffman codes.                                 ||
||----------------------------------------------------------||

bit ::= L | R

hCode == [bit]

table == [ (char,hCode) ]
```

Figure 10.1   The file types.m.

It is interesting to see that the function level definition here gives an exact implementation of the description which precedes it; using partial application and function composition has made the definition clearer.

We now define lookupTable, which is a standard function to look up the value corresponding to a 'key' in a table:

```
lookupTable :: table -> char -> hCode

lookupTable [] c = error "lookupTable"
lookupTable ((ch,n):tb) c
  = n                   , if ch=c
  = lookupTable tb c ,   otherwise
```

Because of the %export directive, this definition is not exported.

 To decode a message, which is a sequence of bits; that is, an element of hCode, we use a tree:

```
decodeMessage :: tree -> hCode -> [char]
```

We saw in Section 10.3 that decoding according to the tree t has two main cases:

- If we are at an internal Node, we choose the sub-tree dictated by the first bit of the code.

- If at a leaf, we read off the character found, and then begin to decode the remainder of the code at the top of the tree t.

When the code is exhausted, so is the decoded message:

```
decodeMessage t
  = decodeByt t
    where
    decodeByt (Node n t1 t2) (L:rest)
      = decodeByt t1 rest
    decodeByt (Node n t1 t2) (R:rest)
      = decodeByt t2 rest
    decodeByt (Leaf c n) l
      = c : decodeByt t l
    decodeByt t1 [] = []
```

The first coding tree and example message of Section 10.3 can be given by

```
exam1 = Node 0 (Leaf 'a' 0)
                (Node 0 (Leaf 'b' 0) (Leaf 't' 0))
mess1 = [R,L,L,R,R,R,R,L,R,R]
```

and decoding of this message proceeds thus

```
decodeMessage exam1 mess1
  = decodeByt exam1 mess1
  = decodeByt exam1 [R,L,L,R,R,R,R,L,R,R]
  = decodeByt (Node 0 (Leaf 'b' 0) (Leaf 't' 0))
                            [L,L,R,R,R,R,L,R,R]
  = decodeByt (Leaf 'b' 0) [L,R,R,R,R,L,R,R]
  = 'b' : decodeByt exam1 [L,R,R,R,R,L,R,R]
  = 'b' : decodeByt (Leaf 'a' 0) [R,R,R,R,L,R,R]
  = 'b' : 'a' : decodeByt exam1 [R,R,R,R,L,R,R]
```

Before looking at the implementation any further, we look how to construct the Huffman coding tree, given a text.

10.7 Complete the calculation of `decodeMessage exam1 mess1` begun above.

10.8 With the table

```
table1 = [ ('a',[L]) , ('b',[R,L]) , ('t',[R,R]) ]
```

give a calculation of

```
codeMessage table1 "battab"
```

10.5 Building Huffman trees

Given a text, such as `"battat"`, how do we find the tree giving the optimal code for the text? We can explain it in a number of stages:[†]

- We first find the frequencies of the individual letters, in this case giving

  ```
  [('b',1),('a',2),('t',3)]
  ```

- The main idea of the translation is to build the tree by taking the two characters occurring least frequently, and making a *single* character (or *tree*) of them. This process is repeated until a single tree results; the steps which follow give this process in more detail.

- Each of `('b',1),` ... is turned into a tree, giving the list of trees

  ```
  [ Leaf 'b' 1 , Leaf 'a' 2 , Leaf 't' 3 ]
  ```

  which is sorted into frequency order.

- We then begin to *amalgamate together* trees: we take the two trees of lowest frequency, put them together, and insert the result in the appropriate place:

  ```
  [ Node 3 (Leaf 'b' 1) (Leaf 'a' 2) , Leaf 't' 3 ]
  ```

[†] The account here is based on that given in Section 17.3 of Cormen *et al.*, *op. cit.*

- This process is repeated, until a single tree results

  ```
  Node 6 (Node 3 (Leaf 'b' 1) (Leaf 'a' 2)) (Leaf 't' 3)
  ```

  which is pictured thus:

- This tree can then be turned into a `table`

  ```
  [ ('b',[L,L]) , ('a',[L,R]) , ('t',[R]) ]
  ```

We now look at how the system is implemented in Miranda.

10.6 Design

Implementing the system will involve us in designing various modules to perform the stages given above. We start by deciding what the modules will be, and the functions they will implement. This is the equivalent at the larger-scale of *divide and conquer*; we separate the problem into manageable portions, which can be solved separately, and which are put together using the `%include` and `%export` directives. We design these **interfaces** before implementing the functions.

The three stages of conversion are summarized in Figure 10.2, which shows the module directives of the three component files. We have added the

```
frequency.m:
  %include "types.m"
  %export  frequency    || [char] -> [ (char,num) ]

makeTree.m:
  %include "types.m"
  %export  makeTree     || [ (char,num) ] -> tree

codeTable.m:
  %include "types.m"
  %export  codeTable    || tree -> table
```

Figure 10.2 Modules for Huffman tree formation.

```
||----------------------------------------------------------||
||                                                          ||
|| makeCode.m                                               ||
||                                                          ||
|| Huffman coding in Miranda.                               ||
||                                                          ||
|| August 1994                                              ||
||                                                          ||
||----------------------------------------------------------||

%include "types.m"
%include "frequency.m"  ||  frequency
%include "makeTree.m"   ||  makeTree
%include "codeTable.m"  ||  codeTable

%export codes codeTable

||----------------------------------------------------------||
|| Putting together frequency calculation and               ||
|| tree conversion                                          ||
||----------------------------------------------------------||

codes :: [char] -> tree

codes = makeTree . frequency
```

Figure 10.3   The module makeCode.m.

types of objects to be exported as comments, so that these directives contain enough information for the exported functions in the files to be used without knowing *how* they are defined.

In fact, the component functions `frequency` and `makeTree` will never be used separately, and so we compose them in the module `makeCode.m` when bringing the three files together. This is given in Figure 10.3.

Our next task is to implement each module, and we turn to that now.

10.7 Implementation – II

In this section we discuss in turn the three implementation modules.

Counting characters – frequency.m

The aim of the function `frequency` is to take a text, such as `"battat"` to a list of characters, in increasing frequency of occurrence, `[('b',1),('a',2),('t',3)]`. We do this in three stages:

- First we pair each character with the count of 1, giving

    `[('b',1),('a',1),('t',1),('t',1),('a',1),('t',1)]`

- Next, we sort the list on the characters, bringing together the counts of equal characters:

    `[('a',2),('b',1),('t',3)]`

- Finally, we sort the list into increasing frequency order, to give the list above.

The function uses two different sorts – one on character, one on frequency – to achieve its result. Is there any way we can define a single sorting function to perform both sorts?

We can give a general merge sort function, which works by **merging**, in order, the results of sorting the front and rear halves of the list:

```
mergeSort :: ([*]->[*]->[*]) -> [*] -> [*]

mergeSort merge x
   = x                                       , if #x < 2
   = merge (mergeSort merge first) (mergeSort merge second)
                                             , otherwise
      where
      first  = take half x
      second = drop half x
      half   = (# x) div 2
```

The first argument to `mergeSort` is the merging function, which takes two sorted lists and merges their contents in order. It is by making this operation a *parameter* that the `mergeSort` function becomes re-usable.

In sorting the characters, we amalgamate entries for the same character:

```
alphaMerge x [] = x
alphaMerge [] y = y
alphaMerge ((a,n):x) ((b,m):y)
   = (a,n+m) : alphaMerge x y           , if a=b
   = (a,n) : alphaMerge x ((b,m):y)     , if a<b
   = (b,m) : alphaMerge ((a,n):x) y     , otherwise
```

whilst when sorting on frequency we compare frequencies; when two pairs have the same frequency, we order according to the character ordering:

```
freqMerge x [] = x
freqMerge [] y = y
freqMerge ((a,n):x) ((b,m):y)
    = (a,n) : freqMerge x ((b,m):y)  , if n<m \/ (n=m & a<b)
    = (b,m) : freqMerge ((a,n):x) y  , otherwise
```

We can now give the top-level definition of `frequency`

```
frequency :: [char] -> [ (char,num) ]
```

```
frequency
    = mergeSort freqMerge . mergeSort alphaMerge . map start
      where
      start ch = (ch,1)
```

which we can see is a direct combination of the three stages listed in the informal description of the algorithm.

Note that of all the functions defined in this module, only `frequency` is exported.

Making the Huffman tree – makeTree.m

We have two stages in making a Huffman tree from a list of characters with their frequencies:

```
makeTree :: [ (char,num) ] -> tree
makeTree = makeCodes . toTreeList
```

where

```
toTreeList :: [ (char,num) ] -> [tree]
makeCodes  :: [tree] -> tree
```

The function `toTreeList` converts each character–number pair into a tree, thus:

```
toTreeList = map toLeaf
                where
                toLeaf (c,n) = Leaf c n
```

and the function `makeCodes` amalgamates trees successively into a single tree:

```
makeCodes [t] = t
makeCodes ts  = makeCodes (amalgamate ts)
```

How are trees amalgamated? We have to pair together the first two trees in the list (since the list is kept in ascending order of frequency) and then insert the result in the correct place in the list. Working top-down, we have

```
amalgamate :: [ tree ] -> [ tree ]

amalgamate (t1:t2:ts) = insert (pair t1 t2) ts
```

When we pair two trees, we need to combine their frequency counts, so

```
pair :: tree -> tree -> tree

pair t1 t2 = Node (v1+v2) t1 t2
             where
             v1 = value t1
             v2 = value t2
```

where the value of a tree is given by

```
value :: tree -> num

value (Leaf c n)    = n
value (Node n t1 t2) = n
```

The definition of `insert`, which is similar to that used in an insertion sort, is left as an exercise. Again, the definition of the exported function uses various others whose definitions are not visible to the 'outside world'.

The code table – codeTable.m

Here we give the function `codeTable` which takes a Huffman tree into a code table. In converting the tree `Node n t1 t2` we have to convert t1, adding L at the front of the code, and t2 with R at the head. We therefore write the more general conversion function

```
convert :: hCode -> tree -> table
```

whose first argument is the 'path so far' into the tree. The definition is

```
convert cd (Leaf c n)
       = [(c,cd)]
convert cd (Node n t1 t2)
       = (convert (cd++[L]) t1) ++ (convert (cd++[R]) t2)
```

The codeTable function is given by starting the conversion with an empty code string

```
codeTable = convert []
```

Consider the calculation of

```
codeTable (Node 6 (Node 3 (Leaf 'b' 1) (Leaf 'a' 2))
                  (Leaf 't' 3))
= convert [] (Node 6 (Node 3 (Leaf 'b' 1) (Leaf 'a' 2))
                     (Leaf 't' 3))
= convert [L] (Node 3 (Leaf 'b' 1) (Leaf 'a' 2)) ++
  convert [R] (Leaf 't' 3)
= convert [L,L] (Leaf 'b' 1) ++
  convert [L,R] (Leaf 'a' 2) ++
  [ ('t',[R]) ]
= [ ('b',[L,L]) , ('a',[L,R]) , ('t',[R]) ]
```

The top-level file

We can now pull all the parts of the system together into a top-level file:

```
%include "types.m"
%include "makeCode.m"    || codes  CodeTable
%include "coding.m"      || codeMessage
                         || decodeMessage
```

In this file we can include representative examples, using the major functions listed in the comments to the %include statements.

The structure of the system is given in Figure 10.4. Modules are represented by boxes, and an arrow from A to B indicates that A.m is included in B.m. An arrow is marked to indicate the functions exported by the included module, so that, for example, codes and codeTable are exported from makeCode.m to top.m.

If this coding system were to be used as a component of a larger system, a %export directive can be used to control which of the four functions and the types are exported. It is important to realize that the types will need to be exported (or be included in the file including top.m) if the functions are to be used.

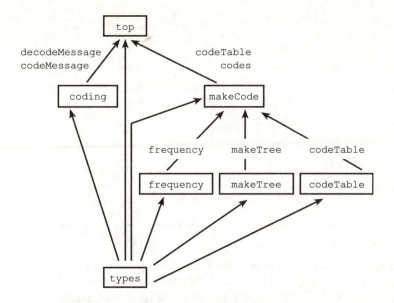

Figure 10.4 The modules of the Huffman coding system.

EXERCISES

10.9 Give a definition of merge sort which uses the built-in ordering '<='.

10.10 Modifying your previous answer if necessary, give a version of merge sort which removes duplicate entries.

10.11 Give a version of merge sort which takes an ordering function as a parameter:

```
ordering :: * -> * -> bool
```

Explain how to implement mergeSort freqMerge using this version of merge sort, and discuss why you *cannot* implement mergeSort alphaMerge this way.

10.12 Define the insert function, used in the definition of makeTree.

10.13 Give a calculation of

```
makeTree  [('b',2),('a',2),('t',3),('e',4)]
```

10.14 Define functions

```
showTree  :: tree  -> string
showTable :: table -> string
```

which give printable versions of Huffman trees and code tables. One general way of printing trees is to use indentation to indicate the structure. Schematically, this looks like:

```
    left sub tree,  indented by 4 characters
value(s) at Node
    right sub tree, indented by 4 characters
```

SUMMARY

When writing a program of any size, we need to divide up the work in a sensible way. The Miranda module system allows one script to be included in another. At the boundary, it is possible to control exactly which definitions are exported or imported.

We gave a number of guidelines for the design of a program into its constituent modules. The most important advice is to make each module perform one clearly-defined task, and for only as much information as is needed to be exported – the principle of **information hiding**. The principle of information hiding is extended in the next chapter, when we examine abstract data types.

The design principles were put into practice in the Huffman coding example. In particular, it was shown for the file makeCode.m and its three sub-modules that design can begin with the design of modules and their *interfaces* – that is, the definitions (and their types) which are exported. Thus the design process starts *before* any implementation takes place.

---

11 Type abstraction

The Miranda module system allows definitions of functions and other objects to be *hidden* when one file is included in another. The hidden definitions are only of use in defining the exported functions, and hiding them makes clearer the exact interface between the two files: only those features of the script which are needed will be visible.

This chapter shows that information hiding is equally applicable for types, giving what are known as **abstract data types**, or ADTs. The Miranda mechanism supporting ADTs is the `abstype`.

11.1 Type representations

We begin our discussion with a scenario, which is intended to show both the purpose and the operation of the `abstype` mechanism.

Suppose we are to build a calculator for numerical expressions, like those given by the `expr` type of Section 9.2, but with variables included. The calculator is to provide the facility to set the values of variables, as well as for variables to form parts of expressions.

As a part of our system, we need to be able to model the current values of the variables, which we might call the *store* of the calculator. How can this be done? A number of models present themselves, including:

- a list of number/variable pairs: `[(num,var)]`; and
- a function from variables to numbers: `(var -> num)`.

Both models allow us to lookup and update the values of variables, as well as set a starting value for the store. These operations have types as follows:

```
initial :: store
lookup  :: store -> var -> num                          (†)
update  :: store -> var -> num -> store
```

but each model allows *more* than that: we can reverse a list, and we can compose a function with others, for instance. In using the type `store` we intend only to use the three operations given, but it is always possible to use the model in unintended ways.

How can we give a better model of a store? The answer is to define a type which *only* has the operations `initial`, `lookup` and `update`, so that we cannot abuse the representation. We therefore hide the information about how the type is actually implemented, and only allow the operations (†) to manipulate items of the type.

Figure 11.1 illustrates the situation, and suggests that as well as giving a natural representation of the type of stores, there are two other benefits of type abstraction:

- The type declarations in (†), which are called the **signature** of the abstract type, form a clearly-defined *interface* between the user of the type and its implementor. The only information that they have to agree on is the signature; once this is agreed, they can work independently. This is therefore another way of breaking a complex problem into simpler parts; another aspect of *divide-and-conquer*.

```
USER

      initial :: store
      lookup :: store -> var -> num
      update :: store -> var -> num -> store


        store == ...     initial = ...

      IMPLEMENTOR
```

Figure 11.1 The `store` abstract data type.

● We can *modify* the implementation of the `store` without having any
  effect on the user. Contrast this with the situation where the
  implementation is visible to the user: we might have used pattern
  matching over a list, for example, and have to re-define *every* function
  using the type.

We shall see both aspects illustrated in the sections to come; first we look at
the details of Miranda `abstype` declarations.

11.2 The Miranda abstype mechanism

Continuing the `store` example, we make the type abstract in Miranda by
typing

```
abstype
  store
with
  initial :: store
  lookup  :: store -> var -> num
  update  :: store -> var -> num -> store
```

The signature is given in the section following the `with`. This is an offside
block, and so is terminated by the first character offside of '`initial`'.

The script must also contain an *implementation* of the `abstype`. This
may appear anywhere in the script, but it is strongly recommended that it
follows the abstype declaration. The implementation consists of a definition

of the type and definitions of the operations in the signature. The implementation of the `store` as a list of pairs is given by

```
store == [ (num,var) ]

initial              = []

lookup []         v = 0
lookup ((n,w):st) v = n              , if v=w
                    = lookup st v    , otherwise

update st v n       = (n,v):st
```

Only in defining the items in the signature can we use the fact that a `store` is of type `[(num,var)]`. Elsewhere in the script, we can only access stores through the signature operations. What happens if we try to break the barrier and deal with stores as lists? Trying to find the length of a store by typing `# initial`, for instance, provokes the type error message

```
cannot unify store with [*]
```

despite the fact that `store` is implemented as `[(num,var)]`. An attempt to print `initial` gets the response

```
<abstract ob>
```

As well as the operations in the signature, equality and the ordering relations (< and so on) are available over the abstype.[†]

A different implementation of `store` is given by the type of functions from variables to numbers.

```
store == (var -> num)

initial v     = 0

lookup st v   = st v

update st v n w = n      , if v=w
                = st w   , otherwise
```

[†] Arguably, this breaks type abstraction, as two different items of the representation type may not behave any differently according to the operations in the signature. They would, of course, be distinguished by the equality operation. In the example, two lists with the same pairs in a different order are indistinguishable, but unequal.

The two implementations are indistinguishable, as far as the operations of the signature are concerned.[†] The store holds the most recent value given to a variable, and zero if the variable has not been given a value.

EXERCISES

11.1 Give an implementation of `store` using lists whose entries are ordered according to the variable names. Discuss why this might be preferable to the original list implementation, and also its disadvantages, if any.

11.2 In this question you should use the polymorphic error type, `err *`. Suppose it is to be an error to `lookup` the value of a variable which does not have a value in the given store. Explain how you would modify the signature of `store` and the two implementations given.

11.3 Rather than giving an error when looking up a variable which does not have a value in the particular store, extend the signature to provide a test of whether a variable has a value in a given store, and explain how you would modify the two implementations to define the test.

11.4 Suppose you are to implement a fourth operation over `store`:

```
setAll :: num -> store
```

so that `setAll n` is the store where every variable has the value n. Can you do this for both the example implementations? Show how if you can, and explain why, if not.

11.5 Design an `abstype` for the library database first examined in Chapter 4.

11.3 Example: Queues

A queue is a 'first in, first out' structure. If first `Flo` and then `Eddie` joins an empty queue, the first person to leave will be `Flo`. As an abstract data type, we expect to be able to add items and remove items as well as there being an empty queue:

[†] Equality can distinguish the two: equality is not available over functions, but it is over lists.

```
abstype
  queue *
with
  emptyQ :: queue *
  addQ   :: * -> queue * -> queue *
  remQ   :: queue * -> ( * , queue * )
```

The function `remQ` returns a pair – the item removed together with the part of the queue that remains – if there are any items in the queue. If not, the standard function `error` is called.

A list can be used to model a queue: we can add to the end of the list, and remove from the front, giving

```
queue * == [*]

emptyQ   = []
addQ a x = x++[a]
remQ x   = (hd x , tl x)        , if x~=[]
         = error "remQ"         , otherwise
```

or we can do the converse,

```
emptyQ   = []
addQ a x = (a:x)
remQ x   = (last x , init x)    , if x~=[]
         = error "remQ"         , otherwise
```

where the built-in functions `last` and `init` take the last element and the remainder of a list.

Although we have not said exactly how to calculate the cost of evaluation (a topic we take up in Chapter 14), we can see that in each implementation one of the operations is 'cheap' and the other is 'expensive'. The 'cheap' functions – `remQ` in the first implementation and `addQ` in the second – can be evaluated in one step, while in both cases the 'expensive' function will have to run along a list x one step per element, and so will be costly if the list is long.

Is there any way of making both operations 'cheap'? The idea is to make the queue out of *two* lists, so that both adding and removing an element can take place at the head of a list. The process is illustrated in Figure 11.2, where the left-hand list grows to the left, and the right-hand to the right. The function `remQ` removes elements from the head of the left-hand list, and `addQ` adds elements to the head of the right. This works until the left-hand list is empty, when the right-hand has to be *reversed* and made into the left (the picture might be misleading here: remember that the two lists grow in opposite directions). This case is expensive, as we have to run

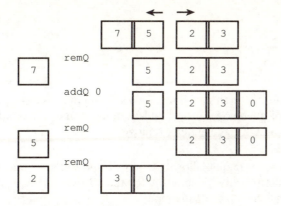

Figure 11.2 A two-list queue in action.

along a list to reverse it, but we will not perform this every time we remove an element from the queue, in general. The Miranda implementation follows:

```
queue == ([*],[*])

emptyQ        = ([],[])
addQ a (l,r)  = (l,a:r)
remQ (a:l,r)  = (a,(l,r))
remQ ([] ,r)  = remQ (reverse r,[])   , if r~=[]
              = error "remQ"           , otherwise
```

As we commented for the store types, the behaviour of this implementation will be indistinguishable from the first two, as far as the operations of the abstype are concerned.[†]

EXERCISES

11.6 Give calculations of

```
"abcde" ++ "f"
init "abcdef"
last "abcdef"
```

[†] Recent work on efficient implementation of queues can be found in 'Simple and Efficient Purely Functional Queues and Deques', C. Okasaki, *Journal of Functional Programming*, Volume 4, 1994.

where

```
init x = take (#x-1) x
last x = x ! (#x-1)
```

11.7 Explain the behaviour of the three queue models if you are asked to perform the following sequence of queue operations: add 2, add 1, remove item, add 3, remove item, add 1, add 4, remove item, remove item.

11.8 A double-ended queue, or deque, allows elements to be added or removed from either end of the structure. Give a signature for the abstype deque ∗, and give two different implementations of the deque type.

11.9 A unique queue can only contain one occurrence of each entry (the one to arrive earliest). Give a signature for the abstype of these queues, and an implementation of the abstype.

11.10 Each element of a priority queue has a numerical priority. When an element is removed, it will be of the highest priority in the queue. If there is more than one of these, the earliest to arrive is chosen. Give a signature and implementation of the abstype of priority queues.

11.4 Design

This section examines the design of Miranda abstypes, and how the presence of this mechanism affects design in general.

General principles

In building a system, the choice of types is fundamental, and affects the subsequent design and implementation profoundly. If we use abstract data types at an early stage we hope to find 'natural' representations of the types occurring in the problem. Designing the abstract data types is a three-stage process:

- First we need to identify and *name* the types in the system.
- Next, we should give an *informal description* of what is expected from each type.
- Using this description we can then move to writing the *signature* of each abstype.

How do we decide what should go in the signature? This is the $64,000 question, of course, but there are some general questions we can ask of any `abstype` signature:

- Can we create objects of the type? For instance, in the `queue *` type, we have the object `emptyQ`, and in a type of sets, we might give a function taking an element to the 'singleton' set containing that element alone. If there are no such objects or functions, something is wrong!

- Can we check what sort of object we have? In a tree abstype we might want to check whether we have a leaf or a node, for instance.

- Can we extract the components of objects, if we so require? Can we take the head of a `queue *`, say?

- Can we transform objects: can we reverse a list, perhaps, or add an item to a queue?

- Can we combine objects? We might want to be able to join together two trees, for example.

- Can we collapse objects? Can we take the sum of a numerical list, or find the size of an object, say?

Not all these questions are appropriate in every case, but the majority of operations we perform on types fall into one of these categories. All the operations in the following signature for binary trees can be so classified, for instance:

```
abstype
   tree *
with
   nil      :: tree *
   isNil    :: tree * -> bool
   isNode   :: tree * -> bool
   leftSub  :: tree * -> tree *
   rightSub :: tree * -> tree *
   treeVal  :: tree * -> *
   insert   :: * -> tree * -> tree *
   delete   :: * -> tree * -> tree *
   join     :: tree * -> tree * -> tree *
```

Other functions might be included in the signature; in the case of `tree *` we might want to include the size function. This function can be defined using the other operations:

```
size :: tree * -> num
size t
  = 0                                      , if isNil t
  = 1 + size (leftSub t) + size (rightSub t)    , otherwise
```

This definition of `size` is *independent* of the implementation, and so would not have to be re-implemented if the implementation type for `tree *` changed. This is a good reason for leaving `size` out of the signature, and this is a check we can make for any signature: are all the functions in the signature needed? We come back to this point, and the tree type, later in the chapter. Now we look at a larger-scale example.

EXERCISES

11.11 Are all the operations in the `tree *` signature necessary? Identify those which can be implemented using the other operations of the signature.

11.12 Design a signature for an abstract type of library databases, as first introduced in Chapter 4.

11.13 Design a signature for an abstract type of indexes, as examined in Section 7.6.

11.5 Example: Simulation

We first introduced the simulation example in Section 9.5, where we designed the algebraic types `inmess` and `outmess`. Let us suppose, for ease of exposition, that the system time is measured in minutes.

The `inmess No` signals no arrival, whilst `Yes 34 12` signals the arrival of a customer at the 34th minute, who will need 12 minutes to be served.

The `outmess Discharge 34 27 12` signals that the person arriving at time 34 waited 27 minutes before receiving their 12 minutes of service.

Our aim in this section is to design the `abstypes` for a simple simulation of queueing. We start by looking at a single queue. Working through the stages, we will call the type `queueState`, and it can be described thus:

There are two main operations on a queue. The first is to add a new item, an `inmess`, to the queue. The second is to process the queue by a one-minute step; the effect of this is to give one minute's further processing to the item at the head of the queue (if there is such a thing). Two outcomes are possible: the item might have its processing completed, in which case an outmess is generated, or further processing may be needed.

Other items we need are an empty queue, an indication of the length of a queue and a test of whether a queue is empty.

This description leads directly to a signature declaration:

```
abstype
  queueState
with
  addMessage  :: inmess -> queueState -> queueState
  queueStep   :: queueState -> ( queueState , [outmess] )
  queueStart  :: queueState
  queueLength :: queueState -> num
  queueEmpty  :: queueState -> bool
```

The queueStep function returns a pair: the queueState after a step of processing, and a *list* of outmess. A list is used, rather than a single outmess, so that in the case of no output an empty list can be returned.

The queueState type allows us to model a situation in which all customers are served by a single processor (or bank clerk). How can we model the case where there is more than one queue? We call this a *server*, and it is to be modelled by the serverState abstype:

A server consists of a collection of queues, which can be identified by the numbers 0, 1 and so on. It is assumed that the system receives one inmess each minute: at most one person arrives every minute, in other words.

There are three principal operations on a server. First, we should be able to add an inmess to one of the queues. Second, a processing step of the server is given by processing each of the constituent queues by one step: this can generate a list of outmess, as each queue can generate such a message. Finally, a step of the simulation combines a server step with allocation of the inmess to the shortest queue in the server.

Three other operations are necessary. We have a starting server, consisting of the appropriate number of empty queues, and we should be able to identify the number of queues in a server, as well as the shortest queue it contains.

As a signature, we have:

```
abstype
 serverState
with
 addToQueue
      :: num -> inmess -> serverState -> serverState
 serverStep
      :: serverState -> ( serverState , [outmess] )
 simulationStep
      :: serverState -> inmess -> ( serverState , [outmess] )
 serverStart    :: serverState
 serverSize     :: serverState -> num
 shortestQueue  :: serverState -> num
```

EXERCISES

11.14 Are there redundant operations in the signatures of the abstypes queueState and serverState?

11.15 Design a signature for *round-robin* simulation, in which allocation of the first item is to queue 0, the second to queue 1, and so on, starting again at 0 after the final queue has had an element assigned to it.

11.6 Implementing the simulation

This section gives an implementation of the abstypes for a queue and a server. The queueState is implemented from scratch, whilst the serverState implementation builds on the queueState abstype. This means that the two implementations are independent; modifying the implementation of queueState has no effect on the implementation of serverState.

The queue

In the previous section, we designed the interfaces for the abstype; how do we proceed with implementation? First we ought to look again at the description of the queueState type. What information does this imply the type should contain?

- There has to be a *queue* of inmess to be processed. This can be represented by a list, and we can take the item at the head of the list as the item currently being processed.

- We need to keep a record of the processing time given to the head item, up to the particular time represented by the state.

- In an outmess, we need to give the waiting time for the particular item being processed. We know the time of arrival and the time needed for processing – if we also know the current time, we can calculate the waiting time from these three numbers.

It therefore seems sensible to define

```
queueState == (time,service,[inmess])
```

where the first field gives the current time, the second the service time so far for the item currently being processed, and the third the queue itself. Now we look at the operations one-by-one. To add a message, it is put at the end of the list of messages:

```
addMessage  :: inmess -> queueState -> queueState

addMessage im (time,serv,ml) = (time,serv,ml++[im])
```

The most complicated definition is of queueStep. As was explained informally, there are two principal cases, when there is an item being processed:

```
queueStep   :: queueState -> ( queueState , [outmess] )

queueStep (time , servSoFar , Yes a serv : inRest)
   = ((time+1, servSoFar+1 , Yes a serv : inRest) , [])
                          , if servSoFar < serv
   = ((time+1, 0 , inRest)
          , [Discharge a (time-serv-a) serv])
                     , otherwise
```

In the first case, when the service time so far (servSoFar) is smaller than is required (serv), processing is not complete. We therefore add one to the time, and the service so far, and produce no output message.

If processing is complete, the otherwise case, the new state of the queue is (time+1, 0 , inRest) – time is advanced by one, processing time is set to zero and the head item in the list is removed. An output message is also produced in which the waiting time is given by subtracting the service and arrival times from the current time.

If there is nothing to process, then we simply have to advance the current time by one, and produce no output:

```
queueStep (time,serv,[]) = ((time+1,serv,[]) , [])
```

The three other functions are given by

```
queueStart :: queueState
queueStart =  (0,0,[])


queueLength :: queueState -> num
queueLength (time,serv,l) = #l


queueEmpty :: queueState -> bool
queueEmpty (t,s,q)  = (q=[])
```

and this completes the implementation.

Obviously there are different possible implementations. We might choose to take the item being processed and hold it separately from the queue, or to use an abstype for the queue part, rather than a 'concrete' list.

The server

The server consists of a collection of queues, accessed by numbers from 0; we choose to use a *list* of queues:

```
serverState == [queueState]
```

Note that the implementation of this abstype builds on another abstype; this is not unusual. Now we take the functions in turn.

Adding an element to a queue uses the function addMessage from the queueState abstract type:

```
addToQueue :: num -> inmess -> serverState -> serverState


addToQueue n im st
  = take n st ++ [newQueueState] ++ drop (n+1) st
    where
    newQueueState = addMessage im (st!n)
```

A step of the server is given by making a step in each of the constituent queues, and concatenating together the output messages they produce:

```
serverStep :: serverState -> ( serverState , [outmess] )

serverStep [] = ([],[])
serverStep (q:qs)
   = (q':qs' , mess++messes)
     where
     (q' , mess)     = queueStep q
     (qs' , messes) = serverStep qs
```

In making a simulation step, we perform a server step, and then add the incoming message, if it indicates an arrival, to the shortest queue:

```
simulationStep
   :: serverState -> inmess -> ( serverState , [outmess] )

simulationStep servSt im
   = (addNewObject im servSt1 , outmess)
     where
     (servSt1 , outmess) = serverStep servSt
```

Adding the message to the shortest queue is done by addNewObject, which is not in the signature. The reason for this is that it can be defined using the operations addToQueue and shortestQueue:

```
addNewObject :: inmess -> serverState -> serverState

addNewObject No servSt = servSt

addNewObject (Yes arr wait) servSt
   = addToQueue (shortestQueue servSt) (Yes arr wait) servSt
```

The other three functions of the signature are standard:

```
serverStart :: serverState
serverStart = rep numQueues queueStart
```

where numQueues is a constant to be defined.

```
serverSize :: serverState -> num
serverSize = (#)
```

In finding the shortest queue, we use the queueLength function from the queueState type:

```
shortestQueue :: serverState -> num
shortestQueue [q] = 0
shortestQueue (q:qs)
   = short+1   , if queueLength (qs!short) <= queueLength q
   = 0         , otherwise
     where
     short = shortestQueue qs
```

This concludes the implementation of the two simulation abstypes. The example is intended to show the merit of designing in stages. First we gave an informal description of the operations on the types, then a description of their signature, and finally an implementation. Dividing the problem up in this way makes each stage easier to solve.

The example also shows that types can be implemented *independently*: since serverState uses only the abstype operations over queueState, we can re-implement queueState without affecting the server state at all.

EXERCISES

11.16 Give calculations of the expressions

```
queueStep (12,3,[Yes 8 4])
queueStep (13,4,[Yes 8 4])
queueStep (14,0,[])
```

11.17 If we let

```
serverSt1 = [ (13,4,[Yes 8 4]) , (13,3,[Yes 8 4]) ]
```

then give calculations of

```
serverStep serverSt1
simulationStep (Yes 13 10) serverSt1
```

11.18 Explain why we cannot use the function type (num -> queueState) as the representation type of serverState. Design an extension of this type which will represent the server state, and implement the functions of the signature over this type.

11.19 Given implementations of the abstypes, is your answer to the question of whether there are redundant operations in the signatures of queues and servers any different?

11.20 If you have not done so already, design a signature for round-robin simulation, in which allocation of the first item is to queue 0, the second to queue 1, and so on.

11.21 Give a version of the round-robin simulation which *uses* the abstype `serverState`.

11.22 Give a different version of the round-robin simulation which *modifies* the implementation of the type `serverState` itself.

11.7 Example: Search trees

A binary search tree is an object of type `itree *`, whose elements are *ordered*:

```
itree * ::= Nil | Node * (itree *) (itree *)
```

(The type is called `itree` because its elements will give the *implementation* of an `abstype` of trees presently.) The tree `Nil` is ordered, and the tree `(Node val t₁ t₂)` is ordered if

- all values in t_1 are smaller than `val`,
- all values in t_2 are larger than `val`, and
- the trees t_1 and t_2 are themselves ordered.

Search trees are used to represent sets of elements, for example. How can we create a type of search trees? The type `itree *` will not serve, as it contains elements like `Node 2 (Node 3 Nil Nil) Nil`, which are not ordered.

The answer is to build elements of the type using only operations which create or preserve order. We ensure that only these 'approved' operations are used by making the type an `abstype`.

The abstype

We gave the signature of the `abstype` in Section 11.4. The implementation type is

```
tree * == itree *
```

and the standard operations to discriminate between different sorts of tree and to extract components are defined by

```
nil :: tree *
nil = Nil

isNil , isNode :: tree * -> bool
isNil  = (=Nil)
isNode = (~=Nil)

leftSub , rightSub :: tree * -> tree *
leftSub Nil            = error "leftSub"
leftSub (Node v t1 t2) = t1

treeVal  :: tree * -> *
treeVal Nil            = error "treeVal"
treeVal (Node v t1 t2) = v
```

Figure 11.3 contains the definitions of the insertion, deletion and join functions. Inserting an element which is already present has no effect, while inserting an element smaller (larger) than the value at the root causes it to be inserted in the left (right) sub-tree. The diagram below shows 3 being inserted in the tree:

```
(Node 7 (Node 2 Nil Nil) (Node 9 Nil Nil))
```

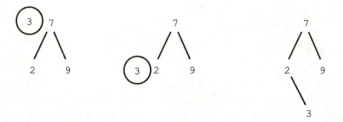

Deletion is straightforward when the value is smaller (larger) than the value at the root node: the deletion is made in the left (right) sub-tree. If the value to be deleted lies at the root, deletion is again simple if either sub-tree is Nil: the other sub-tree is returned. The problem comes when both sub-trees are non-Nil. In this case, the two sub-trees have to be joined together, keeping the ordering intact.

To join two non-Nil trees, t1 smaller than t2, we pick the minimum element, mini, of t2 to be the value at the root. The left sub-tree is t1, and the right is given by deleting mini from t2. The illustration that follows on page 288 shows the deletion of 7 from

```
(Node 7 (Node 2 Nil Nil) (Node 9 (Node 8 Nil Nil) Nil))
```

```
insert :: * -> tree * -> tree *

insert val Nil = (Node val Nil Nil)

insert val (Node v t1 t2)
  = Node v t1 t2              , if v=val
  = Node v t1 (insert val t2)  , if val > v
  = Node v (insert val t1) t2  , if val < v

delete :: * -> tree * -> tree *

delete val (Node v t1 t2)
  = Node v (delete val t1) t2  , if val < v
  = Node v t1 (delete val t2)  , if val > v
  = t1                         , if t2 = Nil
  = t2                         , if t1 = Nil
  = join t1 t2                 , otherwise

join :: tree * -> tree * -> tree *

join t1 t2
  = Node mini t1 newt
    where
    (OK mini) = minTree t2
    newt      = delete mini t2

minTree :: tree * -> err *

minTree t
  = Error     , if isNil t
  = OK v      , if isNil t1
  = minTree t1 , otherwise
    where
    t1 = leftSub t
    v  = treeVal t
```

Figure 11.3 Operations over search trees.

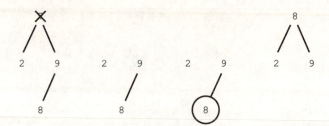

The `minTree` function returns a value of type `err *`, since a `Nil` tree has no minimum. The `OK` constructor therefore has to be removed in the `where` clause of `join`.

Modifying the implementation

Given a search tree, we might be asked for its nth element,

```
indexT :: num -> tree * -> *

indexT n t                                           (†)
    = error "indexT"       , if isNil t
    = indexT n t1          , if n < st1
    = v                    , if n = st1
    = indexT (n-st1-1) t2  , otherwise
      where
      v   = treeVal t
      t1  = leftSub t
      t2  = rightSub t
      st1 = size t1
```

where the `size` is given by

```
size :: tree * -> num
size t
    = 0                                          , if isNil t
    = 1 + size (leftSub t) + size (rightSub t) , otherwise
```

If we are often asked to index elements of a tree, we will repeatedly have to find the `size` of search trees, and this will require computation.

We can think of making the size operation more efficient by *changing the implementation* of `tree *`, so that an extra field is given in an `stree` to hold the size of the tree:

```
stree * ::= Nil | Node * num (stree *) (stree *)
```

What will have to be changed?

- We will have to redefine all the operations in the signature, since they access the implementation type, and this has changed. For example, the insertion function has the new definition:

```
insert val Nil = (Node val 1 Nil Nil)

insert val (Node v n t1 t2)
  = Node v n t1 t2                 , if v=val
  = Node v (n+1) t1 (insert val t2) , if val > v
  = Node v (n+1) (insert val t1) t2 , if val < v
```

- We will have to add `size` to the signature, and redefine it thus:

```
size Nil                = 0
size (Node v n t1 t2) = n
```

to use the value held in the tree.

Nothing else need be changed, however. In particular, the definition of `indexT` given in (†) is unchanged. This is a powerful argument in favour of using `abstype` definitions, and *against* using pattern matching. If (†) had used a pattern match over its argument, then it would have to be re-written if the underlying type changed. This shows that `abstypes` make programs more easily modifiable, as we argued at the start of the chapter.

In conclusion, it should be said that these search trees form a model for a collection of types, as they can be modified to carry different sorts of information. For example, we could carry a count of the number of times an element occurs. This would be increased when an element is inserted, and reduced by one on deletion. Indeed, *any* type of additional information can be held at the nodes – the insertion, deletion and other operations use the ordering on the elements to structure the tree, irrespective of whatever else is held there. An example might be to store indexing information together with a word, for instance. This would form the basis for a re-implementation of the indexing system of Section 7.6.

EXERCISES

11.23 Explain how you would *test* the implementations of the functions over search trees. You might need to augment the signature of the type with a function to print a tree.

11.24 Using the itree implementation, define the functions

```
successor :: * -> tree * -> err *
closest   :: num -> tree num -> num
```

The successor of v in t is the smallest value in t larger than v, whilst the closest
value to v in a numerical tree t is the value in t which has the smallest difference
from v.

   You can assume that closest is always called on a non-Nil tree, so always
returns an answer.

11.25 Re-define the functions of the tree * signature over the stree implementation
type.

11.26 To speed up the calculation of maxTree and other functions, you could imagine
storing the maximum and minimum of the sub-tree at each node. Re-define the
functions of the signature to manipulate these maxima and minima, and redefine
the functions maxTree, minTree and successor to make use of this extra
information stored in the trees.

11.27 You are asked to implement search trees with a count of the number of times an
element occurs. How would this affect the signature of the type? How would you
implement the operations? How much of the previously written implementation
could be re-used?

11.28 Using a modified version of search trees instead of lists, re-implement the indexing
software of Section 7.6.

11.29 Design a polymorphic abstype

```
tree * ** ***
```

so that entries at each node contain an item of type *, on which the tree is
ordered, and an item of type **, which might be something like the count, or a list
of index entries.

   On inserting an element, information of type *** is given (a single index
entry in that example); this information has to be combined with the information
already present. The method of combination can be a functional parameter. There
also needs to be a function to describe the way in which information is
transformed at deletion.

   As a test of your type, you should be able to implement the count trees and
the index trees as instances.

11.8 Case study: Sets

A finite set is a collection of elements of a particular type, which is both like and unlike a list. Lists are, of course, familiar, and examples include

```
[Joe,Sue,Ben]       [Ben,Sue,Joe]
[Joe,Sue,Sue,Ben]   [Joe,Sue,Ben,Sue]
```

Each of these lists is different – not only do the elements of a list matter, but also the *order* in which they occur, and their *multiplicity* (the number of times each element occurs).

In many situations, order and multiplicity are irrelevant. If we want to talk about the collection of people coming to our birthday party, we just want the names; a person is either there or not and so multiplicity is not important, and the order we might list them in is also of no interest. In other words, all we want to know is the *set* of people coming. In the example above, this is the set containing Joe, Sue and Ben.

Like lists and other types, sets can be combined in many different ways: these operations form the signature of the abstype. The search trees we saw earlier provide operations which concentrate on elements of a single set: 'what is the successor of element e in set s?', for instance.

In this section we focus on the combining operations for sets. The abstype signature for sets is as follows. We explain the purpose of the operations at the same time as giving their implementation:

```
abstype
   set *
with
   empty               :: set *
   sing                :: * -> set *
   memSet              :: set * -> * -> bool
   union,inter,diff    :: set * -> set * -> set *
   subSet,eqSet        :: set * -> set * -> bool
   makeSet             :: [*] -> set *
   mapSet              :: (* -> **) -> set * -> set **
   filterSet           :: (*->bool) -> set * -> set *
   foldSet             :: (* -> * -> *) -> * -> set * -> *
   showSet             :: (*->[char]) -> set * -> [char]
   card                :: set * -> num
   setLimit            :: (set * -> set *) -> set * -> set *
```

The implementation we have given represents a set as an *ordered list of elements without repetitions*. The individual functions are described and implemented as follows. We use curly brackets '{', '}', to represent sets in examples – this is *not* part of Miranda notation.

The empty set, { }, is represented by an empty list, and the singleton set {a} consisting of the single element a by a one-element list.

```
empty  = []
sing a = [a]
```

The principal definitions over set * are given in Figure 11.4. To test for membership of a set, we define memSet. It is important to see that we exploit the ordering in giving this definition.

Consider the three cases where the list is non-empty. In (1), the head element of the set, a, is smaller than the element we seek, and so we should check recursively in the tail x. In case (2) we have found the element, whilst in case (3) the head element is *larger* than b; since the list is ordered, *all* elements will be larger than b, so it cannot be a member of the list. This definition would *not* work if we chose to use arbitrary lists to represent sets.

union, inter, diff give the union, intersection and difference of two sets. The union consists of the elements occurring in either set (or both), the intersection of those elements in both sets and the difference of those elements in the first but not the second set. For example,

```
union {Joe,Sue} {Sue,Ben} =  {Joe,Sue,Ben}
inter {Joe,Sue} {Sue,Ben} =  {Sue}
diff  {Joe,Sue} {Sue,Ben} =  {Joe}
```

In making these definitions we again exploit the fact that the two arguments are ordered.

Recall that the brackets '{', '}' are not a part of Miranda; we can see them as shorthand for Miranda expressions as follows:

```
{e₁, ... ,eₙ}
 = {e₁} U ... U {eₙ}
 = sing e₁ $union ... $union sing eₙ
```

To test whether the first argument is a subset of the second, we use subSet; x is a subset of y if every element of x is an element of y.

Two sets are going to be equal if their representations as ordered lists are the same – hence the definition of eqSet as list equality. This would not happen for every representation type: if we chose arbitrary lists to represent sets, the equality test would be more complex, since [1,2] and [2,1,2,2] would be the same set.

To form a set from an arbitrary list, makeSet, the list is sorted, and then duplicate elements are removed.

```
memSet [] b    = False
memSet (a:x) b = memSet x b      , if a<b              (1)
               = True            , if a=b              (2)
               = False           , otherwise           (3)


union [] y         = y
union x []         = x
union (a:x) (b:y) = a : union x (b:y)    , if a<b
                  = a : union x y        , if a=b
                  = b : union (a:x) y    , otherwise


inter [] y = []
inter x [] = []
inter (a:x) (b:y) = inter x (b:y)        , if a<b
                  = a : inter x y        , if a=b
                  = inter (a:x) y        , otherwise


diff [] y = []
diff x [] = x
diff (a:x) (b:y)  = a : diff x (b:y)     , if a<b
                  = diff x y             , if a=b
                  = diff (a:x) y         , otherwise


subSet [] y = True
subSet x [] = False
subSet (a:x) (b:y) = False               , if a<b
                   = subSet x y          , if a=b
                   = subSet (a:x) y      , if a>b


eqSet = (=)


makeSet = remDups . sort
          where
          remDups []    = []
          remDups [a]   = [a]
          remDups (a:b:x) = a : remDups (b:x) , if a < b
                          = remDups (b:x)         , otherwise


mapSet f  = makeSet . (map f)
filterSet = filter
foldSet   = foldr
```

Figure 11.4   Operations over the set abstype.

mapSet, filterSet and foldSet behave like map, filter and foldr except that they operate over sets. The latter two are given by filter and foldr; for mapSet we have to remove duplicates after mapping.

showSet f x gives a printable version of a set, one item per line, using the function f to give a printable version of each element; card x gives the number of elements in x:

```
showSet f = concat . (map ((++"\n") . f))
card      = (#)
```

The final function in the signature is a polymorphic higher-order function of general use. setLimit f x gives the *limit* of the sequence

```
x , f x , f (f x) , f (f (f x)) , ...
```

The limit is the value to which the sequence settles down if it exists. It is found by taking the first element in the sequence whose successor is equal, as a set, to the element itself:

```
setLimit f x = x                , if eqSet x next
             = setLimit f next   , otherwise
               where
               next = f x
```

As an example, take Ben to be Sue's father, Sue to be Joe's mother, who himself has no children. Now define

```
addChildren :: set person -> set person
```

to add to a set the children of all members of the set, so that for instance

```
addChildren {Joe,Ben} = {Joe,Sue,Ben}
```

Now we can give an example calculation of a set limit.

```
setLimit addChildren {Ben}
   ?? eqSet {Ben} {Ben,Sue} = False
 = setLimit addChildren {Ben,Sue}
   ?? eqSet {Ben,Sue} {Ben,Joe,Sue} = False
 = setLimit addChildren {Ben,Joe,Sue}
   ?? eqSet {Ben,Joe,Sue} {Ben,Joe,Sue} = True
 = {Ben,Joe,Sue}
```

EXERCISES

11.30 Define the function

```
symmDiff :: set * -> set * -> set *
```

which gives the **symmetric difference** of two sets. This consists of the elements which lie in one of the sets but not the other, so that

```
symmDiff {Joe,Sue} {Sue,Ben} = {Joe,Ben}
```

11.31 How can you define the function

```
powerSet :: set * -> set (set *)
```

which returns the set of all subsets of a set? Can you give a definition which uses only the operations of the abstype?

11.32 How are the functions

```
setUnion :: set (set *) -> set *
setInter :: set (set *) -> set *
```

which return the union and intersection of a set of sets defined using the operations of the abstype?

11.33 Can infinite sets (of numbers, for instance) be adequately represented by ordered lists? Can you tell if two infinite lists are equal, for instance?

11.34 The abstype set * can be represented in a number of different ways. Alternatives include: arbitrary lists (rather than ordered lists without repetitions), and Boolean-valued functions; that is, elements of the type * -> bool. Give implementations of the type using these two representations.

11.35 Give an implementation of the set abstype using search trees.

11.36 Give an implementation of the tree abstype using ordered lists. Compare the behaviour of the two implementations.

11.9 Relations and graphs

We now use the set abstype as a means of implementing relations and, taking an alternative view of the same objects, graphs.

A binary relation relates together certain elements of a set. A family relationship can be summarized by saying that the isParent relation holds between Ben and Sue, between Ben and Leo and between Sue and Joe. In other words, it relates the *pairs* (Ben,Sue), (Ben,Leo) and (Sue,Joe), and so we can think of this particular relation as the set

```
isParent = {(Ben,Sue) , (Ben,Leo) , (Sue,Joe)}
```

In general we say

```
relation * == set (*,*)
```

This definition means that all the set operations are available on relations. We can test whether a relation holds of two elements using memSet; the union of two relations like isParent and isSibling gives the relationship of being either a parent *or* a sibling, and so on.

Are there any other particular operations over relations? We first set ourselves the task of defining the function addChildren, and then the related problem of finding the isAncestor relation. The functions we define are in Figure 11.5.

Working bottom-up, we first ask how we find all elements related to a given element: who are all Ben's children, for instance? We need to find all pairs beginning with Ben, and then to return their second halves. The function to perform this is image and the set of Ben's children will be

```
image isParent Ben = {Sue,Leo}
```

Now, how can we find all the elements related to a *set* of elements? We find the image of each element separately, and then take the union of these sets. The union of a set of sets is given by folding the binary union operation into the set:

```
unionSet {s₁, ... ,sₙ}
   = s₁ U ... U sₙ
   = s₁ $union ... $union sₙ
```

Now, how do we add all the children to a set of people? We find the image of the set under isParent, and combine it with the set itself. This is given by the function addChildren.

The second task we set ourselves was to find the isAncestor relation – the general problem is to find the **transitive closure** of a relation, the function tClosure of Figure 11.5. We do this by closing up the relation, so we add grandparenthood, great-grandparenthood and so forth to the relation until nothing further is added.

```
image :: relation * -> * -> set *
image rel val = mapSet snd (filterSet ((=val).fst) rel)


setImage :: relation * -> set * -> set *
setImage rel = unionSet . mapSet (image rel)


unionSet :: set (set *) -> set *
unionSet = foldSet union empty


addImage :: relation * -> set * -> set *
addImage rel st = st $union setImage rel st


addChildren :: set people -> set people
addChildren = addImage isParent


compose :: relation * -> relation * -> relation *

compose rel1 rel2
  = mapSet outer (filterSet equals (setProduct rel1 rel2))
      where
      equals ((a,b),(c,d)) = (b=c)
      outer  ((a,b),(c,d)) = (a,d)


setProduct :: set * -> set ** -> set (*,**)
setProduct st1 st2 = unionSet (mapset (adjoin st1) st2)


adjoin :: set * -> ** -> set (*,**)

adjoin st el = mapSet (addEl el) st
              where
              addEl el el' = (el',el)


tClosure :: relation * -> relation *

tClosure rel = setLimit addGen rel
              where
              addGen rel' = rel' $union compose rel' rel
```

Figure 11.5 Functions over the type of relations, relation *.

How do we get the `isGrandparent` relation? We match together pairs like

```
(Ben,Sue)     (Sue,Joe)
```

and see that this gives that `Ben` is a grandparent of `Joe`. We call this relational *composition* of `isParent` with itself. In general,

```
isGrandparent
  = compose isParent isParent
  = { (Ben,Joe) }
```

where we have used the `setProduct` function to give the *product* of two sets. This is formed by pairing every element of the first set with every element of the second. For instance,

```
setProduct {Ben,Suzie} {Sue,Joe}
  = { (Ben,Sue) , (Ben,Joe) , (Suzie,Sue) , (Suzie,Joe) }
```

`setProduct` uses the function `adjoin` to pair each element of a set with a given element. For instance,

```
adjoin Joe {Ben,Sue} = { (Ben,Joe) , (Sue,Joe) }
```

A relation `rel` is *transitive* if for all `(a,b)` and `(b,c)` in `rel`, `(a,c)` is in `rel`. The transitive closure of a relation `rel` is the smallest relation extending `rel` which is transitive. We compute the transitive closure of `rel`, `tClosure rel`, by repeatedly adding one more 'generation' of `rel`, using `compose`, until nothing more is added. To do this, we make use of the `setLimit` function, defined in Section 11.8.

Graphs

Another way of seeing a relation is as a directed *graph*. For example, the relation

```
graph1 = { (1,2) , (1,3) , (3,2) , (3,4) , (4,2) , (2,4) }
```

can be pictured thus:

where we draw an arrow joining a to b if the pair (a,b) is in the relation. What then does the transitive closure represent? Two points a and b are related by tClosure graph1 if there is a *path* from a to b through the graph. For example, the pair (1,4) is in the closure, since a path leads from 1 to 3 then to 2 and finally to 4, while the pair (2,1) is not in the closure, since no path leads from 2 to 1 through graph1.

A problem occurring in many different application areas, including networks and compilers, is to find the (strongly connected) components of a graph. Every graph can have its nodes split into sets or components with the property that every node in a component is connected by a path to all other nodes in the same component. The components of graph1 are {1}, {3} and {2,4}. We solve the problem in two stages:

- we first form the relation which links points in the same component, then
- we form the components (or equivalence classes) generated by this relation.

There is a path from a to b and vice versa if both (a,b) and (b,a) are in the closure, so we define

```
connect :: relation * -> relation *
connect rel = clos $inter solc
          where
          clos = tClosure rel
          solc = inverse clos


inverse :: relation * -> relation *
inverse = mapSet swap
        where
        swap (a,b) = (b,a)
```

Now, how do we form the components given by the relation graph1? We start with the set

```
{{1},{2},{3},{4}}
```

and repeatedly add the images under the relation to each of the classes, until a fixed point is reached. In general this gives

```
classes :: relation * -> set (set *)
```

```
classes rel
  = setLimit (addImages rel) start
    where
      start = mapSet sing (elems rel)
```

where the auxiliary functions used are

```
elems :: relation * -> set *
elems rel = mapSet fst rel $union mapSet snd rel

addImages :: relation * -> set (set *) -> set (set *)
addImages rel = mapSet (addImage rel)
```

Searching in graphs

Many algorithms require us to *search* through the nodes of a graph: we might want to find the shortest path from one point to another, or to count the number of paths between two points.

Two general patterns of search are depth-first and breadth-first. In a depth-first search, we explore all elements below a given child before moving to the next child; a breadth-first search examines all the children before examining the grandchildren, and so on. In the case of searching below node 1 in graph1, the sequence [1,2,4,3] is depth-first (4 is visited before 3), whilst [1,2,3,4] is breadth-first. These examples show that we can characterize the searches as transformations:

```
breadthFirst :: relation * -> * -> [*]
depthFirst   :: relation * -> * -> [*]
```

with breadthFirst graph1 1 = [1,2,3,4], for instance. The use of a list in these functions is crucial – we are not simply interested in finding the nodes below a node (tClosure does this), we are interested in the *order* that they occur.

A crucial step in both searches is to find all the descendants of a node which have not been visited so far. We can write

```
newDescs :: relation * -> set * -> * -> set *
newDescs rel st v = image rel v $diff st
```

which returns the *set* of descendants of v in rel which are not in the set st. Here we have a problem; the result of this function is a set and not a list, but we require the elements in some order. One solution is to add to the set abstype a function

```
flatten :: set * -> [*]                                        (†)
flatten = id
```

which breaks the abstraction barrier in the case of the ordered list implementation. An alternative is to supply as a parameter a function

```
minSet :: set * -> err *
```

which returns the minimum of a non-empty set and which can be used in flattening a set to a list without breaking the abstraction barrier. Unconcerned about its particular definition, we assume the existence of a flatten function of type (†). Then we can say

```
findDescs :: relation * -> [*] -> * -> [*]
findDescs rel l v = flatten (newDescs rel (makeSet l) v)
```

A breadth-first search involves repeatedly applying findDescs until a limit is reached. The generalLimit function finds this:

```
generalLimit :: (* -> *) -> * -> *
generalLimit f x = x                    , if x = next
                 = generalLimit f next  , otherwise
                   where
                   next = f x
```

which works just as setLimit, with = replacing eqSet:

```
breadthFirst rel val
= generalLimit step start
  where
  start = [val]
  step l = l ++ mkset (concat (map (findDescs rel l) l))
```

A step performs a number of operations:

- First, all the descendants of elements in l which are not already in l are found. This is given by mapping (findDescs rel l) along the list l.

- This list of lists is then concatenated into a single list.

- Duplicates can occur in this list, as a node may be a descendant of more than one node, and so any duplicated elements must be removed. This is the effect of the library function mkset :: [*] -> [*] which removes all but the first occurrence of each element in a list.

How does depth-first search proceed? We first generalize the problem to

```
depthSearch :: relation * -> * -> [*] -> [*]
depthFirst rel v = depthSearch rel v []
```

where the third argument is used to carry the list of nodes already visited, and so which are not to appear in the result of the function call:

```
depthSearch rel v used
= v : depthList rel (findDescs rel used' v) used'
  where
  used' = v:used
```

Here we call the auxiliary function depthList which finds all the descendants of a *list* of nodes:

```
depthList rel [] used = []
```

```
depthList rel (val:rest) used
  = next ++ depthList rel rest (used++next)
    where
    next = []                     , if member used val
         = depthSearch rel val used , otherwise
```

The definition has two equations, the first giving the trivial case where no nodes are to be explored. In the second there are two parts to the solution:

- next gives the part of the graph accessible below val. This may be [ ], if val is a member of the list used, otherwise depthSearch is called.

- depthList is then called on the tail of the list, but with next appended to the list of nodes already visited.

This pair of definitions is a good example of definition by *mutual recursion*, since each calls the other. It is possible to define a single function to perform the effect of the two, but this pair of functions seems to express the algorithm in the most natural way.

EXERCISES

11.37 Calculate

```
classes (connect graph1)
classes (connect graph2)
```

where graph2 = graph1 ∪ { (4,3) }.

11.38 Give calculations of

```
breadthFirst graph2 1
depthFirst graph2 1
```

where graph2 is defined in the previous exercise.

11.39 Using the searches as a model, give a function

```
distance :: relation * -> * -> * -> num
```

which gives the length of the shortest path from one node to another in a graph.
For instance,

```
distance graph1 1 4 = 2
distance graph1 4 1 = 0
```

0 is the result when no such path exists, or when the two nodes are equal.

11.40 A weighted graph carries a *weight* with each edge. Design a type to model this.
Give functions for breadth-first and depth-first search which return lists of *pairs*.
Each pair consists of a node, together with the length of the shortest path to that
node from the node at the start of the search.

11.41 A *heterogeneous* relation relates objects of different type. An example might be the
relation relating a person to their age. Design a type to model these relations; how
do you have to modify the functions defined over relation * to work over this
type, if it is possible?

SUMMARY

The abstract data types, or abstypes, of this chapter have three
important and related properties:

- They provide a *natural* representation of a type, which avoids being
  over-specific. An abstype carries precisely the operations which
  are naturally associated with the type, and nothing more.

- The signature of an `abstype` is a firm interface between the user and the implementor: development of a system can proceed completely independently on the two sides of the barrier.

- If the implementation of a type is to be *modified*, then only the operations in the signature need to be changed; any operation using the signature functions can be used unchanged. We saw an example of this with search trees, when the implementation was modified to include size information.

We saw various examples of `abstype` development. Most importantly, we saw the practical example of the simulation types being designed in the three stages suggested. First the types are named, then they are described informally, and finally a signature was written down.

One of the difficulties in writing a signature is being sure that all the relevant operations have been included: we gave a check-list of the kinds of operations which should be present, and against which it is sensible to evaluate any of our signature definitions.

We have not yet said anything about verification of functions over abstypes. This is because there is nothing new to say about the *proof* of theorems: these are proved for the implementation types exactly as we have seen earlier. The theorems valid for an abstype are precisely those which obey the type constraints on the functions in the signature. For a queue type, for instance, we will be able to prove that

```
remQ (addQ a emptyQ) = (a , emptyQ)
```

by proving the appropriate result about the implementation.

12 Lazy evaluation and lists revisited

In our calculations so far, we have said that the order in which we make evaluation steps will not affect the results produced – it may only affect whether the sequence leads to a result. This chapter describes precisely the **lazy evaluation** strategy which underlies Miranda. Lazy evaluation is well named: a lazy evaluator will only evaluate an argument to a function if that argument's value is *needed* to compute the overall result. Moreover, if an argument is structured (a list or a tuple, for instance), only those parts of the argument which are needed will be examined.

Lazy evaluation has consequences for the style of programs we can write. Since an intermediate list will only be generated *on demand*, using an intermediate list will not necessarily be expensive computationally. We examine this in the context of a series of examples, culminating in a case study of parsing.

We also take the opportunity to extend the list comprehension notation. This does not allow us to write any new programs, but does make a lot of list-processing programs – especially those which work by generating and then testing possible solutions – easier to express and understand.

12.1 Introduction

Central to evaluation in Miranda is function application. The basic idea behind this is simple; to evaluate the function f applied to arguments a_1, a_2, ..., a_k, we simply *substitute* the expressions a_i for the corresponding variables in the function's definition. For instance, if

```
egFun1 a b = a+b
```

then

```
egFun1 (9-3) (egFun1 34 3)
= (9-3)+(egFun1 34 3)
```

since we replace a by (9-3) and b by (egFun1 34 3). The expressions (9-3) and (egFun1 34 3) are not evaluated before they are passed to the function.

In this case, for evaluation to continue, we need to evaluate the arguments to '+', giving

```
= 6+(34+3)
= 6+37
= 43
```

In this example, the arguments are evaluated eventually, but this is not always the case. If we define

```
egFun2 a b = a+12
```

then

```
egFun2 (9-3) (egFun1 34 3)
= (9-3)+12
= 6+12
= 18
```

Here (9-3) is substituted for a, but as b does not appear on the right-hand side of the equation, the argument (egFun2 34 3) will not appear in the result, and so *is not evaluated*. Here we see the first advantage of lazy evaluation – an argument which is not needed will not be evaluated. This example is rather too simple: why would we write the second argument if its value is never needed? A rather more realistic example is

```
switch :: num -> * -> * -> *
switch n u v = u    , if n>0
             = v    , otherwise
```

If the number n is positive, the result is u; otherwise it is v. Each of the arguments u and v might be used, but in the first case v is not evaluated and in the second u is not evaluated. A third example is

```
egFun3 a b = a+a
```

so that

```
egFun3 (9-3) (egFun1 34 3)                              (†)
= (9-3)+(9-3)
```

It appears here that we will have to evaluate the argument (9-3) *twice* since it is duplicated on substitution. Lazy evaluation ensures that *a duplicated argument is never evaluated more than once*. This can be modelled in a calculation by doing the corresponding steps simultaneously, thus

```
egFun3 (9-3) 17
= (9-3)+(9-3)
= 6+6
= 12
```

In the implementation, there is no duplicated evaluation because calculations are made over *graphs* rather than trees. For instance, instead of duplicating the argument, as in (i) below, the evaluation of (†) will give a graph in which both sides of the plus there is the *same* expression. This is shown in (ii).

A final example is given by the pattern-matching function,

```
egFun4 (a,b) = a+1
```

applied to the pair (3+2,4-17):

```
egFun4 (3+2,4-17)
= (3+2)+1
= 6
```

The argument is examined, and *part* of it is evaluated. The second half of the pair remains unevaluated, as it is not needed in the calculation.

This completes the informal introduction to lazy evaluation, which shows that

- Arguments to functions are only evaluated when this is necessary for evaluation to continue.
- An argument is not necessarily evaluated fully: only the parts that are needed are examined.
- An argument is only evaluated once, if at all. This is done in the implementation by replacing expressions by *graphs* and calculating over them.

We now give a more formal account of the calculation rules which embody lazy evaluation.

12.2 Calculation rules

As we first saw in Section 2.10, the definition of a function consists of a number of equations. Each equation can have multiple clauses on the right-hand side and may have a number of local definitions given in a `where` clause. Each equation will have on its left-hand side the function under definition applied to a number of patterns:

```
f p₁ p₂ ... pₖ
  = e₁  , if g₁
  = e₂  , if g₂
  ...
  = eᵣ  , otherwise
    where
      v₁  a₁,₁ ... = r₁
      ....
f q₁ q₂ ... qₖ
  = ...
```

In calculating $f\ a_1\ \ldots\ a_k$ there are three aspects.

Calculation – pattern matching

To determine which of the equations is used, the arguments are evaluated. The arguments are not evaluated *fully*, rather they are evaluated sufficiently to see whether they match the corresponding patterns. If they do match the patterns p_1 to p_k, then evaluation proceeds using the first equation; if not, they are checked against the second equation, which may require further evaluation. This is repeated until a match is given, or there are no more equations (which would generate a run-time error 'missing case in definition'). For instance, given the definition

```
f :: [num] -> [num] -> num
f [] y       = 0                    (1)
f (a:x) []   = 0                    (2)
f (a:x) (b:y) = a+b                 (3)
```

the evaluation of f [1..3] [1..3] proceeds thus:

```
  f [1..3] [1..3]                   (4)
= f (1:[2..3]) [1..3]              (5)
= f (1:[2..3]) (1:[2..3])          (6)
= 1+1                              (7)
```

At stage (4), there is not enough information about the arguments to determine whether there is a match with (1). One step of evaluation gives (5), and shows there is not a match with (1).

The first argument of (5) matches the first pattern of (2), so we need to check the second. One step of calculation in (6) shows that there is no match with (2), but that there is with (3); hence we have (7).

Calculation – guards

Suppose that the first equation matches (simply for the sake of explanation). The values a_1 to a_k are substituted for the patterns p_1 to p_k throughout the equation. We must next determine which of the clauses on the right-hand side applies. The guards are evaluated in turn, until one is found which gives the value True; the corresponding clause is then used. If we have

```
f a b c = a    , if a>=b & a>=c
        = b    , if b>=a & b>=c
        = c    , otherwise
```

then

```
  f (2+3) (4-1) (3+9)
    ?? (2+3)>=(4-1) & (2+3)>=(3+9)
      = 5>=3 & 5>=(3+9)
      = True & 5>=(3+9)
        = 5>=(3+9)
        = 5>=12
        = False
```

```
?? 3>=5 & 3>=12
    = False & 3>=12
    = False
?? otherwise = True
= 12
```

Calculation – local definitions

Values in where clauses are calculated on demand: only when a value is needed does calculation begin. Given the definitions

```
f a b = front l     , if notNil l
      = b           , otherwise
        where
        l = [a..b]


front (c:d:y) = c+d
front [c]     = c


notNil []    = False
notNil (a:x) = True
```

the calculation of f 3 5 will be

```
f 3 5
 ?? notNil l
    │    where
    │    l = [3..5]
    │      = 3:[4..5]                           (1)
    │  = notNil (3:[4..5])
    │  = True
    = front l
    │    where
    │    l = 3:[4..5]
    │      = 3:4:[5]                             (2)
 = 3+4                                           (3)
 = 7
```

To evaluate the guard notNil l, evaluation of l begins, and after one step, (1) shows that the guard is True. Evaluating front l requires more information about l, and so we evaluate by one more step to give (2). A successful pattern match in the definition of front then gives (3), and so the result.

Operators

The three aspects of evaluating a function application are now complete; we should now say something about the built-in operators. If they can be given Miranda definitions, such as

```
True  & x = x
False & x = False
```

then they will follow the rules for Miranda definitions. The left-to-right order means that '&' will not evaluate its second argument in case its first is False, for instance. This is unlike many programming languages, where the 'and' function will evaluate both its arguments.

The other operations, such as the arithmetic operators, vary. Plus needs both its arguments to return a result, but the equality on lists can return False on comparing [] and (a:x) without evaluating a or x. In general the language is implemented so that no unnecessary evaluation takes place.

Finally, we turn to the way in which a choice is made between applications to be evaluated.

Evaluation order

What characterizes evaluation in Miranda, apart from the fact that no argument is evaluated twice, is the *order* in which applications are evaluated when there is a choice:

- Evaluation is *from the outside in*. In a situation like

    ```
    f e₁ (f e₂ 17)
    ```

    where one application encloses another, as seen in the expression, the outer one, $f\ e_1\ (f\ e_2\ 17)$, is chosen for evaluation.

- Otherwise, evaluation is *from left to right*. In the expression

    ```
    f e₁ + f e₂
    ```

    the underlined expressions are both to be evaluated. The left-hand one, $f\ e_1$ will be examined first.

These rules are enough to describe the way in which lazy evaluation works. In the sections to come we look at the consequences of a lazy approach.

12.3 List comprehensions revisited

The list comprehension notation does not add any new programs to the Miranda language, but it does allow us to (re-)write programs in a new and clearer way. Building on the introduction in Section 4.5, the notation lets us combine multiple `maps` and `filters` together in a single expression. Combinations of these functions allow us to write algorithms which *generate and test*: all the elements of a particular form are generated, combinations of them are tested, before results depending upon them are returned. We begin the section with a re-examination of the syntax of the list comprehension, before giving some simple illustrative examples. After that we give the rules for calculating with list comprehensions, and we finish the section with a series of longer examples.

Syntax

A list comprehension has the form

$$[\ e \ | \ q_1 \ ; \ \dots \ ; \ q_k \ ]$$

where each *qualifier* q_i has one of two forms:

- It can be a generator, p <- lExp, where p is a *pattern* and lExp is an expression of list type.
- It can be a test, bExp, which is a Boolean expression.

An expression lExp or bExp appearing in qualifier q_i can refer to the variables used in the patterns of qualifiers q_1 to q_{i-1}.

The generator with a multiple pattern $p_1, \dots, p_m$ <- lExp can be used as shorthand for a series of generators, p_1 <- lExp ; ...; p_m <- lExp.

Simpler examples

Multiple generators allow us to combine elements from two or more lists:

```
pairs l m = [ (a,b) | a<-l ; b<-m ]
```

This example is important as it shows the way in which the values a and b are chosen:

```
pairs [1,2,3] [4,5]
= [(1,4),(1,5),(2,4),(2,5),(3,4),(3,5)]
```

The first element of 1, 1, is given to a, and then *for this fixed value* all possible values of b in m are chosen. This process is repeated for the remaining values a in 1, namely 2 and 3.

This choice is not accidental, since if we have

```
triangle n = [ (a,b) | a <- [1..n] ; b <- [1..a] ]
```

the second generator, b <- [1..a] depends on the value of a given by the first generator:

```
triangle 3 = [(1,1),(2,1),(2,2),(3,1),(3,2),(3,3)]
```

For the first choice of a, 1, the value of b is chosen from [1..1]; for the second choice of a, the value of b is chosen from [1..2], and so on.

Three numbers form a *Pythagorean triple* if the sum of squares of the first two is equal to the square of the third. The list of all triples with all sides below a particular bound, n, is given by

```
pyTriple n
  = [ (a,b,c) | a <- [2..n] ; b <- [a+1..n] ;
                c <- [b+1..n] ; a*a + b*b = c*c ]
```

```
pyTriple 100
  = [(3,4,5),(5,12,13),(6,8,10),...,(65,72,97)]
```

Here the test combines values from the three generators.

Calculating with list comprehensions

How can we describe the way in which the results of list comprehensions are obtained? One way is to give a translation of the comprehensions into applications of map, filter and concat. We give a different approach here, of calculating *directly* with the expressions.

Before we do this, we introduce one piece of very helpful notation. We write e{f/x} for the expression e in which every occurrence of the variable x has been replaced by the expression f. This is the *substitution* of f for x in e. If p is a pattern, we use e{f/p} for the substitution of the appropriate parts of f for the variables in p. For instance,

```
[ (a,b) | a<-l ]{[2,3]/l}    = [ (a,b) | a<-[2,3] ]
(a + sum x){(2,[3,4])/(a,x)} = 2 + sum [3,4]
```

since 2 matches a, and [3,4] matches x when (2,[3,4]) is matched against (a,x).

We now explain list comprehensions. The notation looks a bit daunting, but the effect should be clear. The generator v <- $[a_1, ..., a_n]$ has the effect of setting v to the values a_1 to a_n in turn. Setting the value appears in the calculation as *substitution* of a value for a variable:

```
[ e | v <- [a₁,...,aₙ] ; q₂ ; ... ; qₖ ]
= [ e{a₁/v} | q₂{a₁/v} ; ... ; qₖ{a₁/v} ]
  ++ ... ++
  [ e{aₙ/v} | q₂{aₙ/v} ; ... ; qₖ{aₙ/v} ]
```

As a running example for this section we take

```
[ a+b | a <- [1,2] ; isEven a ; b <- [a..2*a] ]
= [ 1+b | isEven 1 ; b <- [1..2*1] ] ++
  [ 2+b | isEven 2 ; b <- [2..2*2] ]
```

where the values 1 and 2 are substituted for a. The rules for tests are simple,

```
[ e | True  ; q₂ ; ... ; qₖ ] = [ e | q₂ ; ... ; qₖ ]
[ e | False ; q₂ ; ... ; qₖ ] = []
```

so that our example is

```
= [ 1+b | False ; b <- [1..2*1] ] ++
  [ 2+b | True ; b <- [2..2*2] ]
= [ 2+b | b <- [2,3,4] ]
= [ 2+2 | ] ++ [ 2+3 | ] ++ [ 2+4 | ]
```

and when there are no qualifiers,

```
[ e | ] = [ e ]
```

Completing the example, we have

```
[ a+b | a <- [1,2] ; isEven a ; b <- [a..2*a] ] = [4,5,6]
```

Now we consider some more examples:

```
[ (a,b) | a <- [1..3] ; b <- [1..a] ]
= [ (1,b) | b <- [1..1] ] ++
  [ (2,b) | b <- [1..2] ] ++
  [ (3,b) | b <- [1..3] ]
```

```
  = [ (1,1) | ] ++
    [ (2,1) | ] ++ [ (2,2) | ] ++
    [ (3,1) | ] ++ [ (3,2) | ] ++ [ (3,3) | ]
  = [(1,1),(2,1),(2,2),(3,1),(3,2),(3,3)]
```

as we argued above. Another example contains a test:

```
  [ m*m | m <- [1..10] ; m*m<50 ]
= [ 1*1 | 1*1<50 ] ++ [ 2*2 | 2*2<50 ] ++ ...
  [ 7*7 | 7*7<50 ] ++ [ 8*8 | 8*8<50 ] ++ ...
= [ 1   | True ] ++ [ 4   | True ] ++ ...
  [ 49  | True ] ++ [ 64  | False ] ++ ...
= [1,4,...49]
```

We now look at two longer examples, whose solutions are aided by the list comprehension style.

EXAMPLE: List permutations ————————————————

A permutation of a list is a list with the same elements in a different order. The perms function returns a list of all permutations of a list:

```
perms :: [*] -> [[*]]
```

The empty list has one permutation, itself. If x is not empty, a permutation is given by picking an element a from x and putting a at the front of a permutation of the remainder x--[a]. (The operation '--' returns the difference of two lists: x--y is the list x with each element of y removed, if it is present.) The definition is therefore

```
perms [] = [[]]
perms x  = [ a:p | a <- x ; p <- perms (x--[a]) ]
```

Example evaluations give, for a one-element list,

```
perms [2]
= [a:p| a <- [2] ; p <- perms [] ]
= [a:p| a <- [2] ; p <- [[]] ]
= [2:p| p <- [[]] ]
= [2:[] | ]
= [[2]]
```

for a two-element list,

```
perms [2,3]
= [ a:p | a <- [2,3] ; p <- perms([2,3]--[a]) ]
= [ 2:p | p <- perms [3] ] ++ [ 3:p | p <- perms [2] ]
= [ 2:[3] ] ++ [ 3:[2] ]
= [ [2,3] , [3,2] ]
```

and finally, for a three-element list,

```
perms [1,2,3]
= [ a:p | a <- [1,2,3] ; p <- perms([1,2,3]--[a]) ]
= [ 1:p | p <- perms [2,3]] ++...++
        [ 3:p | p <- perms [1,2]]
= [ 1:p | p<-[[2,3],[3,2]]] ++...++
        [ 3:p | p<-[[1,2],[2,1]]]
= [[1,2,3],[1,3,2],[2,1,3],[2,3,1],[3,1,2],[3,2,1]]
```

There is another algorithm for permutations: in this, a permutation of a list (a:x) is given by forming a permutation of x, and by inserting a into this somewhere. The possible insertion points are given by finding all the possible *splits* of the list into two halves:

```
perm []    = [[]]
perm (a:x) = [ p++[a]++q | r <- perm x ;
                      (p,q) <- splits r ]
```

We get the list of all possible splits of a list x after seeing that on splitting (a:x), we either split at the front of (a:x), or somewhere inside x, as given by a split of x:

```
splits :: [*]->[ ([*],[*]) ]

splits []    = [ ([],[]) ]
splits (a:x) = ([],a:x) : [ (a:p,q) | (p,q) <- splits x]
```

Vectors and matrices

A vector is a sequence of numbers, $[2, 3, 4]$, say:

```
vector == [num]
```

The scalar product of two vectors (assumed to be the same length) is given by multiplying together corresponding elements and taking the total of the results:

```
scalarProduct [2,3] [4,5] = 2*4 + 3*5 = 23
```

As a first attempt we might write

```
mul l m = sum [ a*b | a<-l ; b<-m ]
```

but this gives

```
mul [2,3] [4,5] = sum [8,10,12,15] = 45
```

since *all* combinations of pairs from the lists are taken. To multiply together corresponding pairs, we first zip the lists together using zip2:

```
scalarProduct :: vector -> vector -> num
scalarProduct l m = sum [ a*b | (a,b) <- zip2 l m ]
```

and a calculation shows that this gives the required result. A matrix like

$$\begin{pmatrix} 2 & 3 & 4 \\ 5 & 6 & -1 \end{pmatrix}$$

can be thought of as a list of rows or a list of columns; we choose a list of rows here:

```
matrix == [vector]
```

The example matrix is [[2,3,4],[5,6,-1]]. Two matrices M and P are multiplied by taking the scalar products of rows of M with columns of P:

$$\begin{pmatrix} 2 & 3 & 4 \\ 5 & 6 & -1 \end{pmatrix} \times \begin{pmatrix} 1 & 0 \\ 1 & 1 \\ 0 & -1 \end{pmatrix} = \begin{pmatrix} 5 & -1 \\ 11 & 7 \end{pmatrix}$$

We therefore define

```
matrixProduct :: matrix -> matrix -> matrix
matrixProduct m p
  = [ [scalarProduct r c | c <- columns p] | r <- m ]
```

where the function `columns` gives the representation of a matrix as a list of columns:

```
columns :: matrix -> matrix
columns y = [ [ z!j | z <- y ] | j<- [0..s] ]
               where
               s = #(hd y)-1
```

The expression `[ z!j | z <- y ]` picks the `j`th element from each row z in y; this is exactly the `j`th column of y. `#(hd y)` is the length of a row in y, and so the indices `j` for the columns will be in the range 0 to s = `#(hd y)-1`.

A pitfall

A problem can arise when patterns are *refutable*; that is, patterns against which a pattern match can fail. If these are used on the left-hand side of an '<-', their effect is to filter out only the elements matching the pattern. For example,

```
[ a | (a:x) <- [[],[2],[],[4,5]] ] = [2,4]
```

The rules for calculation with generators containing a refutable pattern on their left-hand side are similar, except that before performing the substitution for the pattern, the list is filtered for the elements which match the pattern. The details are left as an exercise.

EXERCISES

12.1 Give a calculation of the expression

```
[ a+b | a <- [1..4] ; b <- [2..4] ; a>b ]
```

12.2 Using the list comprehension notation, define the functions

```
subLists,subSequences :: [*] -> [[*]]
```

which return all the sublists and subsequences of a list. A sublist is obtained by omitting some of the elements of a list; a subsequence is a continuous block from a list. For instance, both `[2,4]` and `[3,4]` are sublists of `[2,3,4]`, but only `[3,4]` is a subsequence.

12.3   Give calculations of the expressions

```
perm [2]
perm [2,3]
perm [1,2,3]
```

and of the matrix multiplication

```
matrixProduct [[2,3,4],[5,6,-1]] [[1,0],[1,1],[0,-1]]
```

12.4   Give functions to find the determinant of a square matrix, and if this is non-zero, to invert the matrix.

12.5   The calculation rules for list comprehensions can be re-stated for the two cases [] and (a:x), instead of for the arbitrary list $[a_1, \ldots, a_n]$. Give these rules by completing the equations

```
[ e | v <- []    ; q₂ ; ... ; qk ] = ...
[ e | v <- (a:x) ; q₂ ; ... ; qk ] = ...
```

$$[e \mid v \leftarrow [] \; ; q_2 ; \ldots ; q_k] = \ldots$$
$$[e \mid v \leftarrow (a{:}x) \; ; q_2 ; \ldots ; q_k] = \ldots$$

12.6   Give the precise rules for calculating with a generator containing a refutable pattern, like (a:x) <- lExp. You might need to define auxiliary functions to do this.

12.7   List comprehensions can be translated into expressions involving map, filter and concat by the following equations:

```
[ x | x<-l ]              = l
[ f x | x<-l ]            = map f l
[ e | x<-l ; p x ; ... ] = [ e | x <- filter p l ; ... ]
[ e | x<-l ; y<-m ; .. ] = concat [ [e|y<-m, ..] | x<-l]
```

Translate the expressions

```
[ m*m | m <- [1..10] ]
[ m*m | m <- [1..10] ; m*m<50 ]
[ a+b | a <- [1..4] ; b <- [2..4] ; a>b ]
[ a:p | a <- x ; p <- perms (x--[a]) ]
```

using these equations; you will need to define some auxiliary functions as a part of your translation.

12.4 Data on demand

The data structures manipulated by a program will be generated on demand, and indeed may never appear explicitly. This makes possible a style of programming – *data-directed programming* – in which complex data structures are constructed and manipulated. Take the example of finding the sum of fourth powers of numbers from 1 to n. The data directed solution is to

- build the list of numbers [1..n];
- take the power of each number, giving $[1, 16, \ldots, n^4]$; and
- find the sum of this list.

As a program, we have

```
sumFourthPowers n = sum (map (^4) [1..n])
```

How does the calculation proceed?

```
sumFourthPowers n
= sum (map (^4) [1..n])
= sum (map (^4) (1:[2..n]))
= sum ((^4) 1 : map (^4) [2..n])
= (1^4) + sum (map (^4) [2..n])
= 1 + sum (map (^4) [2..n]) = ...
= 1 + (16 + sum (map (^4) [3..n])) = ...
= 1 + (16 + (81 + ... + n^4))
```

As can be seen, neither of the intermediate lists is created in this calculation. As soon as the head of the list is created, its fourth power is taken, and it becomes a part of the sum which produces the final result.

EXAMPLE: List minimum

A more striking example is given by the problem of finding the minimum of a list of numbers. One solution is to sort the list, and take its head! This would be ridiculous if the whole list were sorted in the process, but in fact we have, writing ins for insert in the definition from Chapter 4,

```
iSort [8,6,1,7,5]
= ins 8 (ins 6 (ins 1 (ins 7 (ins 5 []))))
= ins 8 (ins 6 (ins 1 (ins 7 [5])))
= ins 8 (ins 6 (ins 1 (5 : ins 7 [])))
= ins 8 (ins 6 (1 : (5 : ins 7 [])))
= ins 8 (1 : ins 6 (5 : ins 7 []))
= 1 : ins 8 (ins 6 (5 : ins 7 []))
```

As can be seen from the underlined parts of the calculation, each application of `insert` calculates the minimum of a larger part of the list, since the head of the result of `insert` is given in a single step. The head of the whole list is determined in this case without us working out the value of the tail, and this means that we have a sensible algorithm for minimum given by (hd . iSort).

EXAMPLE: Routes through a graph ─────────────────────

A graph can be seen as an object of type `relation *`, as defined in Section 11.9. How can we find a route from one point in a graph to another? For example, in the graph

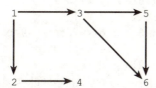

```
graphEx = makeSet [(1,2),(1,3),(2,4),(3,5),(5,6),(3,6)]
```

a route from 1 to 4 is the list [1,2,4].

We solve a slightly different problem: find the list of *all* routes from a to b; our original problem is solved by taking the head of this list. Note that as a list is returned, the algorithm allows for the possibility of there being *no* route from a to b – the empty list of routes is the answer in such a case. This method, which is applicable in many different situations, is often called the 'list of successes' technique: instead of returning one result, or an error if there is none, we return a list; the error case is signalled by the empty list. The method also allows for multiple results to be returned, as we shall see.

How do we solve the new problem? For the present we assume that the graph is *acyclic*: there is no circular path from any node back to itself:

- The only route from a to a is [a].
- A route from a to b will start with a step to one of a's neighbours, c say. The remainder will be a path from c to b.

We therefore look for all paths from a to b going through c, for each neighbour c of a.

```
routes :: relation * -> * -> * -> [*]
routes rel a b
    = [[a]]                           , if a=b
    = [ a:r | c <- nbhrs rel a ;
              r <- routes rel c b ]   , otherwise
```

The nbhrs function is defined by

```
nbhrs :: relation * -> * -> [*]
nbhrs rel a = flatten (image rel a)
```

where flatten turns a set into a list. Now consider the example, where we write routes' for routes graphEx and nbhrs' for nbhrs graphEx, to make the calculation more readable:

```
routes' 1 4
= [ 1:r | c <- nbhrs' 1 ; r <- routes' c 4 ]
= [ 1:r | c <- [2,3] ; r <- routes' c 4 ]
= [ 1:r | r <- routes' 2 4 ] ++
  [ 1:r | r <- routes' 3 4 ]                              (†)
= [ 1:r | r <- [ 2:s | d <- nbhrs' 2 ;
                       s <- routes' d 4 ]]++...
= [ 1:r | r <- [ 2:s | d <- [4] ;
                       s <- routes' d 4 ] ] ++ ...
= [ 1:r | r <- [ 2:s | s <- routes' 4 4 ] ] ++ ...        (‡)
= [ 1:r | r <- [ 2:s | s <- [[4]] ] ] ++ ...
= [ 1:r | r <- [ [2,4] ] ] ++ ...
= [[1,2,4]] ++ ...
```

The head of the list is given by exploring only the first neighbour of 1, namely 2, and its first neighbour, 4. In this case the search for a route leads directly to a result. This is not always so. Take the example of

```
routes' 1 6 = ...
= [ 1:r | r <- routes' 2 6 ] ++
  [ 1:r | r <- routes' 3 6 ]                              (†)
= ...
= [ 1:r | r <- [ 2:s | s <- routes' 4 6 ] ] ++
  [ 1:r | r <- routes' 3 6 ]                              (‡)
```

Corresponding points in the calculations are marked by (†) and (‡). The search for routes from 4 to 6 will *fail*, though, as 4 has no neighbours – we therefore have

```
= [] ++ [ 1:r | r <- routes' 3 6 ] = ...
= [ 1:r | r <- [ 3:s | s <- routes' 5 6 ] ] ++ ...
= [[1,3,5,6]] ++ ...
```

The effect of this algorithm is to *backtrack* when a search has failed: there is no route from 1 to 6 via 2, so the other possibility of going through 3 is explored. This is *only* done when the first possibility is exhausted, though, so lazy evaluation ensures that this search through 'all' the paths turns out to be an efficient method of finding a single path.

We assumed at the start of this development that the graph was acyclic, so that we have no chance of a path looping back on itself, and so for a search to go into a loop. We can make a simple addition to the program to make sure that only paths without cycles are explored, and so that the program will work for an arbitrary graph. We add a list argument for the points not to be visited (again), and so have

```
routesC :: relation * -> * -> * -> [*] -> [*]
routesC rel a b l
  = [[a]]                                    , if a=b
  = [ a:r | c <- nbhrs rel a -- l ;
            r <- routesC rel c b (a:l) ]     , otherwise
```

Two changes are made in the recursive case:

- In looking for neighbours of a we only look for those which are not in the list l;
- in looking for routes from c to b, we exclude visiting both the elements of l and the node a itself.

A search for a route from a to b in rel is given by routesC rel a b [].

EXERCISES

12.8 Defining graphEx2 to be

```
makeSet [(1,2),(2,1),(1,3),(2,4),(3,5),(5,6),(3,6)]
```

try calculating the effect of the original definition on

```
routes graphEx 1 4
```

Repeat the calculation with the revised definition which follows:

```
routes rel a b
  = [[a]]                                    , if a=b
  = [ a:r | c <- nbhrs rel a ;
            r <- routes rel c b ;
            ~ member r a ]                    , otherwise
```

and explain why this definition is not suitable for use on cyclic graphs. Finally, give a calculation of

```
routesC graphEx 1 4 []
```

12.5 Case study: Parsing expressions

We have already seen the definition of `expr`, the type of arithmetic expressions, in Section 9.2.[†]

```
expr ::= Lit num | Var var | Op op expr expr
op   ::= Add | Sub | Mul | Div | Mod
```

and showed there how we could calculate the results of these expressions using the function `eval`. Chapter 11 began with a discussion of how to represent the values held in the variables using the abstract data type `store`. Using these components, we can build a *calculator* for simple arithmetical expressions, but the input is unacceptably crude, as we have to enter members of the `expr` type, so that to add 2 and 3, we are forced to type

```
Op Add (Lit 2) (Lit 3)                                    (†)
```

What we need to make the input reasonable is a function which performs the reverse of `show`: it will take the text `"(2+3)"` and return the expression (†).

The type of parsers: parse

In building a library of parsing functions, we first have to establish the type we shall use to represent parsers. The problem of parsing is to take a list of objects – of type `*`, characters in our example `"(2+3)"` – and from it to extract an object of some other type, `**`, in this case `expr`. As a first attempt, we might define the type of parsers thus

```
parse1 * ** == [*] -> **
```

Suppose that `bracket` and `number` are the parsers of this type which recognize brackets and numbers, then we have

---

[†] Note that here we use the revised version of the type given in Exercise 9.16, augmented with variables.

```
bracket "(xyz" = '('
number  "234"  = 2 or 23 or 234?
bracket "234"  = no result?
```

The problem evident here is that a parser can return more than one result – as in `number "234"` – or none at all, as seen in the final case. Instead of the original type, we suggest

```
parse2 * ** == [*]->[**]
```

where a list of results is returned. In our examples,

```
bracket "(xyz" = ['(']
number  "234"  = [2 , 23 , 234]
bracket "234"  = []
```

In this case, an empty list signals failure to find what was sought, whilst multiple results show that more than one successful parse was possible. We are using the 'list of successes' technique again, in fact.

Another problem presents itself. What if we look for a bracket *followed by* a number, which we have to do in parsing our expressions? We need to know the part of the input which remains after the successful parse. Hence we define

```
parse * ** == [*] -> [(**,[*])]
```

and our example functions will give

```
bracket "(xyz" = [('(' , "xyz")]
number  "234"  = [(2,"34") , (23,"4") , (234,"")]
bracket "234"  = []
```

Each element in the output list represents a successful parse. In `number "234"` we see three successful parses, each recognizing a number. In the first, the number 2 is recognized, leaving `"34"` unexamined, for instance.

Some basic parsers

Now we have established the type we shall use, we can begin to write some parsers. The first is a parser which always fails, so accepts nothing. There are no entries in its output list:

```
fail :: parse * **
fail in = []
```

On the other hand, we can succeed immediately, without reading any input. The value recognized is a parameter of the function:

```
succeed :: ** -> parse * **
succeed val in = [(val,in)]
```

More useful is a parser to recognize a single object or token, t, say. We define

```
token :: * -> parse * *
token t (a:x) = [(t,x)]     , if t=a
              = []          , otherwise
token t []    = []
```

More generally, we can recognize (or spot) objects with a particular property, as represented by a Boolean-valued function:

```
spot :: (* -> bool) -> parse * *
spot p (a:x) = [(a,x)]      , if p a
             = []           , otherwise
spot p []    = []
```

These parsers allow us to recognize single characters like a left bracket, or a single digit,

```
bracket = token '('
dig     = spot digit
```

but we need to be able to combine these simple parsers into more complicated ones, to recognize numbers (lists of digits) and expressions.

Combining parsers

Here we build a library of higher-order polymorphic functions which we then use to give our parser for expressions. First we have to think about the ways in which parsers need to be combined.

Looking at the expression example, an expression is *either* a literal *or* a variable *or* an operator expression. From parsers for the three sorts of expression, we want to build a single parser for expressions. For this we use alt:

```
alt :: parse * ** -> parse * ** -> parse * **

alt p1 p2 in = p1 in ++ p2 in
```

The parser combines the results of the parses given by parsers p1 and p2 into a single list, so a success in either is a success of the result. For example,

```
(bracket $alt dig) "234"
= [] ++ [(2,"34")]
```

the parse by bracket fails, but that by dig succeeds, so the combined parser succeeds.

For our second function, we look again at the expression example. In recognizing an operator expression we see a bracket *then* a number. How do we put parsers together so that the second is applied to the input that remains after the first has been applied?

```
then :: parse * ** -> parse * *** -> parse * (**,***)
```

```
then p1 p2 in
  = [((y,z),rem2) | (y,rem1) <- p1 in ;
                    (z,rem2) <- p2 rem1 ]
```

The values (y, rem1) run through the possible results of parsing in using p1. For each of these, we apply p2 to rem1, which is the input which is unconsumed by p1 in that particular case. The results of the two successful parses, y and z, are returned as a pair.

As an example, assume that number recognizes lists of digits, and look at (number $then bracket) "24(". Applying number to the string "24(" gives two results,

```
number "24)" = [(2,"4(") , (24,"(")]
```

and so (y, rem1) runs through two cases

```
(number $then bracket) "24("
= [((y,z),rem2) | (y,rem1) <- [(2,"4(") , (24,"(")] ;
                  (z,rem2)  <- bracket rem1 ]
= [((2,z),rem2)  | (z,rem2)  <- bracket "4(" ] ++
  [((24,z),rem2) | (z,rem2)  <- bracket "(" ]
```

Now, bracket "4(" = [], so fails, giving

```
= [] ++ [((24,z),rem2) | (z,rem2)  <- bracket "(" ]
```

and `bracket "(" = [('(',"")]` which signals success, gives

```
= [((24,z),rem2) | (z,rem2)  <- [('(',"")] ]
= [ ((24,'(') , "") ]
```

This shows we have one successful parse, in which we have recognized the number 24 followed by ('then') the left bracket ' ('.

Our final operation is to change the item returned by a parser, or to do something to it. Consider the case of a parser, `digList`, which returns a list of digits. Can we make it return the number which the list of digits represents? We apply conversion to the results, thus:

```
do :: parse * ** -> (** -> ***) -> parse * ***
```

```
do p f in = [ (f x,rem) | (x,rem) <- p in ]
```

so in an example, we have

```
(digList $ digsToNum) "21a3"
= [ (digsToNum x,rem) | (x,rem) <- digList "21a3" ]
= [ (digsToNum x,rem)
      | (x,rem) <- [("2","1a3"),("21","a3")]]
= [ (digsToNum "2" , "1a3") , (digsToNum "21" , "a3") ]
= [ (2,"1a3") , (21,"a3")]
```

Using the three operations or *combinators* alt, then and do together with the primitives of the last section, we will be able to define all the parsers we require.

As an example, we show how to recognize a *list* of objects, when we have a parser to recognize a single object. There are two sorts of list:

- A list can be empty, which will be recognized by the parser `succeed []`.
- Any other list is non-empty, and consists of an object followed by a list of objects. A pair like this is recognized by `p $then list p`; we then have to turn this pair `(a,x)` into the list `(a:x)`, for which we use do:

```
list :: parse * ** -> parse * [**]

list p = (succeed []) $alt
         ((p $then list p) $do convert)
         where
         convert (a,x) = (a:x)
```

EXERCISES

12.9 Define the functions

```
neList   :: parse * ** -> parse * [**]
optional :: parse * ** -> parse * [**]
```

so that `neList p` recognizes a non-empty list of objects recognized by p, and `optional p` recognizes such an object *optionally* – it may recognize an object or succeed immediately.

12.10 Define the function

```
nTimes :: num -> parse * ** -> parse * [**]
```

so that `nTimes n p` recognizes n objects recognized by p.

A parser for expressions

Now we can describe our expressions and define the parser for them. Expressions have three forms:

- Literals: 67, ~89, where '~' is used for unary minus.
- Variables: 'a' to 'z'.
- Applications of the binary operations +, *, -, /, %, where % is used for mod, and / gives integer division. Expressions are fully bracketed, if compound, thus (23+(34-45)), and white space not permitted.

The parser has three parts

```
parser :: parse char expr
parser = litParse $alt varParse $alt opExpParse
```

corresponding to the three sorts of expression. The simplest to define is

```
varParse :: parse char expr
varParse = spot isVar $do Var

isVar :: char -> bool
isVar x = ('a' <= x & x <= 'z')
```

(Here the constructor `Var` is used as a function taking a character to the type `expr`.)

An operator expression will consist of two expressions joined by an operator, the whole construct between two brackets.

```
opExpParse
  = (token '(' $then
     parser      $then
     spot isOp $then
     parser      $then
     token ')')
     $do makeExpr
```

where the conversion function takes a nested sequence of pairs, like

```
('(',(Lit 23,('+',(Var 'x',')'))))
```

into the expression Op Add (Lit 23) (Var 'x'), thus:

```
makeExpr (lb,(e1,(bop,(e2,rb))))
  = Op (charToOp bop) e1 e2
```

Defining the functions isOp and charToOp is left as an exercise.

Finally, we look at the case of literals. A number consists of a non-empty list of digits, with an optional '~' at the front. We therefore use the functions from the exercises of the previous section to say

```
litParse
  = ((optional (token '~')) $then
     (neList (spot isDigit))
     $do (charlistToExpr.join)
     where
     join (l,m) = l++m
```

Left undefined here is the function charlistToExpr which should convert a list of characters to a number; this is an exercise for the reader.

EXERCISES

12.11 Define the functions

```
isOp     :: char -> bool
charToOp :: char -> op
```

used in the parsing of expressions.

12.12 Define the function

```
charlistToExpr :: [char] -> num
```

so that

```
charlistToExpr "234" = 234
charlistToExpr "~98" = -98
```

which is used in parsing literal expressions.

12.13 A command to the calculator can be represented thus

```
variable:expr
```

Give a parser for commands.

12.14 How would you change the parser for numbers if decimal numbers are to be allowed in addition to integers?

12.15 How would you change the parser for variables if names longer than a single character are to be allowed?

12.16 Explain how you would modify your parser so that the *whitespace* characters space and tab can be used in expressions, but would be ignored on parsing? (Hint: there is a simple pre-processor which does the trick!)

12.17 *Note:* this exercise is for those familiar with Backus–Naur notation for grammars. Expressions without bracketing and allowing the multiplicative expressions higher binding power are described by the grammar

```
expr  ::= num | var | (expr op expr) |
          lexpr mop mexpr | mexpr aop expr
lexpr ::= num | var | (expr op expr)
mexpr ::= num | var | (expr op expr) | lexpr mop mexpr
mop   ::= '*' | '/' | '%'
aop   ::= '+' | '-'
```

Give a Miranda parser for this grammar.

The top-level parser

The parser defined in the last section, `parser`, is of type

```
[char] -> [ (expr,[char]) ]
```

yet what we need is to convert this to a function taking a string to the expression it represents. We therefore define the function

```
topLevel :: parse * ** -> [*] -> **
topLevel p in
  = hd results                 , if results~=[]
  = error "parse unsuccessful" , otherwise
    where
    results = [ found | (found,[]) <- p in ]
```

The parse p in is successful if the result contains at least one parse (the check on results) in which all the input has been read (the test given by the pattern match to (found,[])). If this happens, the first value found is returned; otherwise we are in error.

We can define the type of commands thus:

```
command ::= Eval expr | Assign var expr | Null
```

This is intended to cause:

- the evaluation of the expression,
- the assignment of the value of the expression to the variable, and
- no effect.

If the assignment command takes the form var:expr, then it is not difficult to design a parser for this type,

```
commandParse :: parse char command
```

We will assume this has been built when we re-visit the calculator example below.

Conclusions

The type of parsers with the signature

```
abstype
  parse * **
with
  fail     :: parse * **
  succeed  :: ** -> parse * **
  token    :: * -> parse * *
  spot     :: (* -> bool) -> parse * *
  alt      :: parse * ** -> parse * ** -> parse * **
```

```
then     :: parse * ** -> parse * *** -> parse * (**,***)
do       :: parse * ** -> (** -> ***) -> parse * ***
topLevel :: parse * ** -> [*] -> **
```

allows us to construct so-called **recursive descent** parsers in a straightforward way. It is worth looking at the aspects of the language we have exploited:

- The type `parse * **` is represented by a function type, so that all the parser combinators are higher-order functions.

- Because of polymorphism, we do not need to be specific about either the input or the output type of the parsers we build.

    In our example we have confined ourselves to inputs which are strings of characters, but they could have been *tokens* of any other type, if required: we might take the tokens to be *words* which are then parsed into sentences, for instance.

    More importantly in our example, we can return objects of any type using the same combinators, and in the example, we returned lists and pairs as well as simple characters and expressions.

- Lazy evaluation plays a role here also. The possible parses we build are generated *on demand* as the alternatives are tested. The parsers will backtrack through the different options until a successful one is found.

EXERCISES

12.18 Define a parser which recognizes strings representing Miranda lists of numbers, like `"[2,3,45]"`.

12.19 Define a parser to recognize simple sentences of English, with a subject, verb and object. You will need to provide some vocabulary: `"cat"`, `"dog"`, and so on, and a parser to recognize a string. Define a function

```
tokenList :: [*] -> parse * [*]
```

so that, for instance,

```
tokenList "Hello" "Hello Sailor" = [ ("Hello"," Sailor") ]
```

12.20 Define the function

```
spotWhile :: (* -> bool) -> parse * [*]
```

whose parameter is a function which tests elements of the input type, and returns the longest initial part of the input all of whose elements have the required property. For instance

```
spotWhile digit "234abc"  = [ ("234","abc") ]
spotWhile digit "abc234"  = [ ([],"abc234") ]
```

SUMMARY

Lazy evaluation of Miranda expressions means that we can write programs in a different style. A data structure created within a program execution will only be created on demand, as we saw with the example of finding the sum of fourth powers. In finding routes through a graph we saw that we could explore just that part of the graph which is needed to reveal a path. In these and many more cases, the advantage of lazy evaluation is to give programs whose purpose is clear and whose execution is efficient.

Also re-introduced in the chapter was the list comprehension notation, which makes many list processing programs easier to express; we saw this in the particular examples of route finding and parsing.

Exploiting higher-order functions, polymorphism and list comprehensions we gave a library of parsing functions, which we saw applied to the type of arithmetical expressions, expr. A design principle exploited here encourages the use of lazy lists: if a function can return multiple results it is possible to represent this as a list; using lazy evaluation, the multiple results will only be generated one-by-one, as they are required. Also, we are able to represent 'no result' by the empty list, []. This 'list of successes' method is useful in a variety of contexts.

13 Infinite lists

As evaluation of data structures is lazy, it is possible for the language to contain *infinite* structures. These would require an infinite amount of time to evaluate fully, but under lazy evaluation only parts of a data structure need to be examined. Any recursive type will contain infinite objects; we concentrate on lists here, as these are by far the most widely-used infinite structures.

After introducing a variety of examples, such as infinite lists of prime and random numbers, we discuss the importance of infinite lists for program design, and see that programs manipulating infinite lists can be thought of as processes consuming and creating 'streams' of data. Based on this idea, we explore how to complete the simulation case study, and explore how **interactive** programs can be written in Miranda.

We build interactive programs from scratch, including giving a front end to the calculator case study, before introducing a family of higher-order polymorphic functions for building interactions.

The chapter concludes with an update on program verification in the light of lazy evaluation and the existence of infinite lists; this section can only give a flavour of the area, but contains further references to more detailed presentations.

13.1 Infinite lists

The simplest examples are constant lists like

```
ones = 1 : ones
```

Evaluation of this in Miranda produces a list of ones, indefinitely. This can be **interrupted** by typing Control-C, which produces

```
[1,1,1,1,1,1,1,1<<...interrupt>>
```

We can sensibly evaluate functions applied to ones. If we define

```
addFirstTwo (a:b:x) = a+b
```

then applied to ones we have

```
addFirstTwo ones
= addFirstTwo (1:ones)
= addFirstTwo (1:1:ones)
= 1+1
= 2
```

Built into the system we have the lists [n..], [n,m..], so that

```
[3..]   = [3,4,5,6,...
[3,5..] = [3,5,7,9,...
```

We can define these ourselves:

```
from :: num -> [num]
from n       = n : from (n+1)

fromStep :: num -> num -> [num]
fromStep n m = n : fromStep (n+m) m
```

and an example evaluation gives

```
fromStep 3 2
= 3 : fromStep 5 2
= 3 : 5 : fromStep 7 2
= ...
```

List comprehensions can also define infinite lists. The list of *all* Pythagorean triples is given by selecting c in [2..], and then selecting suitable values of a and b below that:

```
pythagTriples =
   [ (a,b,c) | c <- [2..] ; b <- [2..c-1] ; a <- [2..b-1] ;
               a*a + b*b = c*c ]
pythagTriples
 = [(3,4,5),(6,8,10),(5,12,13),(9,12,15),(8,15,17),
    (12,16,20),...
```

The powers of a number are given by

```
powers :: num -> [num]
powers n = [ n^x | x <- [0..] ]
```

and this is a special case of the iterate function, which gives the infinite list [x , f x , .. , f^n x , ...

```
iterate :: (* -> *) -> * -> [*]
iterate f x = x : iterate f (f x)
```

EXAMPLE: Generating prime numbers ⎯⎯⎯⎯⎯⎯⎯⎯⎯⎯⎯⎯⎯⎯⎯

A positive integer greater than one is prime if it is divisible only by itself and one. The *Sieve of Eratosthenes* – an algorithm known for over two thousand years – works by cancelling out all the multiples of numbers, once they are established as prime. The primes are the only elements which remain in the list. The process is illustrated in Figure 13.1.

We begin with the list of numbers starting at 2. The head is 2, and we remove all the multiples of 2 from the list. The head of the remainder of the list, 3, is prime, since it was not removed in the sieve by 2. We therefore sieve the remainder of the list of multiples of 3, and repeat the process indefinitely. As a Miranda definition, we write

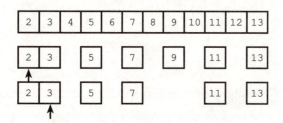

Figure 13.1   The Sieve of Eratosthenes.

```
primes :: [num]

primes     = sieve [2..]
sieve (a:x) = a : sieve [ y | y <- x ; y mod a > 0]
```

where we test whether a divides y by evaluating y mod a; y is a multiple of a if this is zero. Beginning the evaluation, we have

```
primes
= sieve [2..]
= 2 : sieve [ y | y <- [3..] ; y mod 2 > 0]
= 2 : sieve (3 : [ y | y <- [4..] ; y mod 2 > 0])
= 2 : 3 : sieve [ z | z <- [ y | y <- [4..] ;
                        y mod 2 > 0] ; z mod 3 > 0]  = ...
= 2 : 3 : sieve [ z | z <- [5,7,9...] ;
                        z mod 3 > 0]  = ...
= 2 : 3 : sieve [5,7,11,...]  = ...
```

Can we use primes to test for being a prime? If we type member primes 7 to the Miranda prompt we get the response True; while member primes 6 gives no answer. This is because an *infinite* number of elements have to be checked before we conclude that 6 is not in the list. The problem is that member cannot use the fact that primes is ordered. This we do in memberOrd:

```
memberOrd :: [*] -> * -> bool
memberOrd (m:x) n
   = memberOrd x n      , if m<n
   = True               , if m=n
   = False              , otherwise  || i.e. m>n
```

The difference here is in the final case: if the head of the list is greater than the element we seek, the element cannot be a member of the (ordered) list. Evaluating the test again,

```
memberOrd [2,3,5,7,..] 6
= memberOrd [3,5,..] 6  = ...
= memberOrd [7,.] 6
= False
```

EXAMPLE: Generating random numbers

Many computer systems require us to generate 'random' numbers, one after another. Our queueing simulation is a particular example upon which we focus here, after looking at the basics of the problem.

Any Miranda program cannot produce a truly random sequence; after all, we want to be able to predict the behaviour of our programs, and randomness is inherently unpredictable. What we can do, however, is generate a **pseudo-random** sequence of natural numbers, smaller than modulus. This **linear congruential method** works by starting with a seed, and then by getting the next element of the sequence from the previous value, thus:

```
nextRand :: num -> num
nextRand n = (multiplier*n + increment) mod modulus
```

A (pseudo-)random sequence is given by iterating this function,

```
randomSequence :: num -> [num]
randomSequence = iterate nextRand
```

Given the values

```
seed       = 17489
multiplier = 25173
increment  = 13849
modulus    = 65536
```

the sequence produced by randomSequence seed begins

```
[17489,59134,9327,52468,43805,8378,...
```

The numbers in this sequence, which range from 0 to 65535, all occur with the same frequency. What are we to do if instead we want the numbers to come in the (integer) range a to b inclusive? We need to scale the sequence, which is achieved by a map:

```
scaleSequence :: num -> num -> [num] -> [num]
scaleSequence a b
  = map scale
    where
    scale n = n div denom + a
    range   = b-a+1
    denom   = modulus div range
```

The original range of numbers 0 to modulus-1 is split into range blocks, each of the same length. The number a is assigned to values in the first block, a+1 to values in the next, and so on.

In our simulation example, we want to generate for each arrival the length of service that person will need on being served. For illustration, we suppose that they range from 1 to 6 minutes, but that they are supposed to happen with different probabilities:

Waiting time	1	2	3	4	5	6
Probability	0.2	0.25	0.25	0.15	0.1	0.05

We need a function to turn such a distribution into a transformer of infinite lists. Once we have a function transforming individual values, we can map it along the list.

We can represent a distribution of objects of type * by a list of type [(*,num)], where we assume that the numeric entries add up to one. Our function transforming individual values will be

```
makeFunction :: [(*,num)] -> (num -> *)
```

so that numbers in the range 0 to 65535 are transformed into items of type *. The idea of the function is to give the following ranges to the entries for the list above:

Waiting time	1	2	3	...
Range start	0	(m*0.2)+1	(m*0.45)+1	...
Range end	m*0.2	m*0.45	m*0.7	...

where m is used for modulus. The definition follows:

```
makeFunction dist = makeFun dist 0

makeFun ((ob,p):dist) nLast rand
   = ob                       , if nNext >= rand > nLast
   = makeFun dist nNext rand  , otherwise
     where
     nNext = p*modulus + nLast
```

The makeFun function has an extra argument, which carries the position in the range 0 to modulus-1 reached so far in the search; it is initially zero. The transformation of a list of random numbers is given by

```
map (makeFunction dist)
```

and the random distribution of waiting times we require begins thus:

```
map (makeFunction dist) (randomSequence seed)
= [2,5,1,4,3,1,2,5,4,2,2,2,1,3,2,5,...
```

with 6 first appearing at the 35th position.

Pitfall – infinite list generators

The list comprehension `pythagTriples2`, intended to produce the list of all
Pythagorean triples, instead produces *no* output to the prompt

```
pythagTriples2 =
    [ (a,b,c) | a <- [2..] ; b <- [a+1..] ; c <- [b+1..] ;
                a*a + b*b = c*c ]
```

The problem is in the order of choice of the elements. The first choice for a is
2, and for b is 3; given this, there is an infinite number of values to try for
c: 4, 5 and so on, indefinitely.

Two options present themselves. First we can re-define the solution,
as in `pythagTriples`, so that it involves only one infinite list. Alternatively,
we can use the **list diagonalization**, which ensures that when there are infinite
generators all elements of all the lists are examined:

```
pythagTriples3 =
    [ (a,b,c) // a <- [2..] ; b <- [a+1..] ; c <- [b+1..] ;
                a*a + b*b = c*c ]
pythagTriples3 = [(3,4,5),(6,8,10),(9,12,15),(5,12,13),
                 (12,16,20),(8,15,17),...]
```

EXERCISES

13.1 Define the infinite lists of factorial and Fibonacci numbers,

```
factorial = [1,1,2,6,24,120,720,...]
fibonacci = [1,1,2,3,5,8,13,21,...]
```

The corresponding functions were introduced in the exercises in Section 2.2.

13.2 Give a definition of the function

```
factors :: num -> [num]
```

which returns a list containing the factors of a positive integer. For instance,

```
factors 12 = [1,2,3,4,6,12]
```

Using this function or otherwise, define the list of numbers whose only prime
factors are 2, 3 and 5, the so-called **Hamming numbers**

```
hamming = [1,2,3,4,5,6,8,9,10,12,15,...]
```

13.3   Define the function

```
runningSums :: [num] -> [num]
```

which calculates the running sums

$$[0, a_0, a_0+a_1, a_0+a_1+a_2, \ldots$$

of a list

$$[a_0, a_1, a_2, \ldots$$

13.2 Why infinite lists?

Miranda supports infinite lists and other infinite structures, and we saw in the last section that we could define a number of quite complex lists, like the list of prime numbers and lists of random numbers. The question remains, though, of whether these lists are anything other than a curiosity. There are two arguments which show their importance in functional programming.

First, an infinite version of a program can be more abstract, and so simpler to write. Consider the problem of finding the nth prime number, using the Sieve of Eratosthenes. If we work with finite lists, we need to know in advance how large a list is needed to accommodate the first n primes; if we work with an infinite list, this is not necessary: only that part of the list which is needed will be generated as computation proceeds.

In a similar way, the random numbers given by `randomSequence seed` provided an unlimited resource: we can take as many random numbers from the list as we require. There needs to be no decision at the start of programming as to the size of sequence needed. (These arguments are rather like those for **virtual memory** in a computer. It is often the case that predicting the memory use of a program is possible, but tiresome; virtual memory makes this unnecessary, and so frees the programmer to proceed with other tasks.)

The second argument is of wider significance, and can be seen by re-examining the way in which we generated random numbers. We generated an infinite list by means of `iterate`, and we transformed the values using `map`; these operations are pictured in Figure 13.2 as a generator of and a transformer of lists of values. These values are shown in the dashed boxes. These components can then be linked together, giving more complex combinations, as in Figure 13.3. This approach **modularizes** the generation of values in a distribution in an interesting way. We have separated the generation of the values from their transformation, and this means we can change each part independently of the other.

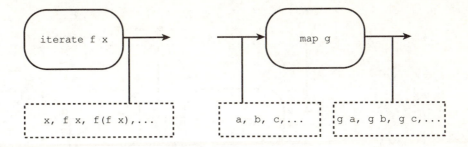

Figure 13.2 A generator and transformer.

Once we have seen the view of infinite lists as the links between processes, other combinations suggest themselves, and in particular we can begin to write process-style programs which involve **recursion**.

Among the exercises in the last section was the problem of finding the running sums

$$[0, a_0, a_0 + a_1, a_0 + a_1 + a_2, \ldots$$

of the list $[a_0, a_1, a_2, \ldots$. Given the sum up to a_k, say, we get the next sum by adding the next value in the input, a_{k+1}. It is as if we *feed the sum back* into the process to have the value a_{k+1} added. This is precisely the effect of the network of processes in Figure 13.4, where the values passing along the links are shown in the dotted boxes.

The first value in the output out is 0; the remaining values are obtained by adding the next value in iList to the previous sum, appearing in the list out. This is translated into Miranda as follows. The output of the function on input iList is out. This is itself obtained by adding 0 to the

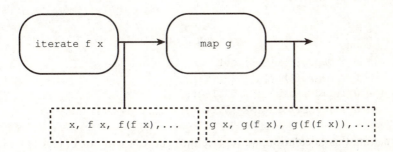

Figure 13.3 Linking together processes.

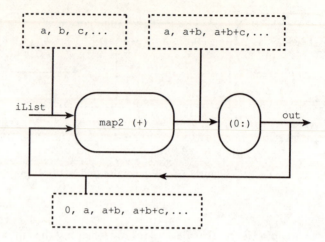

Figure 13.4 Running sums of a list – the process view.

front of the output from the map2 (+), which itself has inputs iList and out. In other words,

```
sums :: [num] -> [num]

sums iList = out
             where
             out = 0 : map2 (+) iList out
```

where map2 is defined by

```
map2 f (a:x) (b:y) = f a b : map2 f x y
map2 f x      y     = []
```

and the function (0:) puts a zero on the front of a list. We give a calculation of an example now:

```
sums [1..]
= out
= 0 : map2 (+) [1..] out
= 0 : map2 (+) [1..] (0:...)                      (1)
= 0 : 1+0 : map2 [2..] (1+0:...)                  (2)
= 0 : 1 : 2+1 : map2 [3..] (2+1:...)   = ...
```

In making this calculation, we replace the occurrence of out in line (1) with the incomplete list (0:...). In a similar way, we replace the tail of out by (1+0:...) in line (2).

The definition of sums is an example of the general function scan',
which combines values using the function f, and whose first output is st:

```
scan' :: (* -> ** -> **) -> ** -> [*] -> [**]
scan' f st iList
  = out
    where
    out = st : map2 f iList out
```

The function sums is given by scan' (+) 0, and a function which keeps a
running sort of the initial parts of list is sorts = scan' insert [], where
insert inserts an element in the appropriate place in a sorted list. The list of
factorial values, [1,1,2,6,...], is given by scan' (*) 1 [1..], and
taking this as a model, any primitive recursive function can be described in a
similar way. (The function is called scan' because of its relation to the scan
function of the standard environment, which is defined in a different way.)

EXERCISES

13.4 Give a definition of the list [2^n | n <- [0..]] using a process network based
on scan'. (Hint: you can take the example of factorial as a guide.)

13.5 How would you select certain elements of an infinite list; for instance, how would
you keep running sums of the *positive* numbers in a list of numbers?

13.6 How would you *merge* two infinite lists, assuming that they are sorted? How
would you remove duplicates from the list which results? As an example, how
would you merge the lists of powers of 2 and 3?

13.7 Give definitions of the lists of Fibonacci numbers [0,1,1,2,3,5,...] and
Hamming numbers [1,2,3,4,5,6,8,9,...] using networks of processes. For
the latter problem, you may find the merge function of the previous question
useful.

13.3 Case study: Simulation

We are now in a position to put together the ingredients of the queue
simulation covered in

- Section 9.5, where we designed the algebraic types `inmess` and `outmess`,

- Section 11.5, where the abstract types `queueState` and `serverState` were introduced, and in

- Section 13.1, where we showed how to generate an infinite list of waiting times from a distribution over the times 1 to 6.

As we said in Section 9.5, our top-level simulation will be a function from a series of input messages to a series of output messages, so

```
doSimulation :: serverState -> [inmess] -> [outmess]
```

where the first parameter is the state of the server at the start of the simulation. In Section 11.5 we presented the function performing one step of the simulation,

```
simulationStep :: serverState ->
                  inmess ->
                  (serverState, [outmess])
```

which takes the current server state, and the input message arriving at the current minute, and returns the state after one minute's processing, paired with the output messages produced by the queues that minute (potentially, every queue could release a customer at the same instant, just as no customers might be released.)

The output of the simulation will be given by the output messages generated in the first minute, and after those the results of a new simulation beginning with the updated state:

```
doSimulation servSt (im:messes)
  = outmesses ++ doSimulation servStNext messes
    where
    (servStNext , outmesses) = simulationStep servSt im
```

How do we generate an input sequence? From Section 13.1 we have the sequence of times given by

```
randomTimes
  = map (makeFunction dist) (randomSequence seed)
  = [2,5,1,4,3,1,2,5,...
```

We are to have arrivals of one person per minute, so the input messages we generate are

```
simulationInput = map2 Yes [1..] randomTimes
= [ Yes 1 2 , Yes 2 5 , Yes 3 1 , Yes 4 4 , Yes 5 3 ,...
```

What are the outputs produced when we run the simulation on this input with four queues, by setting the constant numQueues to 4? The output begins

```
doSimulation serverStart simulationInput
= [Discharge 1 0 2, Discharge 3 0 1, Discharge 6 0 1,
    Discharge 2 0 5, Discharge 5 0 3, Discharge 4 0 4,
    Discharge 7 2 2,...
```

The first six inputs are processed without delay, but the seventh requires a waiting time of 2 before being served.

The infinite number of arrivals represented by simulationInput will obviously generate a corresponding infinite number of output messages. We can make a finite approximation by giving the input

```
simulationInput2 = take 50 simulationInput ++ noes
noes = No : noes
```

where, after one arrival in each of the first fifty minutes, no further people arrive. Fifty output messages will be generated, and we define this list of outputs thus:

```
take 50 (doSimulation serverStart simulationInput2)
```

Experimenting

We now have the facilities to begin experimenting with different data, such as the distribution and the number of queues. The total waiting time for a (finite) sequence of outmess is given by

```
totalWait :: [outmess] -> num
totalWait = sum . map waitTime
            where
            waitTime (Yes t w s) = w
```

For simulationInput2 the total waiting time is 29, going up to 287 with three queues and down to zero with five. We leave it to the reader to experiment with the **round-robin** simulation outlined in the exercises of Section 11.5.

A more substantial project is to model a set-up with a single queue feeding a number of bank clerks – one way to do this is to extend the serverState with an extra queue which feeds into the individual queues: an element leaves the feeder queue when one of the small queues is empty. This should avoid the unnecessary waiting time we face when making the wrong choice of queue, and the simulation shows that waiting times are reduced by this strategy, though by less than we might expect if service times are short.

13.4 Writing interactive programs

An interactive program transforms input into output thus:

where the input and output are sequences of characters

```
input  == [char]
output == [char]
```

so in writing interactive programs, we can use all the resources of Miranda list processing. As a first example we take a program to reverse lines of text: we can use this to recognize English words such as bard which are also words (drab) when reversed, or to spot palindromes, which are the same when reversed:

```
example1 :: input -> output
example1 = lay . map reverse . lines
```

where the standard functions

```
lines :: [char] -> [string]
lay   :: [string] -> [char]
```

split input into lines (at the newlines, '\n') and join a list of strings into a single string, separated by newlines, respectively. For example,

```
lines "hello\nbard" = ["hello","bard"]
lay ["hello","bard"] = "hello\nbard\n"
```

The effect of example1 is to return the lines of input, *reversed*, so that, for instance,

```
example1 "hello\nbard" = "olleh\ndrab\n"
```
(†)

If we evaluate this expression in the Miranda system, recall that it will be printed thus

```
olleh
drab
```

with the '\n' characters becoming real newlines.

In (†) we give the input string directly to the function. How can we make a function take input from the terminal? There are two solutions:

- We can type example1 $- to the Miranda prompt; $- is a way of saying 'standard input' at the Miranda prompt level.

- More generally, we can use the read function,

  ```
  read :: [char] -> [char]
  ```

  which gives the contents of a file as a string, and takes the file name as parameter. On Unix systems the name of the standard input as a file is "/dev/tty", and therefore to use the example on the standard input we write

  ```
  example1 (read "/dev/tty")
  ```

What happens when we evaluate example1 (read "/dev/tty")? An example evaluation is

```
Miranda example1 (read "/dev/tty")
hello
olleh
bard
drab
Control-D
```

where, as we did when we introduced the Miranda system, our input is underlined; Control-D is used to signal the end of the input. The input and the output lines are **interleaved**, so that the reversed version of a line immediately follows its input – why is this?

Lazy evaluation

This interleaving happens because we use lazy evaluation, which means that *part* of the output, a list, can be produced on the basis of *partial* information about the input. The effect of this is that after, say, one line of input we may see one line of output from a program. We can follow this through a calculation, where we use the three dots '. . .' to mean 'not known yet'.

Taking `example1` on the input above, after the first `'\n'` in the input, we can produce the first line,

```
lines "hello\n..." = "hello" : lines "..."
```

Now, we have the head of the input to `map reverse`, so

```
map reverse ("hello" : ...) = "olleh" : map reverse ...
```

and we then have the start of the result string

```
lay ("olleh" : ...) = "olleh\n..."
```

so that putting this together,

```
example1 "hello\n..." = "olleh\n..."
```

This shows how the first line of output can follow the first line of input. Given the definitions of `lines`, `map` and `lay`, this behaviour will be repeated until the end of the file (that is, the end of the input string to `example1`) is reached.

Reading values

Suppose we want to treat the input as representing something other than strings, and in particular, suppose we want the input to consist of one number per line. We can split the input into lines, and then convert each line from a string into a number, either writing a function ourselves, or using the built-in `numval`. The example

```
example2 :: input -> output
example2 = lay . map shownum . map (+1)
                . map numval . lines
```

does this, adding one to each number before outputting the result. Output is in two stages: first the number is converted into a string, and then the strings (or lines) are laid out using `lay`. In the definition we have written three separate `map`s for emphasis; we could have equally well have written

```
example2 = lay . map (shownum . (+1) . numval) . lines
```

to emphasize that we are processing one line at a time.

There is a general mechanism for treating strings as values provided by Miranda. The function

```
readvals :: string -> [*]
```

will read a file and convert each line of a file to a value of the appropriate (*same*) type. In each use of readvals it has to be possible to determine what type is being read. Re-writing our example, we have

```
example2' :: string -> output
example2' = lay . map shownum . map (+1) . readvals
```

where the argument to the function is a filename – to use it interactively, we apply it to "/dev/tty". Alternatively, at the top level, we can write

```
lay (map (shownum . (+1)) $+)
```

where $+ is used to abbreviate readvals "/dev/tty", just as $- is an abbreviation for the corresponding instance of read.

Prompts and messages

Our program to reverse strings can be made to *prompt* for further input, thus:

```
example3
   = lay . map (++"\nAnother?") . map reverse . lines
```

since appended to each reversed string will be the message "Another?". A sample interaction is

```
Miranda example3 $-
hello
olleh
Another?
...
```

but observe that no output is produced until some input has been given. We do this *outside* the loop involving lines, map and lay, all of which examine their input before starting their output. If we write

```
example4 = ("Enter a string or Control-D\n"++) . example3
```

then output of this program will begin with the "Enter..D\n" message, and this can be seen thus:

```
          example4 "..."
        = (("Enter..D\n"++) . example3) "..."
        = ("Enter..D\n"++) (example3 "...")
        = "Enter..D\n" ++ (example3 "...")
```

where the output has its first part defined without any information about the input being available.

EXERCISES

13.8   Modify example4 so that the message "Interaction over." is printed after Control-D is typed. [Hint: this can be done in a similar way to the message at the start of the output.]

13.9   Write a program which checks interactively whether strings are palindromes. Example palindromes are

```
    "abba"
    "Madam I\'m Adam"
```

so that your check will need to remove punctuation and white space, and to be insensitive to the case of letters (capital or small). Your program should print suitable messages at the start and end of the interaction, as well as giving a prompt at each stage.

13.10   To understand some aspects of the implementation of Miranda, it is interesting to write an interactive calculator for expressions like

```
    (2+(3%4))
    (34*23)
```

not involving variables. These expressions can be parsed using the parser of Section 12.5, and the evaluation function of Section 9.2. The messages which your program outputs should provide enough information to make the program usable by a novice.

Scanning

The interactions we have seen so far are special, in that they have *no memory*: each piece of output is determined by the line of input, and nothing else. Many interactions have this form, but most have some sort of memory for what has gone before.

A simple example is an interaction which reads numbers and outputs the total read so far. This form of list processing was given by our scan' of Section 13.2. As an interaction, we write

```
example5 = lay . map shownum . scan' (+) 0
```

and apply it to $+. The main processing is done by the scan'; the other functions, and $+, achieve the conversion to and from strings.

Suppose now that we are asked to keep a running average of the numbers typed in: at each stage we will have to know how many entries there have been, and their total, which we can keep as a (num, num) pair. Given a new value, we apply the function

```
oneStep :: num -> (num,num) -> (num,num)
oneStep val (n,total) = (n+1,total+val)
```

and evaluating

```
example6 = lay . map show . scan' oneStep (0,0)
```

will give an interaction of the form

```
Miranda example6 $+
(0,0)
12
(1,12)
 ...
```

Of course, this is not exactly what we are looking for – instead of printing the pair, we wanted to print the average, so we add an extra function to convert the pair to that:

```
aver (0,total) = 0
aver (n,total) = total/n

example7 = lay . map show . map aver . scan' oneStep (0,0)
```

which gives an interaction like

```
Miranda example7 $+
0
12
12.0
6
9.0
 ...
```

Related to the scanning interactions, we have the full calculator, which we look at now.

Case study: The calculator

The ingredients of the calculator are contained in three places in the text:

- In Section 9.2 we saw the introduction of the algebraic type of expressions, expr, which we subsequently revised in Section 12.5, giving

```
expr ::= Lit num | Var var | Op op expr expr
op   ::= Add | Sub | Mul | Div | Mod
var  ==  char
```

  We revise the evaluation of expressions after discussing the store below.

- In Chapter 11 we introduced the abstract type store, which we use to model the values of the variables currently held. The signature of the abstype is

```
initial :: store
lookup  :: store -> var -> num
update  :: store -> var -> num -> store
```

- In Section 12.5 we looked at how to parse expressions and commands, and defined the ingredients of the function

```
topLevel commandParse :: [char] -> command
```

  which is used to parse each line of input into a command.

Expressions are evaluated by

```
eval :: expr -> store -> num
eval (Lit n) st = n
eval (Var v) st = lookup st v
eval (Op op e1 e2) st
  = opValue op v1 v2
    where
    v1 = eval e1 st
    v2 = eval e2 st
```

where the opValue function, of type op->num->num->num interprets each operator, such as Add, as the corresponding function, like (+).

The list of commands to be interpreted is given by

```
commList = map (topLevel commandparse) (lines $-)
```

and the interpretation itself is given by

```
calculate :: [command] -> store -> [string]
```

which has a clause for each kind of command. First, if we are to evaluate an expression,

```
calculate ((Eval e):cs) st
  = show (eval e st) : calculate cs st
```

the first line of output is the result of the expression; the remainder is given by calculating the effect of the remaining commands, cs, starting from the same state st. Next, if we have an assignment,

```
calculate ((Assign v e):cs) st
= ([v] ++ " = " ++ show val) : calculate cs st'
   where
   val = eval e st
   st' = update st v val
```

we report the value assigned, and then update the state to st', which is used to begin evaluation of the remaining commands. Finally, a null command has no effect,

```
calculate (Null:cs) st
= "Null command" : calculate cs st
```

and at the end of the input, we reach the end of the output

```
calculate [] st = []
```

The definition which gives the calculator is

```
perform = lay (calculate commList initial)
```

where we begin calculation with the initial store.

EXERCISES

The exercises give various extensions of the basic calculator, as well as looking at some of its drawbacks.

13.11 How would you add initial and final messages to the output of the calculator?

13.12 If the calculator is not given a valid command, then an error message will be generated by the function `topLevel`, and evaluation stops. Discuss how you would add an extra argument to `topLevel` to be used in the error case, so that evaluation with the calculator does not halt.

13.13 The form of definition of `calculate` is a generalization of `scan'`: at each stage we output a function of the current state and the value just read, as well as changing the state

```
oneStep :: inVal -> state -> (state,outVal)
```

Define a function

```
mapSide :: (inVal -> state -> (state,outVal)) ->
           state ->
           [inVal] ->
           [outVal]
```

which works like a `map` but changes the value of the `state` at each step. Show how this can be used to define the `calculate` function, where the type `inVal` is `command`, `state` is `store` and `outVal` is `string`.

13.14 Discuss how you would have to modify the system to allow variables to have arbitrarily-long names, consisting of letters and numbers, starting with a letter.

13.15 How would you extend the calculator to deal with decimal numbers as well as integers?

Stylized interactions

The form of the interactions we have seen so far is **stylized** in that we can predict the form the output will take without knowing anything about the values which the program reads. If we want to write more complex interactive systems, where values can determine the 'shape' of the interactions to come, we will have to use different methods. These are the subject of the next section.

13.5 A library for interactions

How can we model what a part of an interactive program does? There are three kinds of action:

- the program can *read* a part of the input;
- the program can *write* a part of the output, or
- the program can modify the value of its *internal state*, and even return a final state of a different type.

We define the abstype `interact * **` of interactions. An interaction starts with a state value of type `*`, does some input and/or output, and terminates with a state value of type `**`.

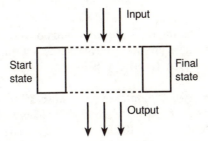

As an example, we might have a program which begins with numeric state, value n say, which reads n lines of input, each of which is echoed reversed, and which terminates with a state containing two numbers, which give the numbers of words and characters in the input which has been read.

The abstype we will implement has the following signature:

```
abstype
   interact * **
with
   apply :: (* -> **) -> interact * **
   readI :: (string -> * -> **) -> interact * **
   write :: (* -> string) -> interact * *
   sq    :: interact * ** -> interact ** *** ->
            interact * ***
   alt   :: condition * ->
            interact * ** -> interact * ** -> interact * **
   run   :: interact * ** -> * -> [char]
```

We will now describe the intended effect of the functions, and build up a series of examples, before giving an implementation of the abstype; readers can, of course, look ahead to the implementation in Section 13.6 if they wish.

The first three functions build the three kinds of interaction: a change to an internal state, a read and a write.

The interaction `apply f`, where `f` is a function from `*` to `**`, applies the function to its state and does not perform any input or output. For instance, `apply (+1)` increases a numerical state by one, and is of type `interact num num`.

An interaction `readI g` takes a line of input, `line`, and the starting state, `st`, and gives a modified state `g line st`. If `g` is the function `(+).numval` the result of reading into the state is to add the numeric value of a line into the state, since

```
((+).numval) "23" 12
= (+) (numval "23") 12
= (+) 23 12
= 35
```

The parameter to `write` takes a state value and converts it to a string, which is output; the state value is unaffected by this interaction. An example would be `write shownum` which returns a string representation of a numerical state.

To write more complex interactions, we have to *combine* the simple interactions. The function `sq` (for 'sequence') takes two interactions, and makes a single interaction of them. `sq inter1 inter2` first performs `inter1` whose final state becomes the starting state for `inter2`. In pictures,

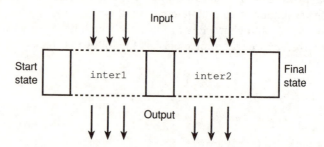

To read, increment and then write a number, we say

```
oneStep :: interact * num
oneStep =
  readI (const . numval) $sq
  apply (+1) $sq
  write shownum
```

using the infix version of sequencing, `$sq`.

We also have to be able to make choices between interactions, depending upon the input and the current state. We define the synonym

```
condition * == (input,*) -> bool
```

for conditions which we use to decide between interactions. The combinator which chooses is `alt`, for 'alternative'. `alt con inter1 inter2` will perform `inter1` if the condition `con` holds of the input and state, otherwise `inter2` is used.

As in any `abstype`, we need a function which takes us out of the `abstype`; this is the purpose of `run`. The list `run inter st` consists of the output produced when the interaction `inter` is run on the standard input, from starting state `st`.

EXAMPLES

To repeatedly read, increment and then write numbers, for instance, we want to define a combinator which does an interaction repeatedly *while* a condition is true. We could make it part of the `abstype`, but in fact it can be defined using the operations of the abstype, and recursion:

```
while ::  condition * -> interact * * -> interact * *

while cond inter
  = whi
    where
    whi = alt cond (inter $sq whi) null
```

The result is the interaction `whi`, which consists of two alternatives. If the condition holds, the interaction is `inter` followed by `whi`; if not, it is the null interaction, which performs no input or output, and which leaves the state unchanged:

```
null :: interact * *
null = apply id
```

How can we test for the end of the input file? It has ended if the input remaining is `[]`, so we define

```
eof :: condition *
eof (in,st) = (in=[])
```

and we now can define a function to perform the operation of repeatedly reading, incrementing and writing:

```
newExample1 = while ((~).eof) oneStep
```

and we can keep a running total of numbers input by writing

```
newExample5
  = while ((~).eof)
          (readI ((+).numval) $sq
           write shownum)
```

This shows we can repeat our earlier examples, but with this model we can go much further. As an example, take the program which reads a positive integer n and the sums the next n numbers.

We design this in two separate phases: first we design the interaction, using an `abstype` for the `state`. The approach take here is to invent the appropriate operation names on the `state`, and then elaborate them into a signature by stating their types:

```
sumN = readI (setBound.numval) $sq
         while underBound
                (readI (addToSum.numval) $sq
                 apply incCount $sq
                 write (shownum.giveSum))
```

We first read in the bound, and set it using `setBound`; next we check whether we are under the bound. If we are, then we add a value to the sum, increase the count and show the sum so far. The `abstype` will have the signature

```
abstype
   state
with
   setBound   :: num -> state -> state
   underBound :: condition state
   addToSum   :: num -> state -> state
   incCount   :: state -> state
   giveSum    :: state -> num
   initialSt  :: state
```

The advantage of this approach is that we can design the interaction *completely separately* from the state, which we do now. Also, the implementation of `state` can be changed without the form of the interaction having to be altered at all. Although the example here is small, this approach will apply and pay dividends in larger-scale systems equally well.

Now we can give a sample implementation of the `abstype` as a triple of three numerical values: the bound to be set, the count of the numbers read so far and the sum accumulated so far:

```
state == (num,num,num)

setBound n (bound,count,sum)        = (n,count,sum)
underBound (in,(bound,count,sum))   = count<bound
addToSum n (bound,count,sum)        = (bound,count,sum+n)
incCount   (bound,count,sum)        = (bound,count+1,sum)
giveSum    (bound,count,sum)        = sum
initialSt                           = (0,0,0)
```

EXERCISES

13.16 Define an interaction which reads the first number, n, adds the numbers it reads until either zero is read, or n numbers have been read. At this stage, the output should be the sum and average of the numbers read.

13.17 [*Harder*] Design an interactive interface for the library database first explored in Chapter 4. You will need to decide on the precise syntax of the queries you can ask and updates you can make to the system, designing types (and perhaps parsers) for them. The system should also provide a sensible response when an invalid or nonsensical input is given to it.

13.18 [*Project*] Design an interactive 'front end' for the simulation system. You should be able to make a choice of the number of servers, the distribution from which the timings come, and so on, as well as offering various sorts of analysis of the output of the simulations (total and average waiting times, and so on).

13.6 Implementing the abstype of interactions

We use the type

```
interact * ** == (input,*) -> (input,**,output)

string == [char]
input  == [string]
output == [string]
```

to model the type interact * **. Note that the input and output types here are lists of lines, rather than the lists of characters given in the earlier definition.

An interaction is modelled as a *function*, whose argument consists of:

- the input before the interaction, paired with
- the value of the state before the interaction: this is an element of type *.

The result consists of three pieces of information:

- what remains of the input after whatever reading is done by the interaction;
- the new state after the interaction: this is a value of type ** (often *, in fact); and
- the output produced by the interaction.

Some example members of this type are the interactions

```
readNumber :: interact * num
readNumber (in,st) = (tl in , numval (hd in) , [])

increaseNumber :: interact num num
increaseNumber (in,st) = (in,st+1,[])

writeNumber :: interact num num
writeNumber (in,st) = (in,st,[shownum st])
```

which read, increase and write a number. In readNumber, the head of the list of input lines is converted to a number, and the *tail* of the input is returned as the remaining input; the other functions are self-explanatory.

What we need to do now is to define of interactions in the interact * ** abstype – the solutions are illustrated in Figure 13.5. We work through these one-by-one.

The apply f function performs as anticipated, applying f to the state component, st, of the argument, producing no output and returning the input unchanged.

To read from the input, readI f takes the head of the list of lines, and applies f to this and the current state, making the result the new state. The remains of the input, rest, is returned in the input position, and no output is generated. Note that a read will only be successful if there is a line of input to be read.

In writing, the write f function generates one piece of output, f st. The state and the input are unchanged. It is not difficult to see increaseNumber, readNumber and writeNumber as examples of apply, readI and write; it is an exercise for the reader.

```
apply :: (* -> **) -> interact * **
apply f (in,st) = (in, f st , [])

readI :: (string -> * -> **) -> interact * **
readI f (line:rest,st) = (rest, f line st, [])

write :: (* -> string) -> interact * *
write f (in,st) = ( in , st , [ f st ] )

sq :: interact * ** -> interact ** *** -> interact * ***

sq inter1 inter2 (in,st)
  = (rest2,st2,out1++out2)
    where
    (rest1,st1,out1) = inter1 (in,st)
    (rest2,st2,out2) = inter2 (rest1,st1)

alt :: condition * ->
       interact * ** -> interact * ** -> interact * **

alt cond inter1 inter2 x
  = inter1 x                , if cond x
  = inter2 x                , otherwise

run :: interact * ** -> * -> [char]

run inter st
  = lay out
    where
    (rest,st',out) = inter (lines (read stdin) , st)

stdin = "/dev/tty"
```

Figure 13.5 Interaction combinators.

The first way of combining two interactions is given by sq (for 'sequence'). When applied to the two interactions inter1 and inter2, and (in,st), the first interaction inter1 is applied to (in,st), to give (rest1,st1,out1). The list out1 will be the first half of the output produced; the remainder is obtained by applying inter2 to the situation *after* inter1, namely the pair (rest1,st1), the part of the input unconsumed by inter1 paired with the state after inter1 finishes. The result then consists of the remains of the input, rest2, the state after performing both interactions, st2, and the combined output, out1++out2.

The second interaction combinator is alt. In defining alt, we simply have to check the condition on the input and initial state – depending on the result, we apply the appropriate interaction.

Finally, we have the function which allows us to use members of the type interact * ** as true interactions. Given the interaction to be performed, inter, and the starting state for the interaction, st, the standard input is split into lines, by lines (read stdin), and paired with st. The interaction inter can now be applied to this, and from the result we then select the output out. Finally, to make the output a string, we apply lay to it.

EXERCISES

13.19 Show that increaseNumber, readNumber and writeNumber are examples of apply, readI and write, respectively.

13.20 Give a definition of the function

```
sqList :: [interact * *] -> interact * *
```

which combines together a list of interactions in sequence; what value do you give to sqList []? Do you need to use the implementation of the abstype, or can you simply use the operations in the signature?

13.21 It is suggested that we define readI thus:

```
readI f (in,st) = (tl in, f (hd in) st, [])
```

Discuss the behaviour of the interaction

```
readI ((+).numval) $sq write (const "Thanks!")
```

which is intended to read a number and then to output the message "Thanks", using the usual and the suggested definitions of the readI function.

13.22 The *trivial* type () has the single member (); that is, () :: (). Define functions

```
makeFun   :: interact * ** -> (* -> interact () **)
makeInter :: (* -> interact () **) -> interact * **
```

so that

```
makeFun . makeInter = id
makeInter . makeFun = id
```

that is, the functions are mutually inverse.[†]

13.7 Proof revisited

After summarizing the effect that lazy evaluation has on the types of Miranda, we examine the consequences for reasoning about programs. Taking lists as a representative example, we look at how we can prove properties of infinite lists, and of the full type of lists, rather than simply the set of finite lists, which was the scope of the proofs we looked at in Chapter 5.

This section cannot give complete coverage of the issues of verification; we conclude with pointers to further reading.

Undefinedness

In nearly every programming language, it is possible to write a program which fails to terminate, and Miranda is no exception. We can deliberately write

```
undef :: *
undef = undef
```

which gives an undefined element of every type, but of course we can write an undefined program without intending to, as in

```
fac n = (n+1) * fac n
```

where we have confused the use of n and n+1 in defining factorial. The 'value' of f n will be the same as undef, as they are both non-terminating.

The existence of these undefined elements has an effect on the type of lists. What if we define, for example, the list

```
list1 = 2:3:undef
```

[†] The functions here show, for the cognoscenti, the relationship between the approach in this chapter, and the *monadic* approach of Moggi, Wadler and others. My type interact () ** is the same as the type of I/O monads over the type **, so the interaction type itself corresponds to a type of **parametric I/O monads** which are combined directly using the bind operation, a close relative of sq.

The list has a well-defined head, 2, and tail 3:undef. Similarly, the tail has a head, 3, but its tail is undefined. The type [num] therefore contains *partial* lists like list1, built from the undefined list, undef. Of course, there are also undefined numbers, so we also include in [num] lists like

```
list2 = undef:[2,3]
list3 = undef:4:undef
```

which contain undefined elements, and might also be partial.

What happens when a function is applied to undef? We use the rules for calculation we have seen already, so that the const function of the standard environment satisfies

```
const 17 undef = 17
```

If the function applied to undef has to pattern match, then the result of the function will be undef, since the pattern match has to look at the structure of undef, which will never terminate. For instance, for the functions first defined in Section 5.2,

```
sumList undef = undef                                          (1)
double  undef = undef                                          (2)
```

In writing proofs earlier in the book we were careful to state that in some cases the results only hold for *defined* elements.

A number is defined if it is not equal to undef; a list is defined if it is a finite list of defined elements; using this as a model, it is not difficult to give a definition of the defined elements of any algebraic type.

A finite list as we have defined it may contain undefined elements. Note that in some earlier proofs we stipulated that the results only hold for (finite) lists of defined elements; that is, for defined lists.

List induction revisited

As we said above, since there is an undefined list, undef, in each list type, lists can be built up from this; there will therefore be *two* base cases in the induction principle.

Proof by structural induction: fp-lists

To prove the property P(x) for all finite and partial lists (*fp-lists*) x we have to do three things:

Base cases	Prove P([]) and P(undef).
Induction step	Prove P(a:x) assuming that P(x) holds already.

Among the results we proved by structural induction in Section 5.2 were the
equations

```
sumList (double x)    = 2 * sumList x                    (3)
x ++ (y ++ z)         = (x ++ y) ++ z                    (4)
member (x++y) b       = member x b \/ member y b         (5)
shunt (shunt x y) [] = shunt y x                         (6)
```

for all *finite* lists x, y and z. For these results to hold for all *fp-lists*, we need
to show that

```
sumList (double undef)    = 2 * sumList undef                 (7)
undef ++ (y ++ z)         = (undef ++ y) ++ z                 (8)
member (undef++y) b       = member undef b \/ member y b  (9)
shunt (shunt undef y) [] = shunt y undef                    (10)
```

as well as being sure that the induction step is valid for all fp-lists. Now, by
(1) and (2) the equation (7) holds, and so (3) holds for all fp-lists. In a
similar way, we can show (8) and (9). More interesting is (10). Recall the
definition of shunt:

```
shunt []    y = y
shunt (a:x) y = shunt x (a:y)
```

It is clear from this that since there is a pattern match on the first parameter,
undef as the first parameter will give an undef result, so

```
shunt (shunt undef y) []
= shunt undef []
= undef
```

whilst an undef as second parameter is not problematic, and we have, for
instance,

```
shunt [2,3] undef
= shunt [3] (2:undef)
= shunt [] (3:2:undef)
= (3:2:undef)
```

This is enough to show that (10) does not hold, and that we cannot infer
that (6) holds for all fp-lists. Indeed, the example above shows exactly that
(6) is not valid.

Infinite lists

Beside the fp-lists, there are *infinite* members of the list types. How can we prove properties of infinite lists? A hint is given by our discussion of lazy evaluation in Section 13.4, where we said that we could use the three dots '...' to mean 'not known yet', when discussing the behaviour of a potentially infinite list. We used the list

```
"hello\n..."
```

as an *approximation* to the list

```
"hello\nthere\n..."
```

which itself can approximate other lists. In fact, we can equate our '...' for 'not known yet' with undef for 'undefined (as yet)', and so we can use the partial lists

$$\text{undef, } a_0\text{:undef, } a_0\text{:}a_1\text{:undef, } a_0\text{:}a_1\text{:}a_2\text{:undef, } \ldots$$

as approximations to the infinite list $[a_0, a_1, a_2, \ldots, a_n, \ldots]$.

Two lists l and m are equal if all their approximants are equal; that is, for all natural numbers n, take n l = take n m. (The take function gives the defined portion of the nth approximant, and so it is enough to compare these parts.) A more usable version of this principle applies to infinite lists only:

Infinite list equality

Two infinite lists l and m are equal if for all natural numbers n, l!n = m!n. A list l is infinite if, for all natural numbers n, take n l $\neq$ take (n+1) l.

Our example here is inspired by the process-based programs of Section 13.2. If fac is the factorial function

```
fac :: num -> num
fac 0     = 1                                                    (1)
fac (n+1) = (n+1) * fac n                                        (2)
```

one way of defining the infinite list of factorials is

```
facMap = map fac [0..]                                          (3)
```

whilst a process-based solution is

```
facs = 1 : map2 (*) [1..] facs                                 (4)
```

Assuming these lists are infinite (which they clearly are), we have to prove
for all natural numbers n that

        facMap!n = facs!n   (5)

Proof: In our proof we will assume for all natural numbers n the results

        (map f l)!n   = f (l!n)   (6)
        (map2 g l m)!n = g (l!n) (m!n)   (7)

which we discuss again later in this section.

Equation (5) is proved by mathematical induction, so we start by
proving the result at zero. Examining the left-hand side first,

        facMap!0
        = (map fac [0..])!0   by (3)
        = fac ([0..]!0)   by (6)
        = fac 0   by def of [0..],!
        = 1   by (1)

The right-hand side is

        facs!0
        = (1 : map2 (*) [1..] facs)!0   by (4)
        = 1   by def of !

establishing the base case. In the induction case we have to prove

        facMap!(n+1) = facs!(n+1)   (8)

assuming (5). The left-hand side of (8) is

        facMap!(n+1)
        = (map fac [0..])!(n+1)   by (3)
        = fac ([0..]!(n+1))   by (6)
        = fac (n+1)   by def of [0..],!
        = (n+1) * fac n   by (2)
        = (n+1) * (facMap!n)   by (5),[0..],!

The right-hand side of (8) is

        facs!(n+1)
        = (1 : map2 (*) [1..] facs)!(n+1)   by (4)
        = (map2 (*) [1..] facs)!n   by def of !
        = (*) ([1..]!n) (facs!n)   by (7)

$$= ([1..]!n) * (facs!n) \qquad \text{by def of } (*)$$
$$= (n+1) * (facs!n) \qquad \text{by def of } [1..],!$$
$$= (n+1) * (facMap!n) \qquad \text{by } (5)$$

The final step of this proof is given by the induction hypothesis, and completes the proof of the induction step and the result itself.

■

Proofs for infinite lists

When are results we prove for all fp-lists valid for *all* lists? If a result holds for all fp-lists, then it holds for all *approximations* to infinite lists. For some properties it is enough to know the property for all approximations to know that it will be valid for all infinite lists as well. In particular, this is true for all *equations*. This means that, for example, we can assert that for *all* lists l,

```
(map f . map g) l = map (f.g) l
```

and therefore by the principle of extensionality for functions,

```
map f . map g = map (f.g)
```

Many other of the equations we proved initially for finite lists can be extended to proof for the fp-lists, and therefore to *all* lists. Some of these are given in the exercises which follow.

Further reading

The techniques we have given here provide a flavour of how to write proofs for infinite lists and infinite data structures in general. We cannot give the breadth or depth of a full presentation, but refer the reader to Paulson (1987) for more details.

EXERCISES

13.23 Show that for all fp-lists y and z,

```
undef ++ (y ++ z)   = (undef ++ y) ++ z
member (undef++y) b = member undef b \/ member y b
```

to infer the results mentioned above.

13.24 Show that when `rev x` is defined to be `shunt x []`,

$$\text{rev (rev undef)} = \text{undef} \qquad (1)$$

In Chapter 5 we proved that

$$\text{rev (rev x)} = x \qquad (2)$$

for all finite lists x.

Why can we not infer from (1) and (2) that `rev (rev x) = x` holds for all fp-lists x?

13.25 Prove for all natural numbers m, n and functions `f :: num-> *` that

```
(map f [m..])!n = f (m+n)
```

[Hint: you will need to choose the right variable for the induction proof.]

13.26 Prove that the lists

```
facMap = map fac [0..]
facs = 1 : map2 (*) [1..] facs
```

are infinite.

13.27 If we define indexing thus

```
(a:x)!0       = a
(a:x) !(n+1) = x!n
[]!n          = error "Indexing"
```

show that for all fp-lists l and natural numbers n,

```
(map f l)!n = f (l!n)
```

and therefore infer that the result is valid for all lists l.

13.28 Show that the following equations hold between functions:

```
filter p . map f     = map f . filter (p.f)
filter p . filter q  = filter (q & p)
concat . map (map f) = map f . concat
```

SUMMARY

Rather than being simply a curiosity, this chapter has shown that we can exploit infinite lists for a variety of purposes:

- In giving an *infinite* list of prime or random numbers we provide an unlimited resource: we do not have to know how much of the resource we need while constructing the program; this *abstraction* makes programming simpler and clearer.

- Infinite lists provide a mechanism for process-based programming in Miranda, which is a useful alternative style, and also leads us into examining how to write interactive programs in the language.

Interaction was first explored form the bottom up, but then an abstype giving a toolkit for interactive programming showed again the power of higher-order, polymorphic functions. We also saw a second important example of the use of abstypes in design: when giving an interaction using a state, the state was described by means of an abstype, so that its implementation and the interaction could be designed completely separately.

The chapter concluded with a discussion of how proofs could be lifted to the partial and infinite elements of the list type: criteria were given in both cases, and we gave examples and counter-examples in illustration.

---

14 Program behaviour

This chapter explores not the values which programs compute, but the way in which those values are reached; we are interested here in program *efficiency* rather than program correctness.

We begin our discussion by asking how we can measure complexity in general, before asking how we measure the time and space behaviour of our functional programs. We work out the time complexity of a sequence of functions, leading up to looking at various implementations of the set abstype.

The **space** behaviour of lazy programs is complex: we show that some programs use less space than we might predict, whilst others use more. This leads into a discussion of **folding** functions into lists, and we introduce the `foldl` function, which folds from the left, and gives more space-efficient versions of folds of operators which need their arguments – the **strict** operations. In contrast to this, `foldr` gives better performance on lazy folds, in general.

In many algorithms, the naive implementation causes re-computation of parts of the solution, and thus a poor performance. In the final section of the chapter we show how to exploit lazy evaluation to give more efficient implementations, by **memoizing** the partial results in a table.

14.1 Complexity of functions

If we are trying to measure the behaviour of functions, one approach is to ask how much time and space are consumed in evaluations for different input values. We might, for example, given a function fred over the natural numbers, count the number of steps taken in calculating the value of fred n for natural numbers n. This gives us a function, call it stepsFred, and then we can ask how complex that function is.

One way of estimating the complexity of a function is to look at how fast it grows for large values of its argument. The idea of this is that a function's essential behaviour becomes clearer for large values. We examine this idea to start with through an example.

How fast does the function

```
f n = 2*n^2 + 4*n + 13
```

grow as n gets large? The function has has three components:

- a constant 13,
- a term 4*n, and
- a term, 2*n^2,

but as the values of n become large, how do these components behave?

- The constant 13 is unchanged;
- the term 4*n grows like a straight line; but
- a square term, 2*n^2, will grow the most quickly.

For 'large' values of n the square term is greater than the others, and so we say that f is of *order* 2, O(^2). In this case the square dominates for any n greater than or equal to 3; we shall say exactly what is meant by 'large' when we make the definition of order precise. As a rule of thumb, we can say that order classifies how functions behave when all but the largest components are removed, and constant multipliers are ignored; the remainder of the section makes this precise, but this rule should be sufficient for understanding the remainder of the chapter.

The notation (^2) is an example of an operator section, in which we partially apply a binary operator to one of its arguments. It gives a very compact notation for 'the function which takes n to n^2', and we shall use these notations in the rest of this chapter without comment. Note, however, the difference between the square function, (^2), and the power function, (2^), both of which are used here.

In the remainder of this section we make the idea of order precise, before examining various examples, and placing them on a scale for measuring complexity.

The big-Oh and theta notation – upper bounds

A function f :: num -> num is O(g), '*big-Oh* g', if there are positive numbers m and d, so that for all n ⩾ m,

    f n ⩽ d*(g n)

The definition expresses the fact that when numbers are large enough (n ⩾ m) the value of f is no larger than a multiple of the function g, namely (d*).g.
For example, f above is O(^2) since, taking m as 1 and d as 19,

    2*n^2 + 4*n + 13 ⩽ 2*n^2 + 4*n^2 + 13*n^2 = 19*n^2

Note that the measure gives an upper bound, which may be an over-estimate; by similar reasoning, f is O(^17) as well. In most cases, we consider the bound will in fact be a tight one. One way of expressing that g is a tight bound on f is that in addition to f being O(g), g is O(f); we then say that f is Θ(g), '*Theta* g'. Our example f is in fact Θ(^2).

A scale of measurement

We say that f ≪ g if f is O(g), but g is not O(f); we also use f ≡ g to mean that f is O(g) and simultaneously g is O(f).
We now give a scale by which function complexity can be measured. Constants (O(^0)) grow more slowly than linear functions (O(^1)), which in turn grow more slowly than quadratic functions (O(^2)). This continues through the powers. All the powers (^n) are bounded by exponential functions, (O(2^)):

    (^0) ≪ (^1) ≪ (^2) ≪ ... ≪ (^n) ≪ ... ≪ (2^) ≪ ...

Two other points ought to be added to the scale. The logarithm function, log, grows more slowly than any positive power, and the product of the functions n and log n, nLog n = n * log n fits between linear and quadratic, thus:

    (^0) ≪ log ≪ (^1) ≪ nLog ≪ (^2) ≪ ...

Counting

Many of the arguments we make will involve counting. In this section we look at some general examples which we will come across in examining the behaviour of functions below.

The first question we ask is, given a list, how many times can we bisect it, before we cut it into pieces of length one? If the length is n, after the first cut, the length of each half is n/2, and after p cuts, the length of each piece is n/(2^p). This number will be smaller than or equal to one when

$$(2^p) \geqslant n > (2^{(p-1)})$$

which, when we take $\log_2$ of each side, gives

$$p \geqslant \log_2 n > p-1$$

The function giving the number of steps in terms of the length of the list will thus be $\Theta(\log_2)$.

The second question concerns trees. A tree is called **balanced** if all its branches are the same length. Suppose we have a balanced binary tree, whose branches are of length n; how many nodes does the tree have? On the first level it has 1, on the second 2, on the kth it has $2^{(k-1)}$, so over all n+1 levels it has

$$1 + 2 + 4 + \ldots + 2^{(k-1)} + \ldots + 2^n = 2^{(n+1)} - 1$$

as can be seen from Figure 14.1.

We thus see that the size of a balanced tree is $\Theta(2^{\wedge})$ in the length of the branches; taking logarithms, a balanced tree will therefore have branches of length $\Theta(\log_2)$ in the size of the tree. If a tree is *not* balanced, the length of its longest branch can be of the same order as the size of the tree itself; see Figure 14.1 for an example.

Our final counting question concerns taking sums. If we are given one object every day for n days, we have n at the end; if we are given n each day, we have n^2; what if we are given 1 on the first day, 2 on the second, and so on? What is the sum of the list [1..n], in other words? Writing the list backwards, as well as forwards, we have

```
1       + 2      + 3      +  ...  + (n-1) + n +
n       + (n-1)  + (n-2)  +  ...  + 2     + 1      =
(n+1)   + (n+1)  + (n+1)  +  ...  + (n+1) + (n+1)
```

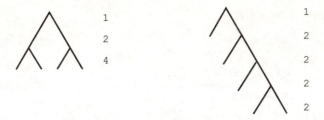

Figure 14.1 Counting the nodes of trees.

adding **vertically** at each point we have a sum of (n+1), and this sum occurs n times, so

    sum [1..n] = n*(n+1) div 2

which makes it Θ (^2), or quadratic. In a similar way, the sum of the squares is Θ (^3), and so on.

EXERCISES

14.1 Show that the example

      f n = 2*n^2 + 4*n + 13

is Θ (^2).

14.2 Give a table of the values of the functions (^0), log, (^1), nLog, (^2), (^3) and (2^) for the values

      0 1 2 3 4 5 10 50 100 500 1000 10000 100000 10000000

14.3 By giving the values of d, m and c (when necessary), show that the following functions have the complexity indicated:

      f1 n = 0.1*n^5 + 31*n^3 + 1000   O(^6)
      f2 n = 0.7*n^5 + 13*n^2 + 1000 Θ(^5)

14.4 Show that (^n) ≪ (2^) for all positive integers n. By taking logarithms of both sides, show that log ≪ (^n) for all positive integers n.

14.5 Show that

      log ≡ ln ≡ log₂

and in fact that all logarithms have the same rate of growth.

14.6 The function `fib` is defined by

```
fib 0     = 0
fib 1     = 1
fib (n+2) = fib n + fib (n+1)
```

Show that $(\wedge n) \ll$ `fib` for all n.

14.7 Show that $\ll$ is transitive – that is, $f \ll g$ and $g \ll h$ together imply that $f \ll h$. Show also that $\equiv$ is an equivalence relation.

14.8 If f is $O(g)$, show that any constant multiple of f is also of the same order. If f1 and f2 are $O(g)$, show that their sum and difference are also $O(g)$.

14.9 If f1 is $O(\wedge k1)$ and f2 is $O(\wedge k2)$, show that their product,

```
f n = f1 n * f2 n
```

is $O(\wedge(k1+k2))$.

14.10 Prove by induction over n that

```
1 + 2 + 4 + ... + 2^n = 2^(n+1) - 1
1^2 + 2^2 + ... + n^2 = n*(n+1)*(2*n+1) div 6
1^3 + 2^3 + ... + n^3 = (n*(n+1) div 2)^2
```

14.2 The complexity of calculations

How can we measure the complexity of the functions we write? One answer is to use the Miranda system itself, with the /count option switched on, to give us various statistics about evaluations. Whilst this gives some information, we opt for a cleaner *model* of what is going on, and we choose to analyse the *calculations* we have been using. There are three principal measures we can use:

- The *time* taken to compute a result is given by the *number of steps* in a calculation which uses lazy evaluation.

- The *space* necessary for the computation can be measured in two ways. First, there is a lower limit on the amount of space we need for a calculation to complete successfully. During calculation, the expression being calculated grows and shrinks; obviously, we need enough space to hold the *largest* expression built during the calculation. This is often called the **residency** of the computation, we shall call it the **space complexity**.

- We can also make a measure of the *total space* used by a computation, which in some way reflects the total area of the calculation; it is of interest to implementors of functional languages, but for users (and for us) the first two are the crucial measures.

How then do we measure the complexity of a function?

Complexity measures

We measure the complexity of the function f by looking at the time and space complexity as described above, as *functions* of the *size* of the inputs to f. The size of a number is the number itself, whilst the size of a list is given by its length, and of a tree by the number of nodes it contains.

EXAMPLES ───

Let us start with the example of fac:

```
fac :: num -> num
fac 0 = 1
fac n = n * fac (n-1)
```

Working through the calculation, we have

```
fac n
= n * fac (n-1)
= ...
= n * (n-1) * ... * 2 * 1 * 1                    (†)
= n * (n-1) * ... * 2 * 1
= n * (n-1) * ... * 2
= ...
= n!
```

The calculation contains 2*n+1 steps, and the largest expression, (†), contains n multiplication symbols. This makes the time and space complexity both $\Theta(\verb|^|1)$, or linear.

Next we look at insertion sort. Recall that

```
iSort []    = []
iSort (a:x) = insert a (iSort x)

insert a [] = [a]
insert a (b:y) = a:b:y          , if a<=b
               = b:insert a y , otherwise
```

A general calculation will be

```
iSort [a₁,a₂,...,aₙ₋₁,aₙ]
= insert a₁ (iSort [a₂,...,aₙ₋₁,aₙ])
= ...
= insert a₁
    (insert a₂ ( ... (insert aₙ₋₁ (insert aₙ []))...))
```

followed by the calculation of the n inserts. What sort of behaviour does insert have? Take the general example of

```
insert a [a₁,a₂,...,aₙ₋₁,aₙ]
```

where we assume that $[a_1, \ldots, a_n]$ is sorted. There are three possibilities:

- In the *best* case, when a<=a₁, the calculation takes 1 step.
- In the *worst* case, when a>aₙ, the calculation takes n steps.
- In an *average* case, the calculation will take n/2 steps.

What does this mean for iSort?

- In the *best* case, each insert will take one step, and the calculation will therefore take a further n steps, making it O(^1) in this case.
- On the other hand, in the *worst* case, the first insert will take one step, the second two, and so on. By our counting argument in Section 14.1 the calculation will take O(^2) steps.
- In an *average* case, the inserts will take a total of

```
1/2 + 2/2 + ... + (n-1)/2 + n/2
```

steps, whose sum is again O(^2).

We therefore see that in most cases, the algorithm takes quadratic time, but in some exceptional cases, when sorting an (almost) sorted list, the complexity is linear in the length of the list. In all cases the space usage will also be linear.

Before looking at another sorting algorithm, we look at the time taken to join together two lists, using ++:

```
[a₁,a₂,...,aₙ₋₁,aₙ] ++ x
= a₁ : ([a₂,...,aₙ₋₁,aₙ] ++ x)
= a₁ : (a₂ : [a₃,...,aₙ₋₁,aₙ] ++ x)
= ... n-3 steps ...
= a₁ : (a₂ : ... : (aₙ:x)...)
```

The time taken is **linear** in the length of the first list.

Our second sorting algorithm, quicksort, is given by

```
qSort []    = []
qSort (a:x)
    = qSort [y|y<-x;y<=a] ++[a]++ qSort [y|y<-x;y>a]
```

When the list is sorted and contains no duplicate elements, the calculation goes thus:

```
qSort [a₁,a₂,...,aₙ₋₁,aₙ]
= ... n steps ...
= [] ++ [a₁] ++ qSort [a₂,...,aₙ₋₁,aₙ]
= ... n-1 steps ...
= a₁ : ([] ++ [a₂] ++ qSort [a₃,...,aₙ])
= ... n-2 steps ...
= ...
= a₁ : (a₂ : (a₃ : ... aₙ:[])
= [a₁,a₂,...,aₙ₋₁,aₙ]
```

Since the number of steps here is $1+2+\ldots+n$, we have **quadratic** behaviour in this sorted case. In the *average* case, we split thus:

```
qSort [a₁,a₂,...,aₙ₋₁,aₙ]
= qSort [b₁,...,bₙ/₂] ++ [a₁] ++ qSort [c₁,...,cₙ/₂]
```

where the list has been bisected. Forming the two sublists will take $O(\verb|^|1)$ steps, as will the joining together of the results. As we argued in Section 14.1, there can be $\log_2 n$ bisections before a list is reduced to one-element lists, so we have $O(\verb|^|1)$ steps to perform $O(\verb|log|)$ many times; this makes quicksort take $O(\verb|nLog|)$ steps, *on average*, although we saw that it can take quadratic steps in the worst (already sorted!) case.[†]

The logarithmic behaviour here is characteristic of a 'divide-and-conquer' algorithm: we split the problem into two smaller problems, solve these and then re-combine the results. The result is a comparatively efficient algorithm, which reaches its base cases in $O(\log_2)$ rather than $O(\verb|^|1)$ steps.

[†]The explanation we have given here depends upon us re-arranging the order of the calculation steps; this is legitimate if we observe that lazy evaluation of combinators is *optimal*, in the sense of taking fewest steps to reach a result; any re-arrangement can only give more steps to our calculation, so the bound of nLog holds.

EXERCISES

14.11 Estimate the time complexity of the reverse functions

```
rev1 []    = []
rev1 (a:x) = rev1 x ++ [a]
```

and

```
rev2          = shunt []
shunt x []    = x
shunt x (a:y) = shunt (a:x) y
```

14.12 We can define multiplication by repeated addition as follows:

```
mult n 0     = 0
mult n (m+1) = mult n m + n
```

'Russian' multiplication is defined by

```
russ n 0 = 0
russ n m =  russ (n*n) (m div 2)       , if m mod 2 = 0
         = (russ (n*n) (m div 2))*n    , otherwise
```

Estimate the time complexity of these two multiplication algorithms.

14.13 Estimate the time complexity of the Fibonacci function.

14.14 Show that the worst-case time behaviour of the merge sort function below is
O(nLog):

```
mSort l = l     , if len < 2
        = merge (mSort (take m l)) (mSort (drop m l))
          where
          len = #l
          m   = len div 2

merge (a:x) (b:y) = a : merge x (b:y)    , if a<=b
                  = b : merge (a:x) y    , otherwise
merge (a:x) []    = (a:x)
merge []    y     = y
```

14.3 Implementations of sets

We first saw the set abstype in Section 11.8, where we gave an implementation based on ordered lists without repetitions. Alternatively, we can write an implementation based simply on lists, whose elements may occur in any order and be repeated:

```
set * == [*]

empty       = []
memSet      = member
inter x y   = filter (member x) y
union       = (++)
subSet x y  = and (map (member y) x)
eqSet x y   = subSet x y & subSet y x
makeSet     = id
mapSet      = map
```

We can also write an implementation based on the search trees of Section 11.7. We now compare the time complexity of these implementations, and summarize the results in the table which follows:

	Lists	Ordered lists	Search trees (average)
memSet	O(^1)	O(^1)	O(log$_2$)
subSet	O(^2)	O(^1)	O(nLog)
inter	O(^2)	O(^1)	O(nLog)
makeSet	O(^0)	O(nLog)	O(nLog)
mapSet	O(^1)	O(nLog)	O(nLog)

As we can see from the table, there is no clear 'best' or 'worst' choice; depending upon the kind of set operation we intend to perform, different implementations make more sense. This is one more reason for providing the abstype boundary beneath which the implementation can change invisibly to suit the use to which the sets are being put.

EXERCISES

14.15 Confirm the time complexities given in the table above for the two list implementations of sets.

14.16 Implement the operations `subSet`, `inter`, `makeSet` and `mapSet` for the search tree implementation, and estimate the time complexity of your implementations.

14.17 Give an implementation of sets as lists without repetitions, and estimate the time complexity of the functions in your implementation.

14.4 Space behaviour

A rule of thumb for estimating the *space* needed to calculate a result is to measure the largest expression produced during the calculation. This is accurate if the result being computed is a number or a Boolean, but it is *not* when the result is a data structure, like a list.

Lazy evaluation

Recall the explanation of lazy evaluation in Section 13.4, where we explained that parts of results are printed as soon as possible. Once part of a result is printed, it need no longer occupy any space. In estimating space complexity, we must be aware of this.

Take the example of the lists `[m..n]`, defined thus:

```
[m..n] = m:[m+1..n]     , if n>=m
       = []             , otherwise
```

Calculating `[1..n]` gives

```
  [1..n]
= 1:[1+1..n]
    ?? n>=1+1
       n>=2
= 1:[2..n]
= 1:2:[2+1..n]
= ...
= 1:2:3:...:n:[]
```

where we have underlined those parts of the result which can be output. To measure the space complexity we look at the non-underlined part, which is of constant size, so the space complexity is `O(^0)`. The calculation has approximately `2*n` steps, giving it linear time complexity, as expected.

Saving values in where clauses

Consider the example of

```
exam1 = [1..n]++[1..n]
```

The time taken to calculate this will be O(^1), and the space used will be O(^0), but we will have to calculate the expression [1..n] *twice*. Suppose, instead, that we compute

```
exam2 = list++list
        where
        list=[1..n]
```

The effect here is to compute the list [1..n] *once*, so that we *save* its value after calculating it in order to be able to use it again. Unfortunately, this means that after evaluating list, the whole of the list is stored, giving an O(^1) space complexity.

This is a general phenomenon: if we save something by referring to it in a where clause we have to pay the penalty of the space that it occupies; if the space is available, fair enough; if not, we have turned a working computation into one which fails for lack of space.

This problem can be worse! Take the examples

```
exam3 = [1..n]++[last [1..n]]
exam4 = list ++[last list]
        where
        list=[1..n]
```

in which last returns the last element of a non-empty list. The space required by exam3 is O(^0), whilst in exam4 it is O(^1), since we hold on to the calculated value of list, even though we only require one value from it, the last. This feature, of keeping hold of a large structure when we only need part of it is called a **dragging problem**. In the example here, the problem is clear, but in a larger system the source of a dragging problem can be most difficult to find.

The lesson of these examples must be that while it is *always* sensible not to repeat the calculation of a simple value, saving a compound value like a list or a tuple can increase the space usage of a program.

Saving space?

As we saw in Section 14.2, the naive factorial function has O(^1) space complexity, as it forms the expression

```
n * ((n-1) * ... * (1 * 1)...)
```

before it is evaluated. Instead, we can perform the multiplications as we go along, using

```
aFac 0 p     = p
aFac (n+1) p = aFac n (p*(n+1))
```

and compute the factorial of n using aFac n 1. Now, we examine the calculation

```
aFac n 1
= aFac (n-1) (1*n)
     ?? (n-1)>0
= aFac (n-2) (1*n*(n-1))
= ...
= aFac 0 (1*n*(n-1)*(n-2)*...*2*1)
= (1*n*(n-1)*(n-2)*...*2*1)                              (†)
```

so that the effect of this program is exactly the same: it still forms a large *unevaluated* expression! The reason that the expression is unevaluated is that it is not clear that its value is needed until the step (†).

How can we overcome this? We need to make the intermediate values *needed*, so that they are calculated earlier. We do this by adding a test; another method is given in Section 14.5:

```
aFac (n+1) p = aFac n (p*(n+1))     , if p=p
```

Now the calculation of the factorial of 4, say, is

```
aFac 4 1
= aFac (4-1) (1*4)
     ?? (4-1)>0 = True
     ?? (1*4)=(1*4) = True                              (‡)
= aFac (3-1) (4*3)
     ?? (3-1)>0
     ?? (4*3)=(4*3) = True                              (‡)
= aFac (2-1) (12*2)
= ...
= aFac 0 (24*1)
= (24*1) = 24
```

The lines (‡) show where the guard p=p is tested, and so where the intermediate multiplications take place. From this we can conclude that this more *strict* version has better (constant) space behaviour.

EXERCISES

14.18 Estimate the space complexity of the function

```
sumSquares :: num -> num
sumSquares n = sumList (map sq [1..n])
```

where

```
sumList = foldr (+) 0
sq n    = n
```

and map and [1..n] have their standard definitions.

14.19 Give an informal estimate of the complexity of the text-processing functions in Chapter 4.

14.5 Folding revisited

One of the patterns of computation which we identified in Chapter 4 is *folding* an operator or function into a list. This section examines the complexity of the two standard folding functions, and discusses how we can choose between them in program design. Before this we make a definition which expresses the fact of a function needing to evaluate an argument. This distinction will be crucial to our full understanding of folding.

Strictness

A function is *strict* in an argument if the result is undefined whenever an undefined value is passed to this argument. For instance, (+) is strict in both arguments, whilst (&) is strict in its first only. Recall that it is defined by

```
True  & x = x
False & x = False
```
(1)

The pattern match in the first argument forces it to be strict there, but equation (1) shows that it is possible to get an answer from (&) when the second argument is undef, so it is therefore not strict in the second.

If a function is not strict in an argument, we say that it is **non-strict** or **lazy** in that argument.

Folding from the right

Our definition of folding was given by

```
foldr :: (* -> ** -> **) -> ** -> [*] -> **

foldr f st []    = st
foldr f st (a:x) = f a (foldr f st x)
```

which we saw was of general application. Sorting a list, by insertion sort, was given by

```
iSort = foldr insert []
```

and indeed, any primitive recursive definition over lists can be given by applying `foldr`.

Writing the function applications as infix operations gives

```
foldr f st [a₁,a₂,...,a_{n-1},a_n]
= a₁ $f (a₂ $f ... $f (a_{n-1} $f (a_n $f st))...)                (2)
```

and shows why the 'r' is added to the name: bracketing is to the right, with the starting value `st` appearing to the right of the elements also. If f is lazy in its second argument, we can see from (2) that given the head of the list, output may be possible. For instance, `map` can be defined thus:

```
map f = foldr ((:).f) []
```

and in calculating `map (+2) [1..n]` we see

```
foldr ((:).(+2)) [] [1..n]
= ((:).(+2)) 1 (foldr ((:).(+2)) [] [2..n])
= 1+2 : (foldr ((:).(+2)) [] [2..n])
= 3 : (foldr ((:).(+2)) [] [2..n])
= ...
```

As in Section 14.4, we see that this will be $O(^0)$, since the elements of the list will be output as they are calculated. What happens when we fold a strict operator into a list? The definition of `fac` in Section 14.2 can be re-written

```
fac n = foldr (*) 1 [1..n]
```

and we saw there that the effect was to give $O(^1)$ space behaviour, since the multiplications in equation (2) cannot be performed until the whole expression is formed, as they are bracketed to the right. We therefore define the function to fold from the *left* now.

Folding from the left

Instead of folding from the right, we can define

```
foldl' :: (** -> * -> **) -> ** -> [*] -> **
foldl' f st []    = st
foldl' f st (a:x) = foldl' f (f st a) x
```

which gives

$$\text{foldl' f st } [a_1, a_2, \ldots, a_{n-1}, a_n]$$
$$= (\ldots((\text{st \$f } a_1) \text{ \$f } a_2) \text{ \$f } \ldots \text{ \$f } a_{n-1}) \text{ \$f } a_n \qquad (3)$$

We can calculate this in the factorial example, the effect being

```
  foldl' (*) 1 [1..n]
= foldl' (*) (1*1) [2..n]
= ...
= foldl' (*) (...((1*1)*2)*...*n) []
= (...((1*1)*2)*...*n)
```

As in Section 14.2, the difficulty is that `foldl'` as we have defined it is not strict in its second argument. In the standard environment, it is made strict using the built-in function seq. The effect of seq x y is to evaluate x before returning y, so that if we write

```
strict f x = seq x (f x)
```

`strict` f is a *strict* version of the function f. We therefore write as the final definition of `foldl`,

```
foldl :: (** -> * -> **) -> ** -> [*] -> **
foldl f st []    = st
foldl f st (a:x) = strict (foldl f) (f st a) x
```

Now, evaluating the example again,

```
  foldl (*) 1 [1..n]
= foldl (*) 1 [2..n]
= foldl (*) 2 [3..n]
= foldl (*) 6 [4..n]
= ...
```

Clearly, this evaluation is in constant space, $O(^0)$. Can we draw any conclusions from these examples?

Designing folds

When we fold in a *strict* function, we will form a list-sized expression with `foldr`, so it will always be worth using `foldl`. This covers the examples of `(+)`, `(*)` and so on.

We saw earlier that when `map` was defined using `foldr` we could begin to give output before the whole of the list argument was constructed. If we use `foldl` instead, we will have to traverse the whole list before giving any output, since any `foldl` computation follows the pattern

```
foldl f st₁ l₁
= foldl f st₂ l₂
= ...
= foldl f stₖ lₖ
= ...
= foldl f stₙ []
= stₙ
```

so in the case of `map`, `foldr` is the clear choice of the two.

A more interesting example is given by the function which is `True` only if a list of Booleans consists of `True` throughout. We fold in `(&)`, of course, but should we use `foldr` or `foldl`? The latter will give a constant-space version, but will examine the *entire* list. Since `(&)` is lazy in its second argument, we might not need to examine the value returned from the remainder of the list. For instance,

```
foldr (&) True (map (=2) [2..n])
= (2=2) & (foldr (&) True (map (=2) [3..n]))
= True & (foldr (&) True (map (=2) [3..n]))
= foldr (&) True (map (=2) [3..n])
= (3=2) & (foldr (&) True (map (=2) [4..n]))
= False & (foldr (&) True (map (=2) [4..n]))
= False
```

This version uses constant space, *and* may not examine the whole list; `foldr` is therefore the best choice.

Beside the examples of `(+)` and `(*)`, there are many other examples where `foldl` is preferable, including:

- Reversing a list. To use `foldr` we have to add an element a to the end of a list, x. The operation x++[a] is strict in x, whilst the 'cons' operation (:) is lazy in its list argument.

- Converting a list of digits "7364" into a number is strict in both the conversion of the front, 736 and the final character, '4'.

Since foldl consumes an entire list before giving any output, it will be of no use in defining functions to work over infinite lists or the partial lists we looked at while writing interactive systems.

EXERCISES

14.20 Define the functions to reverse a list and to convert a digit list into a number using both foldr and foldl, and compare their behaviour using calculations.

14.21 Is it better to define insertion sort using foldr or foldl? Justify your answer.

14.22 How are the results of foldr and foldl related? You may find it useful to use the functions reverse and

```
swap :: (* -> ** -> ***) -> (** -> * -> ***)
swap f a b = f b a
```

in your answers.

14.23 What is the relationship between foldr and foldl when the function to be folded is

- associative: a $f (b $f c) = (a $f b) $f c;
- has st as an identity: st $f a = a = a $f st;
- commutative: a $f b = b $f a;

and what is the relationship when all three hold?

14.6 Avoiding re-computation: Memoization

In this section we look at general strategies which allow us to avoid having to re-compute results during the course of evaluating an expression. This happens particularly in some recursive solutions of problems, where the solutions to sub-problems can be used repeatedly.

We begin the discussion by looking again at the Fibonacci function:

```
fib :: num -> num
fib 0    = 0
fib 1    = 1
fib (n+2) = fib n + fib (n+1)
```

This definition is remarkably inefficient. Computing `fib (n+2)` calls `fib n` and `fib (n+1)` – the latter will call `fib n` again, and within *each* call of `fib n` there will be two calls to `fib (n-1)`. The time complexity of `fib` is greater than any power. How might we avoid this recomputation? We explore two ways of augmenting the definition to make it efficient; in the first we return a complex data structure from each call, and in the second we define an infinite list to hold all the values of the function.

First we observe that to get the value at $(n+2)$ we need the two previous values; we could therefore return *both* values in the result:

```
fibP :: num -> (num,num)
fibP 0    = (0,1)
fibP (n+1) = (b,a+b)
             where
             (a,b) = fibP n
```

A calculation is given in Figure 14.2, where different variables a_1, a_2 etc. have been used for the different occurrences of the local variables a and b; this is not necessary, but does make the different occurrences clearer.

```
fibP 3
= (b,a+b)
  where
  (a,b) = fibP 2
          = (b₁,a₁+b₁)
            where
            (a₁,b₁) = fibP 1
                      = (b₂,a₂+b₂)
                        where
                        (a₂,b₂) = fibP 0
                                  = (0,1)
                      = (1,1)
          = (1,2)
= (2,3)
```

Figure 14.2 Calculating `fibP 3`.

As an alternative strategy, we can try to define the list of Fibonacci values, `fibs`, directly. The values of the function given above now become values at particular indices:

```
fibs       :: [num]
fibs!0     = 0
fibs!1     = 1
fibs!(n+2) = fibs!n + fibs!(n+1)
```

This gives a *description* of the list, but it is not executable in this form. The first two lines tell us that fibs = 0 : 1 : rest, whilst the third equation tells us what the rest is. The (n+2)nd element of fibs is the nth element of rest; similarly, the (n+1)st element is the nth element of (tl fibs). We therefore have, for every n,

```
rest!n = fibs!n + (tl fibs)!n
```

which says that each element is obtained by adding the corresponding elements of two lists; that is,

```
rest = map2 (+) fibs (tl fibs)
```

so that putting the parts together, we have

```
fibs = 0 : 1 : map2 (+) fibs (tl fibs)
```

a **process network** computing the Fibonacci numbers. This gives a linear time, constant space algorithm for the problem, in contrast to the earlier solution which is linear in both time and space, since all the nested calls to `fibP` are built before any result can be given.

Dynamic programming

The example in this section illustrates a general method of solving problems by what has become known as **dynamic programming**. Dynamic programming solutions work by breaking a problem into subproblems, but as in the Fibonacci example, the subproblems will not be independent, in general. A naive solution will therefore contain massive redundancy, which we remove by building a *table* of solutions to subproblems.

The example we consider is to find the length of a maximal common subsequence of two lists – the subsequences need not have all their elements adjacent. In the examples of

```
[2,1,4,5,2,3,5,2,4,3]       [1,7,5,3,2]
```

the length of 4 is given by the subsequence $[1,5,3,2]$. This problem is not simply a 'toy'; a solution to this can be used to find the common lines in two files, which gives the basis of the Unix `diff` program, which is used, for instance, for comparing different versions of programs stored in separate files.

The naive solution is given by `mLen` in Figure 14.3. The interesting part of the definition is given by the third equation. In the case that the lists have equal first elements, these elements must be in a maximal common subsequence, so we find the overall solution by looking in the tails, and

```
mLen :: [*] -> [*] -> num

mLen x []        = 0
mLen [] y        = 0
mLen (a:x) (b:y) = 1 + mLen x y              , if a=b
                 = max2 (mLen x (b:y))
                        (mLen (a:x) y)       , otherwise

maxLen :: [*] -> [*] -> num -> num -> num

maxLen l m 0 j       = 0                                      (1)
maxLen l m (i+1) 0 = 0                                        (2)
maxLen l m (i+1) (j+1)
   = (maxLen l m i j) + 1       , if l!i = m!j                (3)
   = max2 (maxLen l m (i+1) j)
          (maxLen l m i (j+1)) , otherwise                    (4)

maxTab :: [*] -> [*] -> [[num]]

maxTab l m
  = result
    where
    result = [0,0..] : map2 f [0..] result
    f i prev
       = ans
         where
         ans  = 0 : map2 g [0..] ans
         g j v = (prev!j)+1              , if l!i = m!j
               = max2 v (prev!(j+1))     , otherwise
```

Figure 14.3 Maximum common subsequence – three algorithms.

adding one to the result. More problematic is the case when the heads are distinct; we have choice of excluding either a or b; in this algorithm we try both possibilities, and take the maximal result. There, of course, is the source of the redundant computations; each of these may well give rise to a computation of mLen x y. How are we to avoid this situation? We shall store these results in a *table*, which in Miranda will be a list of lists. Once a result appears in the table, we have no need to recompute it.

As an intermediate step, we rewrite the solution as maxLen which uses list indexing, so that

```
maxLen l m u v
```

is the longest common subsequence in the lists take u l and take v m. The function is given in Figure 14.3, and the definition is a straightforward adaptation of mLen.

Now we aim to define the table maxTab l m so that

```
(maxTab l m)!u!v = maxLen l m u v
```

This requirement is made specific by equations (1) to (4). The base case is given by (1), stating that

```
(maxTab l m)!0!v = 0
```

for all v. In other words,

```
(maxTab l m)!0 = [0,0..]
```

so,

```
result = [0,0..] :  ...
```

The equations (2) to (4) tell us how to define the list maxTab!i+1 from the list maxTab!i, and i, so we can define

```
maxTab l m = result
             where
             result = [0,0..] : map2 f [0..] result
```

where f :: num -> [num] -> [num] is the function taking i and the previous value, maxTab!i to maxTab!i+1. Now we have to define this list, which appears in the solution as ans.

Equation (2) tells us that it starts with 0, and g is the function taking maxTab!i+1!j and j to maxTab!i+1!j+1, where we are also able to use the values of maxTab!i, named by prev. Using these insights, the definition of g is a straightforward transliteration of (3) and (4):

```
ans   = 0 : map2 g [0..] ans
g j v = (prev!j)+1              , if l!i = m!j
      = max2 v (prev!(j+1))     , otherwise
```

The top-level result is given by calling

```
maxTab l m (#l) (#m)
```

and this is computed in linear time and space.

Greedy algorithms

A greedy solution to a dynamic programming problem works by building up the optimal solution by making *local* choices of what appear to be the best solutions of sub-problems. In the common subsequence problem, we can think of searching along the two lists in a single sweep, looking successively for the first points of agreement; we search all pairs of indices smaller than n before looking at n. In an example, the greedy solution gives

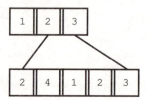

which is *not* optimal: the subsequence [1,2,3] has been missed, since we make the choice of 2 as the first element, as it is the first point of agreement. This local choice is not part of an optimal global solution, but the algorithm gives reasonable performance.

In many situations, where local choices are always part of a global solution, a greedy solution will work. Examples we have seen thus far include

- the line-splitting algorithm we gave in Chapter 4 is optimal in minimizing sum of the inter-word spaces included when the lines are justified;

- the Huffman codes described in Chapter 10 are optimal in the sense of giving the shortest possible codings of files. We did not search all possible sets of codes in giving the Huffman code, rather we built it up from locally sensible choices.

EXERCISES

14.24 Given an implementation of the greedy solution to the maximal common subsequence problem, and show that it behaves as explained above on the lists [1,2,3] and [2,4,1,2,3].

14.25 Can you give an improvement of the maximal common subsequence solution along the lines of fibP, returning a complex (finite) data structure as the result of a function call, rather than simply one value?

14.26 Finding the 'edit distance' between two strings was first discussed in Section 9.5, where we gave a dynamic programming solution to the problem. Show how you can give an efficient implementation of this algorithm using the techniques of this section, and also how you give a greedy solution to the problem. How do the two solutions compare?

14.27 Based on the examples of this section, give a program which gives the difference between two files, matching the corresponding lines, and giving the output in a suitable form, such as a list of the pairs of matching line numbers, or a form copied from the Unix diff program.

SUMMARY

In this chapter we have examined the efficiency of lazy functional programs. We saw that we are able to analyse the time complexity of many of our functions without too much difficulty. To analyse the *space* behaviour is more difficult, but we have shown how the space consumption of lazy programs can be estimated from our calculations.

The introduction of foldl brings the space issue into focus, and the distinction we made between *strict* and lazy functions allows us to analyse the different behaviour of the two folds.

We concluded the discussion with an application of lazy infinite lists to *memoizing* results for re-use; the transition from naive to efficient was done in a systematic way, which can be carried over to other application areas.

APPENDIX A

Functional and imperative programming

Values and states

Consider the example of finding the sum of squares of natural numbers up to a particular number.

A functional program describes the values that are to be calculated, directly:

```
sumSquares :: num -> num
sumSquares 0     = 0
sumSquares (n+1) = (n+1)*(n+1) + sumSquares n
```

These equations state what the sum of squares is. In the first case it is a direct description; in the second it states that the sum to n+1 is got by finding the sum to n and adding the square of n+1.

A typical imperative program might solve the problem thus:

```
s := 0 ;
i := 0 ;
while i<n do begin
    i := i+1 ;
    s := i*i + s ;
end {while}
```

The sum is the final value of the variable s which is changed repeatedly during program execution, as is the 'count' variable, i. The effect of the program can only be seen by following the sequence of changes made to these variables by the commands in the program, whilst the functional program can be read as a series of equations defining the sum of squares. This meaning is *explicit* in the functional program, whereas the imperative program has an overall effect which is not obvious from the program itself.

A more striking algorithm still is one which is completely explicit:

```
To find the sum of squares, build the list of numbers
1 to n,  square each of them, and sum the result.
```

This program, which uses neither complex control flow, as does the imperative example, nor recursion, as seen in the function sumSquares, can be written in a functional style, thus:

```
newSumSq :: num -> num
newSumSq n = sum (map square [1..n])
```

where square x = x*x, the operation map applies its first argument to every member of a list, and sum finds the sum of a list of numbers. More examples of this sort of **data-directed** programming can be seen in the body of the text.

Functions and variables

An important difference between the two styles is what is meant by some of the terminology. Both 'function' and 'variable' have different interpretations.

As was explained earlier, a function in a functional program is simply something which returns a value which depends upon some inputs. In an imperative language like Pascal a function is rather different. It will return a value depending upon its arguments, but in general it will also change the values of variables. Rather than being a pure function it is really a procedure which returns a value when it terminates.

In a functional program a variable stands for an *arbitrary* or *unknown* value. Every occurrence of a variable in an equation is interpreted in the same way. They are just like variables in logical formulas, or the mathematical variables familiar from equations like

$$a^2 - b^2 = (a-b)(a+b)$$

In any particular case, the value of all three occurrences of a will be the same. In exactly the same way, in

```
sumSquares (n+1) = (n+1)*(n+1) + sumSquares n
```

all occurrences of n will be interpreted by the same value. For example

```
sumSquares (7+1) = (7+1)*(7+1) + sumSquares 7
```

The crucial motto is *variables in functional programs do not vary.*

On the other hand, the value of a variable in an imperative program changes throughout its lifetime. In the sum of squares program above, the variable s will take the values $0, 1, 5, \ldots$ successively. Variables in imperative programs *do* vary!

Program verification

Probably the most important difference between functional and imperative programs is logical. As well as being a program, a functional definition is a logical equation describing a **property** of the function. Functional programs are **self-describing**, as it were. Using the definitions, other properties of the functions can be deduced.

To take a simple example, for all n>0, it is the case that

```
sumSquares n > 0
```

To start with,

```
sumSquares 1
= 1*1 + sumSquares 0
= 1*1 + 0
= 1
```

which is greater than 0. In general,

```
sumSquares (n+1) = (n+1)*(n+1) + sumSquares n
```

Now, (n+1)*(n+1) is positive, and if sumSquares n is positive, their sum, sumSquares (n+1), must be. This proof can be formalized using **mathematical induction**; see Chapter 3 for further details and examples.

Program verification is possible for imperative programs as well, but imperative programs are not self-describing in the way functional ones are. To describe the effect of an imperative program, like the 'sum of squares' program above, we need to add to the program logical formulas or assertions which describe the state of the program at various points in its execution. These methods are both more indirect and more difficult, and verification seems very difficult indeed for 'real' languages like Pascal and C. Another aspect of program verification is **program transformation**, in which programs are transformed to other programs which have the same effect but better performance, for example. Again, this is difficult for traditional imperative languages.

Records and tuples

In Section 2.9 the tuple types of Miranda are introduced. In particular, we saw the definition

```
person == (string,string,num)
```

This compares with a Pascal declaration of a record

```
type person = record
   name  : string;
   phone : string;
   age   : integer
end;
```

which has three fields which have to be named. In Miranda the fields of a tuple can be accessed by pattern matching, but it is possible to define functions called **selectors** which behave in a similar way, if required:

```
name  :: person -> string
name (n,p,a) = n
```

and so on. If per :: person then name per :: string, similarly to r.name being a string variable if r is a variable of type person in Pascal.

Lists and pointers

Miranda contains the type of lists built in, and other recursive types such as trees can be defined directly. We can think of the type of linked lists given by pointers in Pascal as an *implementation* of lists, since in Miranda it is not necessary to think of pointer values, or of storage allocation (new and dispose) as it is in Pascal. Indeed, we can think of Miranda programs as *designs* for Pascal list programs. If we define

```
type list = ^node;
type node = record
   head : value;
   tail : list
end;
```

then we have the following correspondence, where the Miranda hd and tl functions give the head and tail of a list.

```
[]                nil
hd l              x^.head
tl l              x^.tail
(a:x)             cons(a,x)
```

where the function cons in Pascal has the definition

```
function cons(b:value;y:list):list;
  var l:list;
  begin
    new(l);
    l^.head := b;
    l^.tail := y;
    cons := l
  end;
```

Functions such as

```
sumList []    = 0
sumList (a:x) = a + sumList x
```

can then be transferred to Pascal in a straightforward way:

```
function sumList(l:list):integer;
  begin
    if l=nil
      then sumList := 0
      else sumList := l^.head + sumList(l^.tail)
  end;
```

A second example is

```
double []    = []
double (a:x) = (2*a) : double x
```

where we use cons in the Pascal definition of the function

```
function double(l:list):list;
  begin
    if l=nil
      then double := nil
      else double := cons( 2*l^.head , double(l^.tail) )
  end;
```

If we define the functions

```
function hd(l:list):value;        function tl(l:list):list;
   begin                             begin
     hd := l^.head                     tl := l^.tail
   end;                              end;
```

then the correspondence is even clearer

```
function double(l:list):list;
   begin
     if l=nil
       then double := nil
       else double := cons( 2*hd(l) , double( tl(l) ) )
   end;
```

This is strong evidence that a functional approach can be useful even if we are writing in an imperative language: the functional language can be the high-level *design* language for the imperative implementation. Making this separation can give us substantial help in finding imperative programs – we can think about the design and the lower-level implementation *separately*, which makes each problem smaller, simpler and therefore easier to solve.

Higher-order functions

Traditional imperative languages give little scope for higher-order programming; Pascal allows functions as arguments, so long as those functions are not themselves higher-order, but has no facility for returning functions as results.

Control structures like if-then-else bear some resemblance to higher-order functions, as they take commands, c_1, c_2 etc. into other commands,

```
if b then c₁ else c₂        while b do c₁
```

just as map takes one function to another. Turning the analogy around, we can think of higher-order functions as **control structures** which we can define ourselves. This perhaps explains why we form libraries of polymorphic functions: they are the control structures we use in programming particular sorts of system. Examples in the text include libraries for building parsers (Section 12.5) and interactive programs (Section 13.6), as well as the built-in list-processing functions.

Polymorphism

Again, this aspect is poorly represented in most imperative languages; the best we can do in Pascal, say, is to use a text editor to copy and modify the list-processing code from one type of lists for use with another. Of course, we then run the risk that the different versions of the programs are not modified in step, unless we are very careful to keep track of modifications, and so on.

As is argued in the text, polymorphism is one of the mechanisms which helps to make programs *re-usable* in Miranda; it remains to be seen whether this will also be true of advanced imperative languages.

Defining types

The algebraic type mechanism of Miranda, explained in Chapter 9, subsumes various traditional type definitions. Enumerated types are given by algebraic types all of whose constructors are 0-ary (take no arguments); variant records can be implemented as algebraic types with more than one constructor, and *recursive* types usually implemented by means of pointers become recursive algebraic types.

Just as we explained for lists, Miranda programs over trees and so on can be seen as *designs* for programs in imperative languages manipulating the pointer implementations of the types.

Abstypes, introduced in Chapter 11, are very like the abstract data types of Modula-2 and so on; the design methods we suggest for use of abstypes mirror the *object-based* approach advocated for modern imperative languages such as Ada.

List comprehensions

List comprehensions provide a convenient notation for *interaction* along lists; the analogue of a `for` loop, which can be used to run through the indices of an array. For instance, to sum all pairs of elements of `l` and `m`, we write

```
[ a+b | a <- l ; b <- m ]
```

The order of the iteration is for a value a from the list l to be fixed and then for b to run through the possible values from m; this is then repeated with the next value from l, until the list is exhausted. Just the same happens for a *nested* `for` loop:

```
for i:=0 to lLen-1 do
   for j:=0 to mLen-1 do                    (†)
      write( l[i]+m[j] )
```

where we fix a value for i whilst running through all values for j.

In the `for` loop, we have to run through the indices; a list generator runs through the values directly. The indices of the list `l` are given by `[0..#l-1]`, and so a Miranda analogue of (†) can be written thus:

```
[ l!i + m!j | i <- [0..#l-1] ; j <- [0..#m-1] ]
```

if we so wish.

Lazy evaluation

Lazy evaluation and imperative languages do not mix well. In Pascal, for instance, we can write the function definition

```
function succ(x : integer):integer;
begin
  y    := y+1;
  succ := x+1
end;
```

This function adds one to its argument, but also has the *side-effect* of increasing y by one. If we evaluate `f(y,succ(z))` we cannot predict the effect it will have:

- If f evaluates its second argument first, y will be increased before being passed to f; on the other hand,
- if f needs its first argument first (and perhaps its second argument not at all), the value passed to f will not be increased, even if it is increased before the function call terminates.

In general, it will not be possible to predict the behaviour of even the simplest programs. Since evaluating an expression can cause a change of the state, the order of expression evaluation determines the overall effect of a program, and so a lazy implementation can behave differently (in unforeseen ways) from the norm.

State and infinite lists

Section 13.1 introduces infinite lists, and one of the first examples given there was an infinite list of random numbers. This list could be supplied to a function requiring a supply of random numbers; because of lazy evaluation, these numbers will only be generated on demand.

If we were to implement this imperatively, we would probably keep in a variable the last random number generated, and at each request for a number we would update this store. We can see the infinite list as supplying *all the values that the variable will take* as a single structure; we therefore do not need to keep the state, and hence have an *abstraction* from the imperative view.

Conclusion

Clearly, there are parallels between the functional and the imperative, as well as clear differences. The functional view of a system is often higher-level, and so even if we ultimately aim for an imperative solution, a functional *design* or *prototype* can be most useful.

Some languages offer imperative features within a functional framework. Chief among these are Standard ML (Milner *et al.*, 1990), and the Imperative/Functional extension of Haskell (Peyton Jones and Wadler, 1993). If use of the imperative is controlled, many of the benefits of the functional approach carry over, although it remains to be seen whether larger-scale verification is still possible.

APPENDIX B

Further reading

This textbook introduces the fundamentals of lazy functional programming, and from here we can set off in many different directions. This appendix gives some signposts; others are to be found on the World Wide Web page

```
http://www.ukc.ac.uk/computer_science/Miranda_craft/
```

Miranda

The Miranda language was introduced in Turner (1985), and an overview can be found in Turner (1990a). Miranda has been used in a number of larger-scale projects:

- An experimental operating system developed using Miranda is described in Turner (1987) and Cupitt (1989).
- Researchers at the National Institute of Health in Bethesda, Maryland, have developed in Miranda a suite of programs called MC-SYM for computing the three-dimensional structure of protein molecules by energy minimization; details are given in Major *et al.* (1991).
- Engineers at the Logica company in Cambridge, England, have been using Miranda to describe integrated circuits. By a series of transformations these programs can be turned into actual circuit designs. A complete microprocessor called Viper 2 was developed using this method. For an overview see Dettmer (1989).

Underpinning the work on proving properties of Miranda programs are the papers by Thompson (1989, 1995), which present a method of translating Miranda scripts into logical formulas, and give some example proofs. (Texts on logic and discrete mathematics abound; two serviceable texts on logic for computer scientists are Galton (1990), and Reeves and Clarke (1990), each of which provides sufficient background to make sense of this logical rendering of Miranda.)

Other functional programming languages

Haskell is a recently developed lazy functional language, similar to Miranda in many respects. Its major innovation is the notion of type classes (Wadler and Blott, 1989), which allow names to be overloaded, meaning different things at different types (just as show in Miranda). A description of Haskell is given in Hudak *et al.* (1992), and in the same volume can be found a tutorial (Hudak and Fasel, 1992) on the language. Gofer (Jones, 1994) can be seen as based on a subset of Haskell, but with a rather more sophisticated class system.

A functional language is *strict* if arguments are evaluated before being passed to functions. The most widely-used strict but strongly-typed functional programming language is Standard ML (Milner *et al.*, 1990), for which Paulson (1991) provides an introduction.

A different style of functional programming, eschewing variables as much as possible, was introduced in Backus (1978). An imperative language, used for telephone switching and other real-time applications, with functionally-inspired features is ERLANG (Armstrong *et al.*, 1993).

More advanced topics

Turner (1990b) is a useful survey of research topics in functional programming. In that volume, Bird (1990) gives examples in the 'Bird-Meertens' style of program transformation, Hughes (1990) argues powerfully for the advantages of a lazy programming style, and Thompson (1990) explores the foundations of interactive programming as discussed in this text. Another source of program transformation examples is Darlington (1982), which is also a part of a useful collection of papers.

A novel approach to I/O and programming systems with state is given by **monads**, as suggested by Moggi, and developed by Wadler, who (1992) gives a readable introduction to the issues involved. How programs like these can be verified is a topic of Gordon (1994), which also contains a useful survey of the field, showing its tortuous history. A general reference on verification of functional programs is provided by Paulson (1987), while Sanella (1986) investigates how functional programs can best have their properties specified.

Foundations and future developments

Type polymorphism was first introduced in Milner (1978), and the field of more advanced type systems is surveyed in the useful Cardelli and Wegner (1985). The lambda calculus is one of the historical roots of functional programming; Barendregt (1993) gives an overview of the foundations of the typed lambda calculus, as well as of more recent innovations, which are also surveyed in Huet (1990). Constructive type theories can be seen as simultaneously functional languages and logics; Thompson (1991), Girard *et al.* (1989) and Luo (1994) give three complementary perspectives.

Functional programming in education

A special edition of the *Journal of Functional Programming* (Thompson, 1993) explores ways in which functional programming can be taught.

Implementation techniques

In the last ten years, powerful techniques of implementation of lazy functional languages have been developed. The twin texts Peyton Jones (1987) and Peyton Jones and Lester (1992) describe these in lucid detail; the latter uses Miranda as its description vehicle.

APPENDIX C

Glossary

We include this glossary to give a quick reference to the most widely-used terminology in the book. Words appearing in **bold** in the descriptions have their own entries. Further references and examples are to be found by consulting the index.

Abstract Type An abstract type definition consists of the type name, the **signature** of the type, and the implementation equations for the names in the signature.

Algebraic Type An algebraic type definition states what are the **constructors** of the type. For instance, the declaration

```
tree ::= Leaf num |
         Node tree tree
```

says that the two constructors of the tree type are Leaf and Node, and that their types are, respectively,

```
Leaf :: num->tree
Node :: tree->tree->tree
```

Application This means giving values to (some of) the arguments of a function. If an n-argument function is given fewer than n arguments, this is called a **partial application**.

Argument A **function** takes one or more arguments into an **output**. Arguments are also known as **inputs** and **parameters**.

Base Types The types of numbers, num, **Booleans**, bool, and characters, char.

Booleans The type containing the two 'truth values' True and False.

Calculation A calculation is a line-by-line **evaluation** of a Miranda **expression** on paper. Calculations use the **definitions** which are contained in a **script**, as well as the built-in definitions.

Cancellation The rule for finding the type of a partial application.

Character A single letter, such as 's' or '\t', the tab character.

Clause A clause is one of the alternatives lying on the right-hand side of an **equation**. A clause consists of an **expression**, and in some cases a **guard**. When evaluating a function application, the first clause whose guard evaluates to True is chosen.

Combinator Another name for a **function**.

Comment Part of a **script** which plays no computational role; it is there for the reader to read and observe.

Complexity A measurement of the time or space behaviour of a function.

Composition The combination of two functions by passing the **output** of one to the **input** of the other.

Constructor An **algebraic type** is specified by its constructors, which are the functions which build elements of the algebraic type.

In the example in the entry for algebraic types, elements of the type are constructed using Leaf and Node; the elements are Leaf n where n::num and Node s t, where s and t are trees.

Curried Function A function of two arguments which takes its arguments one at a time

    t1 -> t2 -> t

in contrast to the **uncurried** version

    (t1,t2) -> t

The name is in honour of Haskell B. Curry.

Declaration A **definition** can be accompanied by a statement of the **type** of the object defined; these are often called **type declarations**.

Definition A definition associates a **value** or a **type** with a **name**.

Design In writing a system, the effort expended *before* implementation is started.

Directive A directive is an instruction to the Miranda system. These begin with the '%' character, and include %export and %include.

Enumerated Type An **algebraic type** with each constructor having no arguments.

Equation A **definition** in Miranda consists of a number of equations. On the left-hand side of the equation is a **name** applied to zero or more **patterns**; on the right-hand side are one or more **clauses**.

Evaluation Every **expression** in Miranda has a value; evaluation is the process of finding that value. A **calculation** evaluates an expression, as does the Miranda system when that expression is typed to the Miranda prompt.

Expression An expression is formed by applying a **function** or **operator** to its arguments; these arguments can be **literal** values, or expressions themselves. A simple numerical expression is (2+8)-10, in which the operator '-' is applied to two arguments.

Extensionality The principle of proof which says that two functions are equal if they give equal results for every input.

Filter To pick out those elements of a list which have a particular property, represented by a Boolean-valued function.

Fold To combine the elements of a list using a binary **operation**.

Fraction A number which is given in decimal (e.g. 456.23) or exponent (e.g. 4.5623e+2) form; not an **integer**, in other words.

Function A function is an object which returns a **value**, called the **output** or **result** when it is applied to its **inputs**. The inputs are also known as its **parameters** or **arguments**.

Examples include the square root function, whose input and output are numbers, and the function which returns the borrowers (output) of a book (input) in a database (input).

Function Types The type of a **function** is a function type, so that, for instance, the function which checks whether its argument is even has type num->bool. This is the type of functions with **input** type num and **output** type bool.

Generalization Replacing an object by something of which the original object is an instance.

This might be the replacement of a function by a polymorphic function from which the original is obtained by passing the appropriate parameter, or replacing a logical formula by one which implies the original.

Guard The **Boolean** expression appearing to the right of if in the **clauses** on the right-hand side of an **equation** in a Miranda **definition**.

Higher-order Function A **function** is higher-order if either one of its **arguments** or its **result**, or both, are functions.

Identifier Another word for **name**.

Implementation The particular **definitions** which make a design concrete; for an **abstract data type**, the definitions of the objects named in the **signature**.

Induction The name for a collection of methods of proof, by which statements of the form 'for all x ...' are proved.

Infix An **operation** which appears between its **arguments**.

Input A **function** takes one or more inputs into an **output**. Inputs are also known as **arguments** and **parameters**. The 'square' function takes a single numerical input, for instance.

Instance An instance of a type is given by **substituting** a type expression for a type **variable**. For example, [(bool,**)] is an instance of [*], given by substituting (bool,**) for the variable *.

Integers The positive and negative whole numbers. In Miranda these are represented exactly, so that evaluating 2 to the power 1000 will give a result consisting of some three hundred digits.

Interactive Program A program which reads from and writes to the terminal; reading and writing will be *interspersed*, in general.

Interface The common information which is shared between two program modules.

Lazy Evaluation The type of expression **evaluation** in Miranda. In a function application only those arguments whose values are *needed* will be evaluated, and moreover, only the parts of structures which are needed will be examined.

Linear Complexity Order 1, $O(^1)$, behaviour.

Lists A list consists of a collection of elements of a particular type, given in some order. The list $[2,1,3,2]$ is of type $[num]$, for example.

Literal Something that is 'literally' a value: it needs no **evaluation**. Examples include 34, $[23]$ and $"string"$.

Local Definitions The definitions appearing in a where clause. Their **scope** is the equation to which the clause is attached.

Map To apply an operation to every element of a list.

Mathematical Induction A method of proof for statements of the form 'for all natural numbers n, the statement $P(n)$ holds for n'.

   The proof is in two parts: the base case, at zero, and the induction step, at which $P(n+1)$ is proved on the assumption that $P(n)$ holds.

Memoization Keeping the value of a sub-computation in a list, so that it can be re-used rather than re-computed, when it is needed.

Module Another name for a **script**; used particularly when more than one script is used to build a program.

Monomorphic A type is **monomorphic** if it is not **polymorphic**.

Most General Type The most general type of an expression is the type t with the property that every other type for the expression is an **instance** of t.

Mutual Recursion Two definitions, each of which depends upon the object defined in the other.

Name A **definition** associates a name or **identifier** with a value. Names of **constructors** must begin with capital letters, names of other values and types must begin with small letters. After the first letter, any letter, digit, '$'$' or '$\_$' can be used.

Natural Numbers The non-negative whole numbers: $0, 1, 2, \ldots$.

Offside Rule The way in which the end of a part of a definition is expressed using the *layout* of a **script**, rather than an explicit symbol for the end.

Operation Another name for **function**.

Operator A **function** which is written in infix form, between its **arguments**. The function f is made infix thus: $\$f$.

Operator Section A partially applied operator.

Output When a **function** is applied to one or more **inputs**, the resulting value is called the output, or **result**. Applying the 'square' function to (-2) gives the output 4, for example.

Overloading The use of the same **name** to mean two (or more) different things, at different types. The equality operation, $=$, is an example. This is different from **polymorphism**, where the *same* definition applies at different types.

Parameter A **function** takes one or more parameters into an **output**. Parameters are also known as **arguments** and **inputs**, and applying a function to its inputs is sometimes known as 'passing its parameters'.

Parsing Revealing the structure of a sentence in a formal language.

Partial Application A **function** of type $t_1 \rightarrow t_2 \rightarrow \ldots \rightarrow t_n \rightarrow t$ can be applied to n arguments, or less. In the latter case, the **application** is partial, since the result can itself be passed further parameters.

Pattern A pattern is either a **variable** or the application of a **constructor** to other patterns. Over the natural numbers 0 and '+k' for **literal** k are treated as constructors.

Polymorphism A type is polymorphic if it contains type **variables**; such a type will have many **instances**.

Prefix An **operation** which appears before its **arguments**.

Primitive Recursion Over the natural numbers, defining the values of a function outright at zero, and at $(n+1)$ using the value at n.

   Over an **algebraic type** defining the function by cases over the constructors; recursion is permitted at constructors which are themselves recursive.

Proof A logical argument which leads us to accept a logical statement as being valid.

Quadratic Complexity Order two, $O(^2)$, behaviour.

Recursion Using an object (value or type) in its own **definition**.

Result When a **function** is applied to one or more **inputs**, the resulting value is called the result, or **output**.

Scope The area of a program in which a **definition** or definitions are applicable.

The scope of top-level definitions in Miranda is by default the whole **script** in which they appear; it may be extended by %include directives, for example. More limited scopes are given by **local definitions**.

Script A script is a file containing **definitions**, **declarations** and compiler **directives**.

Set A collection of objects for which the order of elements and the number of occurrences of each element are irrelevant.

Signature A sequence of type **declarations**. These declarations state what are the types of the operations (or functions) over an **abstract type** which can be used to manipulate elements of that type.

String The type string is a **synonym** for lists of characters, [char].

Structural Induction A method of proof for statements of the form 'for all lists l, the statement P(l) holds of l'. The proof is in two parts: the base case, at [], and the induction step, at which P(a:x) is proved on the assumption that P(x) holds.

Also used of the related principle for any algebraic type.

Substitution The replacement of a **variable** by an **expression**. For example, (9+12) is given by substituting 12 for n in (9+n).

Synonym Naming a type is called a type synonym. The symbol == is used for synonyms.

Syntax The description of the properly formed programs (or sentences) of a language.

Transformation Turning one program into another program which computes identical results, but with superior behaviour in other respects.

Tuples A tuple type is built up from a number of component types. Elements of the type consist of elements of the component types, so that

    (2,True,3) :: (num,bool,num)

for instance.

Type A collection of data values. Types can be built from the **base** types using **tuple**, **list** and **function types**. New types can be defined using the **algebraic** and **abstract** type mechanisms, and types can be named using the type **synonym** mechanism.

Undefinedness The result of an expression whose evaluation continues forever, rather than giving a *defined* result.

Unification The process of finding a common **instance** of two (type) expressions containing (type) variables.

Value A value is a member of some **type**; the value of an **expression** is the result of **evaluating** the expression.

Variable A variable stands for an *arbitrary* value, or in the case of type variables, an arbitrary type. Variables have the same syntax as **names**; type variables are denoted by sequences of stars, *, ** and so on.

Verification Proving that a function or functions have particular logical properties.

Where clause Another term for a **local definition**.

APPENDIX D

Understanding programs

This appendix is included to offer help to readers confronted with an unfamiliar function definition. There are various things we can do with the definition, and these are examined in turn here. Given a functional program like

```
mapWhile :: (* -> **) -> (* -> bool) -> [*] -> [**]

mapWhile f p []    = []                            (1)
mapWhile f p (a:x) = f a : mapWhile f p x   , if p a    (2)
                   = []                      , otherwise (3)
```

we can understand what it means in various complementary ways. We can read the program itself, we can write *calculations* of examples using the program, we can *prove* properties of the program, and we can estimate its space and time complexity,

Reading the program

Besides any comments which might accompany a program, the program itself is its most important documentation.

The type declaration gives information about the input and output types: for `mapWhile`, we have to supply three arguments:

- a function, f say, of arbitrary type, * -> **;
- a *property* of objects of type *; that is, a function taking a * to a Boolean value; and
- a list of items of type *.

The output is a list of elements of type ** – the output type of f.

The function definition itself is used to give values of mapWhile, but can also be read directly as a description of the program:

- On [], the result is [].

- On a non-empty list, if the head a has property p, then according to (2), we have f a as the first element of the result, with the remainder given by a recursive call on x.

- If the property p fails of a, the result is terminated, as it were, by returning the empty list [].

In the definition we have a complete description of how the program behaves, but we can animate this by trying specific examples.

Calculating with the program

A more concrete view of what the program does is given by calculating particular examples. For instance,

```
mapWhile (2+) (>7) [9,12,3,13,16]
= 2+9 : mapWhile (2+) (>7) [12,3,13,16]          by (2)
= 11 : 2+12 : mapWhile (2+) (>7) [3,13,16]       by (2)
= 11 : 14 : []                                   by (3)
= [11,14]
```

Other examples include

```
mapWhile (2+) (>2) [9,12,3,13,16] = [11,14,5,15,18]
mapWhile (2+) (>2) [] = []
```

Reasoning about the program

We can get a deeper understanding about a program by *proving* properties that the program might have. For mapWhile, we might prove that for all f, p and finite lists x,

```
mapWhile f p x                = map f (takewhile p x)
mapWhile f (const True) x = map f x
mapWhile id p x                = takewhile p x
```

where we can, in fact, see (5) and (6) as consequences of the characterization of mapWhile given by property (4).

Program behaviour

It is not hard to see that the program will at worst take time linear (that is $O(^\wedge 1)$) in the length of the list argument assuming $O(^\wedge 0)$ behaviour of f and p, as it runs through the elements of the list once, if at all.

The *space* behaviour is more interesting; because we can output the head of a list once produced, the space required will be constant, as suggested by underlining the parts which can be output in the calculation above:

```
  mapWhile (2+) (>7) [9,12,3,13,16]
= 2+9 : mapWhile (2+) (>7) [12,3,13,16]
= 11 : 2+12 : mapWhile (2+) (>7) [3,13,16]
= 11 : 14 : [] = [11,14]
```

Getting started

Each view of the program gives us a different understanding about its behaviour, but when we are presented with an unfamiliar definition we can begin to understand what its effect is by calculating various small examples. If we are given a collection of functions, we can test out the functions from the bottom up, building one calculation on top of another.

The important thing is to realize that rather than being stuck, we can get started by calculating representative examples to show us the way.

APPENDIX E

Miranda operators

The Miranda operators are listed below in increasing order of binding power: operators lower in the table bind more tightly than the ones above. See Section 2.3 for a discussion of associativity and binding power.

Operator	Associativity
: ++ --	right
\/	associative
&	associative
~	prefix
> >= = ~= <= <	
+ -	left
-	prefix
* / div mod	left
^	right
.	associative
#	prefix
!	left
$ident $Ident	right

APPENDIX F

Miranda errors

The programs we write all too often contain errors. On encountering an error, the Miranda system either halts, and gives an **error message**, or continues, but gives a **warning message** to tell us that something unusual has happened, which might signal we have made an error. In this appendix, we look at a selection of the messages output by Miranda; we have chosen the messages which are both common and require some explanation; messages like

```
"otherwise" must be last case
ATTEMPT TO TAKE hd OF []
```

are self-explanatory. The messages are classified into roughly distinct areas. Syntax errors show up malformed programs, whilst type errors show well-formed programs in which objects are used at the wrong types. In fact, an ill-formed expression can often show itself as a type error and not as a syntax error, so the boundaries are not clear.

Syntax errors

The Miranda system attempts to match the input we give to the syntax of the language. Commonly, when something goes wrong, we type something *unexpected*. Typing '2=3)' will provoke the error message

```
syntax error - unexpected token ')'
```

Missing parts of a definition are signalled in the obvious way, with messages like

```
missing guard
```

while the inclusion of type declarations or definitions in a where clause are signalled by

```
'==' encountered in local defs
```

An important error message from the definition syntax is

```
syntax error: unreachable case in defn of "fishcake"
```

which points to a situation like

```
fishcake x (b:y) = ...                              (1)
fishcake x []    = ...                              (2)
fishcake z w     = ...                              (3)
```

in which (1) deals with a non-empty list as second argument, and (2) with an empty list; these cover all the possibilities and so the equation (3) can never be 'reached'. Errors like this often come from mis-typing: perhaps in (2) we meant to type fishcake (a:x) [] on the left-hand side.

The syntax of patterns is more restricted than the full expression syntax, and so we get error messages like

```
inappropriate use of "+" in pattern
```

when we give an over-complicated pattern involving numbers.

In specifying constants, we can make errors: floating point numbers can be too large, and characters specified by an out-of-range ASCII code:

```
syntax error: out-of-range char const ('\999')
floating point number out of range
```

Not every string can be used as a name; some words in Miranda are *keywords*, and will give an error if used as an identifier. The keywords are

```
abstype div if mod otherwise readvals show type where with
```

Other definitions are built into the *standard environment* – see Appendix G – and so if re-defined will give error messages, thus:

```
syntax error: type of ... already declared
 (in standard environment)
```

The final restriction on names is that names of constructors must being with a capital letter; nothing else can do so, and hence we get error messages like

```
upper case identifier cannot be used as typename
```

Type errors

As we have seen in the body of the text, the main type error we meet is exemplified by the response to typing 4 + True:

```
type error in expression
cannot unify bool with num
```

which is provoked by using a bool where a num is expected. To locate the source of such an error in general, we have to look for a function which expects a num, but is supplied with a bool.

As we said before, we can get type errors from syntax errors. For example, writing abs -2 instead of abs (-2) gives the error message

```
cannot unify num->num with num
```

because it is parsed as 2 subtracted from abs::num->num, and the operator '−' expects a num, rather than a function of type num->num. Other common errors are

```
cannot unify num with [*]
cannot cons [num] to [num]
```

given by 2++[2] and [2]:[2], which confuse the roles of ':' and '++'.

We always give type declarations for our definitions; one advantage of this is to spot when our definition does not conform to its declared type. For example,

```
myCheck :: num -> bool
myCheck n = n+0
```

gives the error message

```
incorrect declaration (line ... of script ...)
specified, myCheck::num->bool
inferred,  myCheck::num->num
```

Without the type declaration the definition would be accepted, only to give an error (presumably) when it is used.

The show function, which will give a printable version of objects that are not functions, must always be used in a *monomorphic* way; failure to do so will give the message

```
use of "show" at polymorphic type
```

A final error related to types is given by definitions like

```
tree == (num,tree,tree)                              (†)
```

a *recursive* type synonym; these are signalled by

```
error: cycle in type "==" definition
```

The effect of (†) can be modelled by the algebraic type definition

```
tree ::= Node num tree tree
```

which introduces the *constructor* Node to identify objects of this type.

Program errors

Once we have written a correct script, and asked for the value of an expression which is itself acceptable, other errors can be produced during the *evaluation* of the expression.

The first class of errors comes from missing cases in definitions. If we have written the definition ourself, we get

```
program error: missing case in definition of ...
```

whilst some of the functions in the standard environment have their own error messages:

```
foldl1 applied to []
ATTEMPT TO TAKE tl OF []
```

Other errors happen because an *arithmetical constraint* has been broken. These include an out-of-range list index, division by zero, using a fraction where an integer is expected and floating point calculations which go out of range:

```
subscript out of range
attempt to divide by zero
program error: fractional number where integer expected
floating point number out of range
```

If we make a conformal definition, like

```
[a,b] = [1..10]
```

this will fail with

```
program error: lhs of definition doesn't match rhs
```

if the left-hand side fails to match the value on the right; that is clearly the situation here, where the right-hand side has ten elements.

Evaluation in Miranda is by need, and so a script which uses a name with no corresponding definition for the name will not be in error; only if the value of that name is required will we get the message

```
UNDEFINED NAME - ...
```

Finally, if we write a definition like c=c, an attempt to evaluate c gives no result; some recursions, such as

```
c = d where d=d
```

can be *detected* as being circular, and an attempt to evaluate c gives

```
BLACK HOLE
```

before halting evaluation.

Module errors

The %include and %export statements can provoke a variety of error messages: files may not be present, or may contain errors; names may be included more than once, or an alias on inclusion may cause a name clash. The error messages for these and other errors are self-explanatory.

Warnings

Various situations are acceptable, but may indicate that something is wrong with a script. Among these are:

- Specifying the type of an object, but giving it no definition. This is signalled by the message SPECIFIED BUT NOT DEFINED: ....
- Failing to give any information about an object. This is signalled by the message WARNING, SCRIPT CONTAINS UNDEFINED NAMES: ....

- Local definitions which are not used. The combination of this with an 'UNDEFINED' message often signals that a name has been mis-typed: the name we *should* use is unused, whilst the name we *do* use is undefined.

Various warnings are also generated by the module system; their meaning is clear.

Top-level errors

Apart from the syntax errors of mis-typed commands, and commands with missing arguments, like '??', readvals and $+ give rise to various errors if the type of the input expressions is incorrect. Typical messages are

```
data has wrong type ::
readvals: bad data in file "%s"
```

System messages

In response to some commands and interrupts, the system generates messages, including

```
<<compilation interrupted>>
<<interrupt>>
```

signalling the interruption of the current task,

```
<<not enough heap space -- task abandoned>>
```

which shows that the space consumption of the evaluation exceeds that available. One way around this is to increase the size of the heap. Typing /heap gives the current size, and

```
/heap 100000
```

changes the heap size to 100000, if possible, replying with

```
heaplimit = 100000 cells
```

If not, the message

```
illegal value (heap unchanged)
```

will be returned.

If the /count command is performed, after each evaluation the system prints diagnostic information of the form

```
reductions = 2004, cells claimed = 530564,
no of gc's = 5, cpu = 19.02
```

The number of reductions corresponds to the number of steps in our calculations, the cells claimed to the total space usage and the cpu to the time (in seconds) used by the central processing unit of the computer system. Space can be re-cycled after it is no longer used; the *garbage collector* performs this task when it is necessary, and the no of gc's indicates how many garbage collections have taken place during evaluation.

A measure of the space complexity of a function, as described in Chapter 14, is given by the size of the smallest heap in which the evaluation can take place; there is no direct measure of this given by the system.

Some useful functions

abs takes the absolute value of a number – abs (-3) is 3, abs 3.5 is 3.5.

```
abs::num->num
abs x = -x, if x<0
      =  x, otherwise
```

Applied to a list of truth values and gives their logical conjunction:

```
and::[bool]->bool
and = foldr (&) True
```

cjustify applied to a number and a string, centre-justifies the string in a field of the specified width. See also ljustify, rjustify, spaces:

```
cjustify::num->[char]->[char]
cjustify n s = spaces lmargin++s++spaces rmargin
               where
               margin = n - #s
               lmargin = margin div 2
               rmargin = margin - lmargin
```

concat applied to a list of lists, joins them together into a single list with ++. For example, concat [[1,2],[],[3,4]] is [1,2,3,4]:

```
concat::[[*]]->[*]
concat = foldr (++) []
```

const is a combinator for creating constant-valued functions – (const 3) is the function that always returns 3:

```
const::*->**->*
const x y = x
```

converse is a combinator for inverting the order of arguments of a two-argument function:

```
converse::(*->**->***)->**->*->***
converse f a b = f b a
```

digit is a predicate on characters which returns True if the character is a digit; see also letter:

```
digit::char->bool
digit x = '0'<=x<='9'
```

drop, applied to a number and a list, returns the list with that many elements removed from the front. If the list has less than the required number of elements, drop returns []. For example,

```
drop 2 [1,2,3,4] = [3,4]
```

See also take.

```
drop::num->[*]->[*]
drop (n+1) (a:x) = drop n x
drop n x = x, if integer n
         = error "drop applied to fraction", otherwise
```

dropwhile, applied to a predicate and a list, removes elements from the front of the list while the predicate is satisfied. An example is

```
dropwhile digit "123gone" = "gone"
```

See also takewhile.

```
dropwhile::(*->bool)->[*]->[*]
dropwhile f [] = []
dropwhile f (a:x) = dropwhile f x, if f a
                  = a:x, otherwise
```

error applied to a string creates an error value with the associated message. Error values are all equivalent to the undefined value – any attempt to access the value causes the program to terminate and print the string as a diagnostic. It is defined internally:

```
error::[char]->*
```

filter, applied to a predicate and a list, returns a list containing only those elements that satisfy the predicate. Example:

```
filter (>5) [3,7,2,8,1,17] = [7,8,17]

filter::(*->bool)->[*]->[*]
filter f x = [a | a<-x; f a]
```

foldl folds up a list, using a given binary operator and a given start value, in a left-associative way. Example:

```
foldl op r [a,b,c] = (((r $op a) $op b) $op c)
```

But note that to run in constant space, foldl forces op to evaluate its first parameter by means of the built-in seq operator. See the definitions of product, reverse, sum for examples of its use, and see also foldr:

```
foldl::(*->**->*)->*->[**]->*
foldl op r [] = r
foldl op r (a:x) = foldl op (strict op r a) x
                   where
                   strict f x = seq x (f x)
```

foldl1 folds left over non-empty lists. See the definitions of max, min for examples of its use:

```
foldl1::(*->*->*)->[*]->*
foldl1 op (a:x) = foldl op a x
foldl1 op [] = error "foldl1 applied to []"
```

foldr folds up a list, using a given binary operator and a given start value, in a right-associative way. Example:

```
foldr op r [a,b,c] = a $op (b $op (c $op r))
```

See the definitions of and, concat, or, for examples of its use:

```
foldr::(*->**->**)->**->[*]->**
foldr op r [] = r
foldr op r (a:x) = op a (foldr op r x)
```

`foldr1` folds right over non-empty lists:

```
foldr1::(*->*->*)->[*]->*
foldr1 op [a] = a
foldr1 op (a:b:x) = op a (foldr1 op (b:x))
foldr1 op [] = error "foldr1 applied to []"
```

`fst` returns the first component of a pair. See also `snd`:

```
fst::(*,**)->*
fst (a,b) = a
```

`hd` applied to a non-empty list, returns its first element. It is an error to apply `hd` to the empty list, `[]`; see also `tl`:

```
hd::[*]->*
hd (a:x) = a
hd [] = error "hd []"
```

`id` is the identity function – applied to any object it returns that object:

```
id::*->*
id x = x
```

`index` applied to a (finite or infinite) list, returns a list of its legal subscript values, in ascending order.

```
index "hippopotamus" is [0,1,2,3,4,5,6,7,8,9,10,11].
```

```
index::[*]->[num]
index x = f 0 x
          where
          f n [] = []
          f n (a:x) = n:f(n+1)x
```

`init` is dual to `tl`, it returns a list without its last component. For instance,

```
init [1,2,3,4] = [1,2,3].
```

See also `last`. [Note, by the dual of a list-processing function we mean the function which does the same job in a world where all lists have been reversed.]

```
init::[*]->[*]
init (a:x) = [], if x=[]
           = a:init x, otherwise
init [] = error "init []"
```

iterate – iterate f x returns the infinite list [x, f x, f(f x), ...].
Example, iterate (2*) 1 yields a list of the powers of 2:

```
iterate::(*->*)->*->[*]
iterate f x = x:iterate f(f x)
```

last applied to a non-empty list returns its last element. This function is the
dual of hd. Note that for any non-empty list x:

```
(init x ++ [last x]) = x

last::[*]->*
last x = x!(#x-1)
```

lay, applied to a list of strings, joins them together after appending a
newline character to each string. Example:

```
lay ["hello","world"] = "hello\nworld\n"
```

Used to format output thus, lay(map show x) as a top level expression,
causes the elements of the list x to be printed one per line; see also layn,
lines:

```
lay::[[char]]->[char]
lay [] = []
lay (a:x) = a++"\n"++lay x
```

layn is similar to lay, but produces output with numbered lines:

```
layn::[[char]]->[char]
layn x
  = f 1 x
    where
    f n [] = []
    f n (a:x) = rjustify 4 (show n) ++ ") " ++
                a ++ "\n" ++ f (n+1) x
```

letter is a predicate on characters which returns True if the character is a
letter:

```
letter::char->bool
letter c = 'a'<=c<='z' \/ 'A'<=c<='Z'
```

limit, applied to a list of values, returns the first value which is the same as
its successor. Useful in testing for convergence. For example, the following

Miranda expression computes the square root of 2 by the Newton–Raphson method:

```
limit [x | x<-1, 0.5*(x + 2/x).. ]

limit::[*]->*
limit (a:b:x) = a, if a=b
              = limit (b:x), otherwise
limit other = error "incorrect use of limit"
```

lines applied to a list of characters containing newlines, returns a list of lists, by breaking the original into lines. The newline characters are removed from the result. Example, lines applied to

```
"hello world\nit's me,\neric\n"
```

returns ["hello world","it's me","eric"]. Note that lines treats newline as a terminator, not a separator (although it will tolerate a missing '\n' on the last line):

```
lines::[char]->[[char]]
lines [] = []
lines (a:x) = []:lines x, if a='\n'
            = (a:x1):xrest, otherwise
              where
              (x1:xrest) = lines x, if x~=[]
                         = []:[], otherwise
                                    || handles missing '\n'
                                    || on last line
```

Note that the inverse of lines is the function lay, in that applying lay to the output of lines will restore the original string (except that a final newline will be added, if missing in the original string).

ljustify, applied to a number and a string, left-justifies the string in a field of the specified width:

```
ljustify::num->[char]->[char]
ljustify n s = s++spaces(n - #s)
```

map applied to a function and a list returns a copy of the list in which the given function has been applied to every element:

```
map::(*->**)->[*]->[**]
map f x = [f a | a<-x]
```

map2 is similar to map, but takes a function of two arguments, and maps it along two argument lists. We could also define map3, map4 etc., but they are much less often needed:

```
map2::(*->**->***)->[*]->[**]->[***]
map2 f x y = [f a b | (a,b)<-zip2 x y]
```

max applied to a list returns the largest element under the built-in ordering of >. Example:

```
max "hippopotamus" = 'u'
```

See also min, sort:

```
max::[*]->*
max = foldl1 max2
```

max2 applied to two values of the same type returns the larger under the built-in ordering of >; see also min2:

```
max2::*->*->*
max2 a b = a, if a>=b
         = b, otherwise
```

member applied to a list and a value returns True or False as the value is or not present in the list:

```
member::[*]->*->bool
member x a = or (map (=a) x)
```

merge applied to two sorted lists merges them to produce a single sorted result. Used to define sort, see below:

```
merge :: [*]->[*]->[*]
merge [] y = y
merge (a:x) [] = a:x
merge (a:x) (b:y) = a:merge x (b:y), if a<=b
                  = b:merge (a:x) y, otherwise
```

min applied to a list returns its least member under <:

```
min::[*]->*
min = foldl1 min2
```

min2 returns the smaller of its two arguments under the built-in ordering <:

```
min2::*->*->*
min2 a b = b, if a>b
         = a, otherwise
```

mkset applied to a list returns a copy of the list from which any duplicated elements have been removed. A list without duplications can be used to represent a set, whence the name. Works even on an infinite list, but (beware) takes a time quadratic in the number of elements processed:

```
mkset::[*]->[*]
mkset [] = []
mkset (a:x) = a:filter (~=a) (mkset x)
```

or applied to a list of truth values, takes their logical disjunction:

```
or::[bool]->bool
or = foldr (\/) False
```

postfix takes an element and a list and adds the element to the end of the list. This is the dual of the prefix operator (:):

```
postfix::*->[*]->[*]
postfix a x = x ++ [a]
```

product applied to a list of numbers returns their product; see also sum:

```
product::[num]->num
product = foldl (*) 1
```

rep applied to a number and a value, returns a list containing the specified number of instances of the value. (The name is short for replicate.) For example:

```
rep 6 'o' = "oooooo"
```

See also repeat.

```
rep::num->*->[*]
rep n x = take n (repeat x)
```

`repeat` applied to a value returns an infinite list, all of whose elements are the given value:

```
repeat::*->[*]
repeat x = xs
          where xs = x:xs
```

`reverse` applied to any finite list returns a list of the same elements in reverse order:

```
reverse::[*]->[*]
reverse = foldl (converse(:)) []
```

`rjustify`, applied to a number and a string, right-justifies the string in a field of the specified width:

```
rjustify::num->[char]->[char]
rjustify n s = spaces(n - #s)++s
```

`scan op r` applies `foldl op r` to every initial segment of a list. For example `scan (+) 0 x` computes running sums of the numbers in the list x:

```
scan::(*->**->*)->*->[**]->[*]
scan op = g
          where
          g r [] = [r]
          g r (a:x) = r:g (op r a) x
```

There is another way to explain `scan`, which makes it clearer why it is useful. Let s_0 be the initial state of an automaton, whose state transition function is `f::state->input->state`. The function `scan f` s_0 then takes a list of inputs for the automaton and returns the resulting list of states, starting with s_0.

`snd` returns the second component of a pair:

```
snd::(*,**)->**
snd (a,b) = b
```

`sort` applied to any finite list sorts the elements of the list into ascending order on the built-in < relation. Note that you cannot sort a list of functions. Example:

```
sort "hippopotamus" = "ahimoopppstu"
```

The following definition uses merge-sort, which has $O(nLog)$ worst-case behaviour:

```
sort::[*]->[*]
sort x = x, if n<=1
       = merge (sort(take n2 x)) (sort(drop n2 x))
                                          , otherwise
          where
          n = #x
          n2 = n div 2
```

spaces applied to a number returns a list of that many spaces:

```
spaces::num->[char]
spaces n = rep n ' '
```

sum applied to a list of numbers returns their sum:

```
sum::[num]->num
sum = foldl (+) 0
```

take applied to a number and a list returns the specified number of elements from the front of the list. If the list has less than the required number of elements, take returns as many as it can get. For example:

```
take 2 [1,2,3,4] = [1,2]

take::num->[*]->[*]
take (n+1) (a:x) = a:(take n x)
take n x = [], if integer n
         = error "take applied to fraction", otherwise
```

takewhile applied to a predicate and a list, takes elements from the front of the list while the predicate is satisfied. For instance,

```
takewhile digit "123gone" = "123"

takewhile::(*->bool)->[*]->[*]
takewhile f [] = []
takewhile f (a:x) = a:takewhile f x, if f a
                  = [], otherwise
```

tl applied to a non-empty list returns the list without its first element. Example, tl "snow" is "now":

```
tl::[*]->[*]
tl (a:x) = x
tl [] = error "tl []"
```

`transpose` applied to a list of lists, returns their transpose (in the sense of matrix transpose – rows and columns are interchanged). Example:

```
transpose [[1,2,3],[4,5,6]] = [[1,4],[2,5],[3,6]]
```

The following definition is slightly more subtle than is at first sight necessary, in order to deal correctly with *upper triangular* matrices. Example:

```
transpose [[1,2,3],[4,5],[6]] = [[1,4,6],[2,5],[3]]

transpose :: [[*]]->[[*]]
transpose x = [], if x'=[]
            = map hd x':transpose(map tl x'), otherwise
              where
              x' = takewhile (~=[]) x
```

It might be thought that this function belongs in a specialized library of matrix-handling functions, but it has been found useful as a general purpose list-processing function, whence its inclusion in the standard environment.

`undef` is a name for the completely undefined value. Any attempt to access it results in an error message. Note that `undef` belongs to every type:

```
undef::*
undef = error "undefined"
```

`until` applied to a predicate, a function and a value, returns the result of applying the function to the value the smallest number of times necessary to satisfy the predicate. Example:

```
until (>1000) (2*) 1 = 1024

until::(*->bool)->(*->*)->*->*
until f g x = x, if f x
            = until f g (g x), otherwise
```

`zip2` applied to two lists returns a list of pairs, formed by tupling together corresponding elements of the given lists. Example:

```
zip2 [0..3] "type" = [(0,'t'),(1,'y'),(2,'p'),(3,'e')]
```

This function is often useful in list comprehensions, where it provides an idiom for accessing two generators simultaneously. For example, the following expression returns the scalar product of the lists of numbers x and y:

```
sum [ a*b | (a,b) <- zip2 x y ]

zip2::[*]->[**]->[(*,**)]
zip2 (a:x) (b:y) = (a,b):zip2 x y
zip2 x y = []
```

Note that if the lists being zipped are of different lengths, the length of the result is that of the shorter list.

Bibliography

Armstrong J., Virding R. and Williams M.
(1993). *Concurrent Programming in
ERLANG*. Englewood Cliffs, NJ: Prentice
Hall

Backus J. (1978). Can programming be
liberated from the Von Neumann style?
Comm. ACM, **21**(8)

Barendregt H. (1993). Lambda calculi with
types. In *Handbook of Logic and Computer
Science*, Vol. 2 (Abramsky S. *et al.*, eds).
Oxford: Oxford University Press

Bird R.S. (1990). A calculus of functions for
program derivation. In *Research Topics in
Functional Programming* (Turner D.A., ed.).
Reading, MA: Addison-Wesley

Cardelli L. and Wegner P. (1985). On
understanding types, data abstraction and
polymorphism. *Computing Surv.*, **17**

Cupitt J. (1989). The design and
implementation of an operating system in a
functional programming language. *PhD
thesis*, Computing Laboratory, University of
Kent

Darlington J. (1982). Program transformation.
In *Functional Programming and its
Applications* (Darlington J., Henderson P.
and Turner D.A., eds). Cambridge:
Cambridge University Press

Dettmer R. (1989). Formal chip design: a
functional approach. *IEE Review*, May

Galton A. (1990). *Logic for Information
Technology*. Chichester: Wiley

Girard J.-Y., Lafont Y. and Taylor P. (1989).
Proofs and Types. Volume 7 of *Cambridge
Tracts in Theoretical Computer Science*.
Cambridge: Cambridge University Press

Gordon A.J. (1994). *Functional Programming
and Input/Output*. British Computer Society
Distinguished Dissertations in Computer
Science. Cambridge: Cambridge University
Press

Hudak P. and Fasel J.H. (1992). A gentle
introduction to Haskell. *ACM SIGPLAN
Notices*, **27**(5)

Hudak P., Peyton Jones S. and Wadler P., eds.
(1992). Report on the programming language
Haskell, version 1.2. *ACM SIGPLAN
Notices*, **27**(5)

Huet G., ed. (1990). *Logical Foundations of
Functional Programming*. Reading, MA:
Addison-Wesley

Hughes J. (1990). Why functional programming
matters. In *Research Topics in Functional
Programming* (Turner D.A., ed.). Reading,
MA: Addison-Wesley

Jones M. (1994). *A Theory of Qualified Types*.
British Computer Society Distinguished
Dissertations in Computer Science.
Cambridge: Cambridge University Press

Luo Z. (1994). *Computation and Reasoning: A
Type Theory for Computer Science*. Oxford:
Oxford University Press

Major F., Turcotte M. *et al.* (1991). The
combination of symbolic and numerical
computation for three-dimensional modelling
of RNA. *Science*, **253**

Milner R. (1978). A theory of type
polymorphism in programming. *J. Computer
and System Sciences*, **17**

Milner R., Tofte M. and Harper R. (1990). *The
Definition of Standard ML*. Cambridge, MA:
MIT Press

Paulson L.C. (1987). *Logic and Computation – Interactive Proof with Cambridge LCF*. Cambridge: Cambridge University Press

Paulson L.C. (1991). *ML for the Working Programmer*. Cambridge: Cambridge University Press

Peyton Jones S. (1987). *The Implementation of Functional Programming Languages*. Englewood Cliffs, NJ: Prentice Hall

Peyton Jones S. and Lester D. (1992). *Implementing Functional Languages*. Englewood Cliffs, NJ: Prentice Hall

Peyton Jones S. and Wadler P. (1993). Imperative functional programming. In *Twentieth Annual Symposium on Principles of Programming Languages (POPL)*. ACM

Reeves S. and Clarke M. (1990). *Logic for Computer Science*. Wokingham: Addison-Wesley

Sanella D. (1986). Formal specification of ML programs. *Technical Report ECS-LFCS-86-15*, Laboratory for Foundations of Computer Science, Edinburgh University

Thompson S.J. (1989). A Logic for Miranda. *Formal Aspects of Computing*, **1**

Thompson S.J. (1990). Interactive functional programs: a method and a formal semantics. In *Research Topics in Functional Programming* (Turner D.A., ed.). Reading, MA: Addison-Wesley

Thompson S.J. (1991). *Type Theory and Functional Programming*. Wokingham: Addison-Wesley

Thompson S.J. (1993). Functional programming in education – introduction. *J. Functional Programming*, **3**(1), 3–4

Thompson S.J. (1995). A logic for Miranda, revisited. *Formal Aspects of Computing*, forthcoming

Turner D.A. (1985). Miranda: a non-strict functional language with polymorphic types. In *Functional Programming Languages and Computer Architecture* (Jouannaud J.P., ed.). Berlin: Springer-Verlag

Turner D.A. (1987). Functional programming and communicating processes. In *PARLE Conference: Vol. 258 of Lecture Notes in Computer Science*. Berlin: Springer-Verlag

Turner D.A. (1990a). An overview of Miranda. In *Research Topics in Functional Programming* (Turner D.A., ed.). Reading, MA: Addison-Wesley

Turner D.A. (1990b). *Research Topics in Functional Programming*. Reading, MA: Addison-Wesley

Wadler P. (1992). The essence of functional programming. In *Nineteenth Annual Symposium on Principles of Programming Languages (POPL)*. ACM

Wadler P. and Blott S. (1989). Making *ad hoc* polymorphism less *ad hoc*. In *Proc. 16th ACM Symposium on Principles of Programming Languages*. ACM Press

Index